When Your Child Dies

When Your Child Dies

Tools for Mending Parents' Broken Hearts

Avril Nagel and
Randie Clark, MA, CCC

New Horizon Press
Far Hills, NJ

Mississippi Mills
Public Library

Requests for permission should be addressed to:
New Horizon Press
P.O. Box 669
Far Hills, NJ 07931

Description of intuitive and instrumental grievers from *Men Don't Cry... Women
Do: Transcending Gender Stereotypes of Grief* by Terry L. Martin and Kenneth J.
Doka, Copyright © 2011. Reproduced with permission of Taylor & Francis Group
LLC and Brunner/Mazel.

Avril Nagel and Randie Clark
When Your Child Dies: Tools for Mending Parents' Broken Hearts

Cover design: Wendy Bass
Interior design: Scribe Inc.

Library of Congress Control Number: 2012932039

ISBN-13: 978-0-88282-391-1

New Horizon Press

Manufactured in the U.S.A.

16   15   14   13   12   1   2   3   4   5

For Bereaved Parents—
and for our sons, David and Alden

When we hold back our feelings and ignore our pain
we are committing violence against ourselves.

—THICH NHAT HAHN,
CREATING TRUE PEACE

AUTHORS' NOTE

This book is based on the authors' research, personal experiences and bereaved parents' real life experiences. In order to protect privacy, names have been changed and identifying characteristics have been altered except for contributing experts.

For purposes of simplifying usage, the pronouns s/he and his/her are sometimes used interchangeably. The information contained herein is not meant to be a substitute for professional evaluation and therapy with mental health professionals.

CONTENTS

x   *Contents*

INTRODUCTION

No parents imagine that their children will die before them. When the unthinkable happens, there is no preparation for the new, consuming reality that overtakes them on life's journey.

When our sons died, our life paths were profoundly changed. The unbearable grief stunned us into immobility—then, as the pain softened, we both tried to find our way back to ourselves. Our search for guiding information was overwhelming, lonely and disjointed at times; sometimes we found a piece here, a bit there. It was hard to find comprehensive information that was specific to the different circumstances in which each of our children died. Our experiences taught us that there is no roadmap for navigating the death of a child. Slowly we began to recognize that grieving parents need a resource that can help them understand the tragedy that has happened to them, recover from the trauma and begin to move forward.

This book is a work of love that we offer with honor in our hearts for those you have lost. We hope the information and tools you find in this book will guide you on your journey toward healing. We encourage you to remember that although nothing can fill the absence of your child or erase your terrible loss, you will get better, little by little. You will discover new ways of being in the world and once again feel engaged in your life.

The main sources of this book are personal experience, research and interviews. We interviewed more than thirty parents whose children died in a variety of circumstances. Randie has worked with bereaved parents for over ten years through her counseling practice and bereavement support groups. The silent backbone of the book is drawn from what we each learned following the traumatic and sudden loss of our sons.

This book is written for parents, but it also offers valuable insight for professionals and others who are helping bereaved parents. If you are a professional, educator or concerned friend, we welcome and support your interest in learning how to better serve and assist bereaved parents.

Since losing a child involves so many different kinds of experiences, we address the psychological, emotional and spiritual experiences related to grieving that loss. Chapters in the book are devoted to the interplay between trauma and grief and how it influences your bereavement. With this information we hope to empower you to be active and healthy in your journey of grieving, mourning and rebuilding your life.

A BOOK JUST FOR PARENTS

The relationship between parent and child is like no other. Parents feel a deep sense of responsibility to protect and nurture their children. Their roles are to love and guide their children to maturity and beyond. But when a child dies, a parent's heart is shattered. The shock can flood a parent's body and mind with a complex combination of overwhelming trauma responses, which mix with searing grief emotions, complicating the parent's reactions and influencing his or her recovery. The sharp loss touches and challenges every aspect of a parent's life and identity, including his or her understanding of the world. The complexities of the loss of a child cause a bereaved parent's healing journey to be multi-layered.

Although our cultural and social responses to grief and loss have many valuable supports to offer, after experiencing our own losses and realizing the conflicts of heart and mind of many to whom we spoke, we felt the need to go beyond the general and delve into the specific heartaches and deeper issues with which grieving parents struggle. This book speaks directly to parents whose children have died.

If you are a bereaved parent, our hearts reach out to you. Though there are no two losses alike, what bereaved parents share is a common knowing. In this book we try to illuminate the issues specific to child loss as well as provide information, support, strategies and tools to guide you on your journey. Within the text we use the terms *parent(s)* and *you* to mean anyone in a parental role, such as a mother, father, stepparent or caretaker.

TASKS OF MOURNING

Grief and mourning do not progress in direct, predictable lines and the experience of loss is different for each person. All parents must do their own work to grieve in healthy ways and to incorporate the death into their ongoing lives. The Tasks of Mourning are guidelines that help to contextualize the journey of grief. These steps do not occur in any special order. Our four Tasks of Mourning are based on those outlined by J. W. Worden in his book *Grief Counseling and Grief Therapy: A Handbook for the Mental Health Practitioner.* We have adapted the wording of the tasks to reflect the unique nature of each parent's bereavement.

- **Coming to terms with the reality of your loss**

  When the shock and numbness of the immediate death of your child begins to diminish, you may feel the sharp pain of grief. This is a time when the reality of the death and loss begins to penetrate your awareness and comprehension. Though you may have moments of absolute disbelief, there will be daily reminders of your child's absence. Acknowledging the reality of the death will help define your next steps along the path.

- **Experiencing the pain of your loss**

  The emotions of grieving a loss are natural, human responses. If grieving is to be healthy, you must allow yourself to express and release your feelings. Attempting to suppress, avoid, numb or deny your feelings can hinder, complicate and prolong grief. Some mourners believe that holding onto the pain will defer a child's absence or sustain their love for their deceased children, but the pain needn't be held onto. Pain will dissipate as you release it. You'll learn in the process that you are capable of deep emotions and strong enough to give voice to them.

- **Learning what it means to live without your child**

  As months pass you will begin to adjust to the reality that your child is no longer among the living. Though the place your child held in your life can never be filled in the same way, your work is to discover what your life is now and what it can be in her or his absence. You will need to reflect on how this experience has changed your identity and roles in life. Ask yourself: What do I wish to create from the remains of my old life? How can I incorporate this tragic experience into my life in ways that have meaning?

  Despite the fact that it seems impossible at first, with the passage of time we believe you can discover what matters to you in your life. To do this, you need to reevaluate, explore and reinvent your way of living in the world. By doing these things, you may experience new perspectives, develop new interests and redirect your energies in entirely new ways. With these changes will come a deeper understanding of yourself and a new awareness of your emotional capacity and strength.

- **Emotionally accommodating your child's death and moving forward**

  The agony of your child's death can leave you grasping at the hopelessness that she or he will never return. As time passes, allow yourself to bring your child into your life in new traditions: through storytelling, rituals and memorials. The love you shared with your daughter or son is infinite and can be expressed in many ways. Gradually, your relationship with your child will transform from one of grieving in the present to one of treasured memory. Your love can go with you wherever you are, whatever you do. Knowing this can help you choose actions that represent your daughter or son as you move forward in your life.

We hope you will use this book as a guide to move through these tasks of mourning. Each task is relevant to the journey upon which you are embarking and will ultimately move you toward healing your wounds and reengaging in your life.

HOW TO USE THIS BOOK

Circumstances surrounding every death are unique and all parents grieve and cope with their losses differently. In recognition of this, the chapters of this book are designed to work both independently and consecutively, with some chapters covering the possible scenarios that might surround the event of your child's death. The chapters are designed to make it easy for you to access the information you need, as you need it. The first three chapters provide information that is important for gaining a general understanding of your grief and how the cause of death will influence your journey. From there, let your emotions, challenges or struggles guide you. Consult the table of contents and index and read the chapters that apply to your present needs, issues or questions.

Randie's Story: When David Was Killed

It was an ordinary Wednesday evening. I had just returned home after a meeting and I was pleased to find a voicemail from my son David, who lived in another state with his wife. In his message he told me how relieved, excited and happy he and his wife were about the new apartment they had just moved into. (Their first child was to be born in two months.) The last words on the message were, "I love you, Mom; I'll try to call you later." I sat down with my fifteen-year-old daughter to watch our favorite high school TV drama.

Just before 10 P.M. the phone rang. My daughter ran to answer it. She shouted to me to come to the phone, saying it was one of David's close friends calling. *Why in the world would he be calling me?* I thought. *I wonder what might be wrong.* I took the phone and asked David's friend what was going on. His voice said, "David was robbed tonight. There was a knife and he was stabbed and he's dead."

I experienced a strange feeling creeping through my body; everything froze as if the molecules of air around me had thickened and solidified. It felt as if the world had ceased to turn on its axis. My vision shifted and the scene around me became surreal. The words he had spoken trailed away and I could not remember what he'd said. I asked, "What . . . what did you say?" I forced him to repeat his words over and over, asking, "Why are you saying this to me?" I could not understand what reason he would have to say such a terrible thing to me. But no matter how many times I asked him, the words did not change. I demanded to speak to my daughter-in-law. He put her on the phone and she uttered, "I'm so sorry." Those words and the tone in her voice broke through the fog and pierced my brain.

In that moment, reality shattered before me and from somewhere far off I could hear my own terrible screaming. My vision collapsed into a narrow tunnel that sharpened every detail to a painful edge. As time stretched out and then froze, I lost all sensation in my body except a searing, crushing pain in my heart. I could see my daughter across the room in a corner, curled up in a ball, her eyes pleading, her voice wailing, "No, not David, no, not my brother." I was helpless to stanch her pain.

A strange feeling came over me: I felt weightless, as if I had stepped next to myself. I could see a threshold before me and I knew that all I had to do was step across it and I could be with my son, with the promise of all the pain and horror ending in one instant. I was aware of my daughter grabbing my shoulders and shouting, "Don't leave! I'm here; I won't leave you. I need you, Mom." In that brief moment I faced two clear choices: step across to oblivion or stay and face a new, awful reality that included acknowledging that my twenty-six-year-old son was dead. I grasped my daughter in my arms and we sobbed together as we began a journey for which we had no roadmap and from which there was no turning back.

My mind was flooded with images of what might have happened to my son: the scene of his struggle, the doctors working on him, the emergency room at the hospital—my heart was pounding. Everything felt strange to me; my world no longer made any sense. The first forty-eight hours following that phone call were a blur to me. What I remember most clearly is an intense compulsion to see my son and touch him. I had to have proof he was dead.

After a five-hour drive to the city where he was killed, I was able to find out the details of what had happened. David and his wife had walked downtown with another friend after David had agreed to help the friend sell a small amount of marijuana to some local acquaintances. I later found out David had gone along with the idea because he and his wife had spent all their money acquiring the new apartment and the friend had promised to share the profits with them. Two teens had decided to "go downtown to rob a hippie of his pot," because they wanted to raise some money for a motel party with their girlfriends. David was targeted and confronted at knifepoint. He chose to defend himself; there was a struggle and he was stabbed fourteen times. He died in his wife's arms.

David's death sent ripples of shock throughout his community. He was loved by many and known as a big brother to the street kids. He was an accomplished musician and deeply excited about becoming a father. David was my firstborn and we shared a very special bond of friendship and mutual love. What I enjoyed most about him was his wise and philosophical spirit. He treasured his little sister and she adored him.

Since his death, my life has changed entirely. At first I just had to survive and help my daughter, though at times I did not believe I could live through it. I found some solace and direction through a support group for homicide vistims' relatives and through therapy. I also tried to immerse myself in pursuing a graduate degree. Many years have passed since that December night. Sometimes the feelings are as raw and intense as they were that night and sometimes I am able to feel deep gratitude and love toward my son, for the gift of grace he brought to my life, for the beauty of this present moment and for the depth of love it holds. I will always miss him, yet I have found ways to have him in my life every day.

Avril's Story: A Glimpse of Alden

On October 3, 2006, my labor pains started. My husband and I were filled with excitement, anticipation and nervousness. The pregnancy had gone smoothly to this point; we had no reason to suspect anything would go wrong.

After almost twenty-four hours of labor, my delivery was still going well. I was working through the contractions and was in a steady birth rhythm. The nursing staff was monitoring the baby's heart rate, keeping an eye on something, but I was oblivious to the details and focused on the task at hand. I was feeling confident and strong.

My husband and I were in the bath when the nurse asked me to get out, so she could hook me up to the heart rate monitor. I had decided to use gas to manage my pain, so I was quite disoriented. The nurse suddenly called, "Decel! Decel!" which means deceleration. I later learned that Alden's heart went from 120 to 60, then silent. The room filled with nurses and resident doctors. They stood, mouths agape, staring at my naked body, noting the silence on the heart monitor. I felt alone, confused and afraid.

The doctor broke my water, which intensified the labor pains; an immense pressure took over my body. I was trying to figure out what was happening as I managed the contractions. Nurses gave me oxygen to reduce the disorienting effects of the gas. Because the pregnancy was "low risk," the staff had put us on the second floor of the hospital, above the operating rooms. Wheeling me down the corridor and onto the elevators, they all knew what I didn't yet understand; my baby was dead. By the time the emergency caesarian section began, crucial time had already passed. Hospital staff denied my husband entry to the operating room. He waited in anguish, not knowing what was happening or if either of us would survive.

When I awoke from the surgery, the pediatric doctor informed me that they had been able to resuscitate our son, but the brain damage was too extensive for survival.

My husband and I had one day in the neonatal intensive care unit with our son. When I first met him I was awestruck by how this tiny body, hooked up to machines, could contain such a huge, present soul. I was overcome by an unknown love and heartbreak. Friends and family came to meet him and say their goodbyes. In the end his body and mind were not strong enough to survive, even with the help of the machines. He died in his father's arms. His name, Alden, means old friend and we found that in him.

We never found out the cause of his death.

Alden was our first child. After he died, I found myself returning to an old life that suddenly felt empty. All of my dreams and plans for the future depended on his entry into my life. They were lost to the reality and pain of his death.

As time passed, I was slowly able to rebuild my vision of the future and find ways to express love for and connect with Alden. Even though he was only with us for a day, my love will last my lifetime. My whole being has forever changed.

MOVING FORWARD THROUGH THIS BOOK

Losing a child is a life-changing event. The grief of a bereaved parent is a layered and ongoing journey. The interplay between trauma and grief adds complexity to the loss. This book aims to demystify, normalize and help you navigate your experience. As bereaved parents ourselves and through

CHAPTER ONE

When Trauma and Grief Combine

Losing a child is unlike any other loss because of its inherently traumatic nature. Not only are parents plunged into grief following the death of a child, but also they experience symptoms related to trauma response. Understanding the differences between your feelings of grief and your trauma symptoms can be a powerful tool in your healing process. Acknowledging the traumatic nature of your loss sheds new light on the emotions and reactions you are experiencing. The ability to separate grief from trauma and address both, piece by piece, brings a new sense of understanding to the experience and contributes to a more holistic healing process.

To help you sort through the multitude of responses you may be experiencing, we will explore some tough questions: What is grief? What is mourning? What is trauma? What is the human stress response? How are trauma responses different from grief responses? Why is it important to know the difference?

Later in the chapter we address serious complications and symptoms that might arise when you experience a particularly traumatic loss.

WHAT IS GRIEF?

Grief is the emotional response to a loss. *The Merriam-Webster Dictionary* defines grief as an "intense emotional suffering caused by loss; sorrow; regret." The grief one feels after losing a child has a strong impact on the spiritual, emotional, physical and psychological facets of one's life.

Grief follows no timeline or set order of emotional responses and each parent's grief is unique. The experience of grief depends on many things: the nature of a parent's relationship with the child, how the child died, emotional and spiritual predispositions, life circumstances and loss history. Grief also differs when death is anticipated versus when death is sudden.

In anticipated loss, a parent may experience "anticipatory grief." When parents realize their child's life will be foreshortened, the process of emotionally preparing for and grieving their child's death begins. There is time for goodbyes and resolutions, which influences the aftermath of the loss.

When a child's death is sudden, the onset of grief is abrupt. There is no opportunity to prepare for the loss. There is no time for goodbyes. Circumstances surrounding sudden death are often violent, unexpected and difficult to absorb, adding complexity to a grieving parent's journey.

Grief is a natural, human response to a loss. It is a journey that leads to full acknowledgement of the fact that your loved one is gone and to the emotional and psychological integration of that reality.

WHAT IS MOURNING?

Mourning involves the external expressions and actions of the internal emotions of grief. *The Merriam-Webster Dictionary* defines it as, "to feel or express grief or sorrow; to grieve; to be sorrowful." Mourning is a series of tasks carried out by an individual over time. Some examples of mourning include enacting personal and cultural rituals, weeping, wearing black and marking anniversaries.

WHAT IS TRAUMA?

Psychological trauma occurs following exposure to an extraordinary stressor outside the usual realm of human experience. *The Merriam-Webster Dictionary* defines trauma as "an emotional experience or shock, which has a lasting psychic effect." A child's death, no matter what the circumstances or cause, is a traumatic experience for the parent. When a traumatic event occurs, the human stress response is automatically triggered.

WHAT IS THE HUMAN STRESS RESPONSE?

In the first few moments following the shocking realization that your child is dying or has died, a series of psychological, neurological, emotional and physical reactions occurs. This series of natural autonomic actions is called the human stress response or the "fight, flight or freeze" response.

The human stress response occurs instantaneously when we are exposed to something out of the ordinary that is perceived as life threatening, out of our control, shocking or startling. The human stress response is an innate preservation mechanism. It is a basic function of the nervous system that is hardwired to a part of the brain called the neocortex. In evolutionary terms, the response activates signals throughout the body to assure the person's ability to survive a real or perceived threat.

We have all felt this response many times in our lives. When there is an unexpected loud noise, when someone jumps out to surprise us or when we unwittingly touch a hot surface, we react before having time to think about our choice of actions. Our brains take over and prime us to take corrective action. Only after the threat has passed do we begin to analyze what took place in order to determine future actions or behaviors that will prevent the same thing from happening again.

The next chart outlines the basic sequences of the human stress response. It shows what happens inside the brain and body in the first instants following exposure to a stressor event.

The Human Stress Response

Stressor Event
Threat or Danger Perceived
Brain Floods with Neurochemical Signals
Central Nervous System Activates (muscles/heart/heightened sensory response)
Rational Thinking Deactivates
Neocortex Activates (judgement and memory for survival)
Action/Inaction (fight, flight or freeze)
Perceived Threat Is Gone
Interpretation/Resolution (analysis logic)

Human stress response is intense, powerful and usually brief—but when the stressor event is traumatic, such as the death of your child, the stress response can be unremitting. Your mind can become stuck in a pattern of arousal, replaying the events over and over as you try to make sense of what has happened and regain a sense of meaning and control in your world, as seen in the next chart.

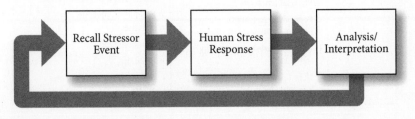

In this book, we refer to the characteristics of the *human stress response* interchangeably with *trauma responses.*

HOW ARE TRAUMA RESPONSES DIFFERENT FROM GRIEF?

We have compiled a list that outlines responses common to grief (left column) in contrast with responses found in trauma (right column). You may be experiencing some or many of these feelings and reactions. It is helpful to note that there are differences as you reflect upon what you are going through. Remember, this list is to help you identify some of what you are experiencing and does not suggest that there is a right or wrong way to grieve.

Grief Responses Versus Trauma Responses

	Common and Natural Grief Responses	*Common Responses Following Traumatic Loss*
FEELINGS	• Irritability, feeling "on edge" • Recurrent feelings of guilt or remorse • Anger • Resentment • Without feeling • Longing • Sadness • Loneliness and social isolation • Worsening of existing mental illness symptoms • Exhaustion	• Fear, anxiety, panic • Emotional numbness, detachment • Wanting to hurt someone as much as you have been hurt • Vulnerability • Intense and contradictory emotions (e.g., rage/sorrow, fear/relief) • A sense of emptiness • Feeling overwhelmed or immobilized • Dissociation (feeling out-of-body)
BEHAVIORS	• Crying at unanticipated times • Restlessness • Overactivity, taking care of others' grief • Physical lethargy • Loss of interest in other responsibilities • Loss of interest in grooming, self-care • Urge to retell the details of the loss repeatedly	• Frequent and uncontrollable pacing or restlessness • Hypervigilance, on guard all the time • Exaggerated startle response • Inability to perform normal activities • Immobilization • Isolation • Increased dependence on others

	Common and Natural Grief Responses	Common Responses Following Traumatic Loss
BEHAVIORS (continued)	• Sleeplessness • Sleeping more than usual	• Increased substance use, abuse of pharmaceutical or recreational substances • Uncontrollable urges or actions of violence toward others • Avoidance of thinking or talking about what has happened, of places and people associated with the incident
THOUGHT PATTERNS	• Poor concentration and focus • Forgetfulness • Loss of time perception • Periods of "blankness" • Sense of unreality • Visualizing life "like it was" • Imagining hearing, smelling or seeing deceased loved one • Denial of the reality of the loss	• Inability to concentrate • Problems with memory • Confusion or mental paralysis • Mental fragmentation, scattered thoughts • Ruminating or obsessing • Recurring imagery of the death • Nightmares • Fear for safety • Thoughts of suicide or self-harm • Unrelenting self-blame
PHYSICAL SENSATIONS	• Tightness in the throat • Pounding of the heart • Fatigue, weakness, lack of energy • Frequent sighing • Heaviness in the chest, "heavy heart" • Lack of appetite • Dry mouth • Excess nervous energy • Sensitivity to noise, bright lights • Weak, vulnerable immune system • Worsening of existing illness or condition	• Recurring feelings as if the loss has just happened • Exaggerated startle response, jumpiness • Anxiety, panic attacks (heart palpitations, sweating, shortness of breath) • Lack of energy or fatigue • Extreme/enduring changes in appetite • Inability to fall or stay asleep • Oversensitivity to noise • Difficulty settling down, restlessness • Lack of physical sensation or numbness • Sensory overload or shutdown

	Common and Natural Grief Responses	Common Responses Following Traumatic Loss
SPIRITUAL RESPONSES	• Anger at God/the universe • Loss of hope • Creating false justification (making a saint of the deceased) • Faith is shaken by doubt • Finding strength in faith • Epiphany, awe (burst open)	• Worldview is shattered • Loss of sense of self • "Nothing has meaning anymore" • Forced unknowing • Feeling bereft of faith or hope • Feeling punished/abandoned by higher power

To continue exploring these emotions and responses see chapter 2: *A Dictionary of Emotions for the Grieving Parent.*

KNOWING THE DIFFERENCE BETWEEN TRAUMA RESPONSE AND GRIEF

Trauma responses are separate and different from the emotional and physical characteristics of grief. Initially, the intensity of the stress response is appropriate to the overwhelming nature of coping with the loss of a child. Grief emotions occur simultaneously with the trauma response, which can be further compounded by a profound sense of helplessness. If these reactions do not abate over a reasonable period of time, they will negatively impact your ability to interpret the experience intellectually and process your emotions toward resolution.

Without resolution, the trauma response can become stuck in a loop and become the overriding function operating in your body and mind. If you are experiencing prolonged trauma responses, you will need to attend to them before you can move naturally through your grieving process. Often this requires professional assistance to help prevent the trauma responses you are experiencing from becoming a chronic condition and to guide you toward healthy recovery from the trauma.

COMPLICATIONS OF GRIEVING

Grieving is exhausting, but what if you are picking up signs that your grieving has become complicated and significantly unhealthy? Maybe you wonder why falling asleep is so difficult and when you finally fall asleep, you are awakened by nightmares. Perhaps during the day you are unable to focus or concentrate and your physical sensations range from jumpy to weak and exhausted. Emotionally you feel pervasive numbness and loss of interest in activities that once gave you pleasure. Without warning, sounds, sights, images or smells trigger a reaction that plummets you back to the intensity you felt at the time of your child's death. You may be asking, "What has happened to me? Why is this happening?"

In the remainder of this chapter we address "tricky responses" or conditions that can influence your ability to process your grief and move forward in the healing process. We will discuss the impacts of a prolonged trauma response and the chronic condition known as post-traumatic stress disorder (PTSD). Conditions that might restrain you from grieving healthily also include complicated grief and depression.

When a chronic condition exists, intervention is essential to progress and heal. It's important to realize that factors such as PTSD, complicated grief or depression can combine with your grief and that getting help is the first step toward shifting unhealthy patterns in your healing process. Because of the complexity of responses related to the trauma of your child's death, each aspect of your experience must be addressed in turn.

POST-TRAUMATIC STRESS DISORDER

We hear the term post-traumatic stress disorder used often in today's world, but what does it mean?

In this chapter we have already explored how traumatic events arouse a series of instantaneous and automatic responses in your body and mind. In a flash your body ramps up into full alert as your mind struggles to make sense of the death. Over time, your shock will decrease and your mental and emotional acceleration will tone down. For some, this natural toning down does not happen and the emotional and physical responses related to the trauma remain in a heightened state. Weeks or months later, you may find yourself still struggling with feelings, bodily sensations and thoughts that seem to have a will of their own and stand in the way of your grief.

Susan shared her story of when her only child, Amelia, died when her car careened off an icy road into a tree. Several months later Susan was experiencing physical and emotional reactions that made normal daily functioning difficult for her. She talked to her physician, who diagnosed her with post-traumatic stress disorder, and she began appropriate treatment.

> *I'm normally a pretty easygoing person, but months after Amelia died I felt as if I was a stranger to myself. I couldn't understand what was happening to me. I kept making movies in my head of what might have happened that night when her car left the road. When those pictures came into my mind, my emotions were blindingly intense, as if it were happening all over again. I was*

afraid to go to sleep because of the nightmares. I avoided driving and couldn't stand to be a passenger, because I felt such panic.

A diagnosis of PTSD is warranted when the trauma response continues longer than thirty days after the initial exposure. PTSD prolongs the human stress response, which is designed to help the mind and body cope with stressors. When individuals suffer from PTSD, they are trapped in the cycle of the *fight, flight or freeze* response and the struggle to comprehend what has happened. The mind recalls the event repetitively and sometimes unrelentingly, which keeps the individual aroused and hypersensitive to stimuli. Flashbacks of the event can be so intense that it feels as if it is real or happening again, which can be exhausting and debilitating.

Experiencing the traumatic loss of your child does not mean you will develop PTSD, which can only be diagnosed by a health professional. Correct diagnoses of PTSD usually identify specific symptoms that affect cognitive functioning, mood and behaviors, such as arousal, avoidance and re-experiencing the event. If you are concerned that you might have PTSD, read our checklist of the features of PTSD to help determine if it is appropriate for you to talk with your doctor or a clinician regarding the symptoms you are experiencing and to discuss treatments that can help you. If it is less than thirty days since the traumatic event and you are experiencing these symptoms, it is also appropriate to see a health professional. The sooner intervention occurs, the less likely it is that PTSD will develop.

There are three categories of PTSD:

☐ ACUTE: Duration is fewer than three months.
☐ CHRONIC: Duration is three months or more.
☐ DELAYED ONSET: Onset is at least six months after trauma event.

FEATURES OF PTSD

Arousal

Arousal is part of the trauma response mechanism, which gives you the ability to escape danger and protect yourself. Normally, arousal concludes shortly after the danger has passed. With PTSD, arousal becomes stuck at higher than normal levels and remains active for prolonged periods of time. Arousal experienced by individuals with PTSD manifests as hyperarousal or hypervigilance. Common characteristics are:

☐ Feeling alert, wound up, on edge/jumpy.
☐ Irregular or racing heart rate, heart palpitations.
☐ Sensitivity to stimuli (sights, sounds, smells).

☐ Exaggerated startle response.
☐ Difficulty falling or staying asleep.
☐ Irritable mood.
☐ Unpredictable angry outbursts or misdirected rage.
☐ Problems with concentration, focus and memory.
☐ Feeling protective, guarded and fearful.
☐ Expecting danger or disaster.
☐ Significant distress or impairment in social and/or work environments.
☐ Feeling numb emotionally.

Avoidance

Healthy avoidance instincts protect us when we are threatened and help secure safety and survival. They also help us cope when we are distressed, providing a break that allows us to problem solve or rest and refresh. When an individual suffers from PTSD, avoidance behaviors interfere with his or her ability to carry out daily life with flexibility and a sense of control. Avoidance prevents a person from processing emotional and psychological wounds because emotions and healing are blocked by fear. Common variations of avoidance include:

☐ ACTIVE AVOIDANCE: Avoiding people, conversations, thoughts, places, objects and/or activities that remind the person of the child's death.
☐ PASSIVE AVOIDANCE: Emotional and psychological detachment and disassociation or self-medication in an attempt to prevent experiencing feelings associated with the loss. Self-medication can include drug and alcohol abuse, self-harm or eating disorders.
☐ ISOLATION: Compulsive unwillingness or inability to participate in social and work relationships or activities.
☐ EMOTIONAL/PSYCHOLOGICAL NUMBING: Ongoing sense of feeling unresponsive, empty, emotionally flat. Prolonged numbing is a sign that the sensory response system is not functioning appropriately. It can signal the onset of depression.
☐ MEMORY LOSS: Difficulty remembering events related to the trauma. Memory loss following a traumatic event is normal to some degree, but individuals eventually do begin to recall details of the event. In cases of PTSD, memories may be suppressed or inaccessible but continue to affect the psyche.

Reexperiencing the Event

☐ FLASHBACKS: Spontaneously experiencing images, perceptions or thoughts of the trauma that intrude upon the person's inner life

and which are as vivid and intense as the actual experience. Can
include acting or feeling as if it is actually happening.

☐ DISTRESS RESPONSE: An intense psychological response to an
internal or external cue that reminds the person of the trauma.

☐ NIGHTMARES: Distressing, recurrent dreams related to the
trauma disturb sleep patterns.

Each of us has a unique way of coping and of healing from traumatic loss.
The checklists are meant to offer information and help you to determine if you
need additional support to cope with your loss and initiate further healing.

It can be hard to break the cycle of PTSD. If you have identified with any
of the characteristics we just discussed, consider seeking help from a medical
professional for treatment and intervention. By addressing the symptoms of
PTSD and reducing the impacts on your psyche and your ability to function,
you will be able to focus more energy toward healing your grief and pain.

COMPLICATED GRIEF

As with trauma, internal and external factors may also influence the experience of grief. For example, if a parent has an unresolved loss from the past, this
loss may combine with and influence the grief for his or her child. When losses
from a person's past and present meld in this way, the grieving process is prolonged and professionals describe it as *complicated grief*. This kind of grieving
process often feels confusing, stagnant and seemingly without direction or
end. It can be hard to determine who or what you are grieving at any given
time. If you identify with any of the scenarios listed next, it may be that your
grief experience has been complicated by factors beyond the loss of your child.

Some of the circumstances and influences that can complicate the
grieving process include:

☐ Multiple losses close together without adequate time to grieve
each loss individually.

☐ A historically difficult relationship and/or unfinished emotional
"business" with the deceased.

☐ Sudden and difficult circumstances as a result of the death
such as loss of financial stability, housing or social identity,
involvement with the judicial system and injury or health issues.

☐ Circumstances associated with the loss that create social stigma
(e.g., crime-related death, homicide, suicide, overdose, combat
fatality).

☐ Feeling guilt or responsibility for the death.

☐ Difficulty adapting to the absence of the person(s) who died.

☐ Survivor guilt.

☐ Single or multiple trauma experiences.
☐ Self-imposed postponement of grief due to emotional blocking or fulfilling obligations such as work or raising children.
☐ A sense of loss of identity and purpose (e.g., "I feel I am no longer a whole person").
☐ Involvement in the death (e.g., being the driver of the car that crashed, deciding to end life support).
☐ Preexisting mental health issues.
☐ Substance abuse, addictions.
☐ Isolation from support systems (geographic, economic, emotional, physical).

Complicated grief can present itself in many forms. The next list outlines some of the mixed thoughts, feelings and behaviors with which you may be dealing. Some of these experiences are a natural part of the grieving process, but when compounded with complicating factors, they could be signs that you are struggling with complicated rather than simple grief:

☐ Lacking energy or motivation to attend to normal daily tasks.
☐ Feeling exhausted even upon waking.
☐ Difficulty falling asleep and/or staying asleep.
☐ Recurring emotions that are not related to the loss or that have unreasonable intensity (e.g., crying, panic, anger, numbness).
☐ Inability to grasp or acknowledge that the child is gone.
☐ Intense, relentless longing for the child.
☐ Floods of memories from past losses or traumas.
☐ Unrelenting guilt or shame.
☐ Experiencing obsessive or compulsive thoughts and behaviors.
☐ Difficulty concentrating or paying attention.
☐ Feeling as if life is meaningless, pointless and empty.
☐ Using nonprescription drugs or alcohol to "medicate" emotions.
☐ Losing the ability to trust others or to experience intimacy with loved ones.
☐ Losing a sense of future.
☐ A distorted sense of linear time (none has gone by or it is racing by).

Perhaps your child's death has unleashed memories of past losses that remain unresolved or perhaps you are suddenly revisiting a past trauma with fresh intensity. It may be that months have passed and your longing and sadness have not lessened; you may feel haunted by impressions of being incomplete, purposeless or hopeless.

It is important to recognize that each loss and each complicating factor has an influence upon the whole of your grief. To foster your healing, you must pull apart and address the individual elements in order to navigate along your path of grief. It is best to seek help with this process. A professional counselor or grief therapist can offer the appropriate treatment approach that will safely and gently guide you as you unravel the tangled web of emotions that hold you in a frozen state. (For suggestions on how to choose a therapist see chapter 13: *Tools for Healing.*)

DEPRESSION

Grief and depression have many similarities and can sometimes be confused. After suffering the death of a child, a parent can expect to feel sad, full of longing and without the energy to do even simple tasks. These feelings are a natural part of grief and mourning. Grief has an ebb and flow, with periods of intensity and periods of relief from the emotions of sadness and longing.

In contrast, depression has a persistent nature. One's mood remains low most of the day, nearly every day, without lifting. One experiences a general feeling of heaviness and an inability to feel responsive to previously pleasurable activities. Thinking may feel clouded and negative, with a sense of hopelessness, detachment and absence of resilience, affecting one's perspective toward life.

If you are concerned that you might have depression, this checklist contains some of the primary signs of depression:

- ☐ LOSS OF INTEREST: In activities, relationships or behaviors that were previously important.
- ☐ SENSE OF MEANINGLESSNESS: A feeling that there is no future; pointlessness.
- ☐ FEELING ESTRANGED, DETACHED: Loss of connection with others, isolation.
- ☐ ANHEDONIA: Not experiencing one's normal range of emotions and responses. Lack of humor, pleasure, joy, anger, etc.
- ☐ TIREDNESS: Lack of energy, unmotivated, excessive sleeping and exhaustion.
- ☐ CHANGE OF APPETITE: Inability to eat or overeating.
- ☐ LOSS OF LIBIDO: Reduction or absence of sexual interest or desire.
- ☐ CHANGE IN SLEEP PATTERN: Wakefulness, restlessness or excessive sleeping.
- ☐ SENSE OF WORTHLESSNESS: Unrealistic negative evaluation of one's worth.
- ☐ SUICIDAL THOUGHTS OR THOUGHTS OF SELF-HARM: Active or passive.
- ☐ PREOCCUPATION WITH PAST FAILINGS: Blaming and shaming oneself.

The onset of an episode of depression can be sudden or gradual; the episode can be brief or prolonged. If you think you are experiencing depression rather than your natural grief and mourning process, be reassured that depression is treatable. The first step is to discuss your concerns with a doctor. (For exercises and ideas to help you address your emotions as well as choose a therapist, see chapter 13: *Tools for Healing.*)

CHAPTER TWO

A Dictionary of Emotions for the Grieving Parent

After your child dies you may experience a flood of unfamiliar emotions, all kinds of feelings and sensations that you haven't learned how to handle yet. In this chapter we focus on the most common reactions and emotional responses you may be experiencing and provide guidance for how to cope and heal.

Emotional reactions and responses have been organized in alphabetical order for easy access; leafing through the chapter is encouraged, as you may be feeling some of these emotions more strongly than others. In addition to the ideas for emotional release in this section, also see chapter 13: *Tools for Healing* for more exercises and techniques.

Emotions of grief and child loss do not follow any particular pattern and they are not predictable. Many individual and unique factors will affect how you react to your loss, factors such as your personality, your relationship with your child, the circumstances of the death and your experience during the rituals after your loss such as the funeral. As you move forward, pay close attention to recurring feelings and sensations in your grieving; they may be telling you where to focus your energies for healing.

Anger

Among parents who have lost their children, it is common for them to experience emotions of anger. Paul recalled:

> *Some days it seemed like everything made me enraged, I*
> *couldn't stop thinking about how unfair it all was, how nothing*

15

went right, how it shouldn't have happened. Sometimes I just
wanted to scream at everyone and everything.

You may be feeling anger toward a number of people or things,
including:

- Your deceased child
- Your husband, wife or partner
- Family members
- Friends
- Perpetrator(s)
- Justice system
- Hospital system or staff
- Police
- Yourself
- God/higher power

In child loss, anger is natural: your child has died and that is not okay.
Anger expressed in a healthy way promotes healing of emotional wounds.
Physical exercise, purgative crying, writing, going somewhere private to
scream and talking about your anger with someone you trust are all effective methods of release. (See chapter 13: *Tools for Healing* for more emotional release exercises.)

Anger arises in many ways and can be illogical at times. You may be
directing anger toward your spouse or your surviving children when in
fact you are angry with the drunk driver who has taken your child from
you. Anger can be hurtful and can manifest through physical, verbal or
emotional violence. These forms of anger are very destructive and can
cause damage to relationships with people you love. If you find yourself
acting out toward people unexpectedly, take the time to reflect on the root
of your anger. This is a positive step toward ensuring that you do not unintentionally hurt those around you.

Anger can also function as a cover-up to mask other, more vulnerable emotions. When this happens it can become a dysfunctional coping
mechanism. Are you creating surface issues to hide what is really going on
or to make yourself unapproachable?

Anger is a physical as well as an emotional response creating tension in the body. If left unresolved, anger can manifest in physical symptoms such as anxiety, stomach ulcers, the inability to sleep and stiff or sore
muscles. Unexpressed anger has the potential to engender self-destructive
behaviors. Make an effort to express your anger in healthy ways.

Anxiety

Death reminds us that the world is not a benign and safe place. The worst possible thing has happened and your senses of normalcy and safety have been challenged. You may be experiencing feelings of uneasiness or apprehension regarding what could happen in the future. Grieving parents who attend counseling often report, "My stomach is in knots, I feel so hyped up all the time and I constantly worry that something else might happen to my family." This is a form of anxiety.

You may also experience increased anxiety about domestic and family matters such as finances, how clean the house is or what your relatives might be thinking. You may be dealing with additional financial pressures due to the need to travel or funeral costs. It is important to acknowledge the impact these situations may have on your stress levels. Reach out and ask family and friends for help.

When confronted with your child's traumatic or violent death, the arousal of anxiety is a natural, involuntary physiological response. Sometimes that natural response lingers and worsens as your imagination continues to create images of possible threats that you feel powerless to control. This anxiety can intensify to a level of emotional paralysis and physical inaction. If your anxiety is becoming chronic, it is important to address it with a trained psychologist or counselor. See chapter 13: *Tools for Healing* for techniques to manage anxiety.

Bargaining

In the aftermath of loss, grieving parents are often troubled by recurring, insistent questions, like, "What if I had contacted the doctor earlier?"

This is a form of bargaining and it is your way of seeking to undo what has happened. Other forms may sound like, "If only . . . What if . . . If I could change . . . If s/he comes back I promise to . . ." Bargaining is a part of processing your loss. The degree to which you believe that the loss could have been prevented can have an influence on the intensity of bargaining. "What if" scenarios can become strong obsessions, played over in the mind without rest.

This questioning is a natural part of the grieving process. You are attempting to reverse or rewrite the events as a means to dull the pain and the reality of the loss. After the mind exhausts all possibilities, you realize that despite all potential outcomes, the loss has happened and is real. You may need to exhaust every possibility before you can begin acknowledging the reality of your loss.

Blame

Your mind might deliberate common questions when your child has died, like "Who is responsible for this? Why did this happen? Whose fault is this?" These questions represent the need to find a reason for what has occurred.

In the process of trying to find reasonable causes, you might question what you did and could have done differently; you might blame yourself for your child's death. Many who come to grief counseling express mental scenarios such as, "I can't count the times that I thought: If only I had been home to receive his phone call, if only I had been there to talk to him, he would not have walked into the robbery and would still be alive."

The circumstances of your child's death are unique and the thought process of blame varies according to experience. Seeking a cause for the tragedy is a normal part of the process. But blame can be irrational; it might make you overlook the facts as you replay potential scenarios in your mind.

Your blame might also manifest in guilt, shame or anger. It is important to recognize when you are feeling burdened with self-blame and work through your uncertainty. Talking with someone you trust (e.g., a friend, minister, counselor) can help to sort through your thoughts and feelings. See chapter 13: *Tools for Healing* for exercises to help you work through these difficult emotions.

Crazy, Feeling As If

After the loss of a child, even simple tasks may seem complicated and difficult. You may feel as if you are losing your mind. Confusion, disorientation, lack of concentration and unanticipated mood swings are common symptoms of trauma and grief. Some grievers complain, "I can't concentrate; I can't even read. Nothing seems to make sense anymore. I feel like I am losing my mind." Some cognitive responses can be startling, such as memory loss, recurring flashbacks or nightmares and a feeling of disconnection with reality. You may be asking yourself: *Am I going crazy?* You're not.

You have experienced an extreme shock and your brain is working hard to process and understand what has happened to you. The effort of absorbing the full shock of what has happened all at once is just too overwhelming. It is okay to give yourself (and your brain) time by being gentle and patient with yourself.

If the symptoms of memory loss or recurring flashbacks, nightmares and panic attacks are becoming chronic rather than diminishing, consult the checklists in chapter 1: *When Trauma and Grief Combine.*

Crying

CRYING UNCONTROLLABLY

Some parents who grieve their children often come to therapy reporting, "I can't seem to control my tears. I wake up crying, fall asleep crying; everything seems to trigger more tears."

Crying is a natural and healthy release of pain and sorrow. Tears are your body's unique release mechanism when you are under stress. When you feel overrun with the experience of grief and sadness, you may find that you cannot or do not wish to control your tears as you once could. All personal or social boundaries you have placed on yourself regarding the expression of tears may be broken by the depth of sadness and grief you are experiencing.

Allow this process to happen. Tears release stress hormones and function to externalize the sadness and pain you feel in your heart. Crying will come in cycles with breaks in between that allow you to regroup and rest. Try not to let the reactions of others or perceived social boundaries influence you. Repressing these feelings can impede your healing progress.

INABILITY TO CRY

Shock and numbness can make your body and mind seem like a stranger to you. You may say, along with many other grieving parents, "I can't seem to cry even though I feel so much pain and sorrow." Your way of coping may be to arrest your tears. Perhaps you are afraid that if you start crying you may never stop or perhaps you feel nothing emotionally. It is helpful to be patient with yourself and seek counsel with someone who can listen and support you confidentially and without judgment. The safety of that connection can provide the space you need to release the emotions inside of you.

Denial

When you've lost your child, your mind searches to understand something inconceivable, incomprehensible and unbelievable. Your heart and mind cannot fully process the event and denial allows for moments away from the pain. Denial often takes the form of thoughts such as, *This can't be real. I can't believe this is happening. Tomorrow when I wake up, he'll be here.* Denying what has happened means that you refuse to accept the loss and its implications and have placed a protective wall between yourself and your emotions.

Denial manifests as emotional and cognitive disconnect and can appear in many forms, depending on personal patterns. Some individuals may withdraw completely from those around them, while others will act like nothing has happened and everything is as it was before. Though denial is an adaptive coping mechanism and a natural step in the grieving process, it can also inhibit your ability to move forward in your grief. Take small steps as you move toward acknowledging the reality of your child's death.

Despair

If you are experiencing thoughts such as, *I have no reason to go on. I can't bear this pain any longer,* then you may be feeling despair that your child has died.

Throughout the grieving process moments of despair will come. At times you may feel overwhelmed by emotion; your endurance might be stretched to the breaking point and you might lose confidence in your ability to survive the tragedy or to go on without your child. Despair can manifest as a loss of interest in life and in others, low motivation and an extreme desire to be with your child.

Remember to be gentle with yourself in these moments, reach out to someone you can trust and share your feelings. If you are having thoughts of suicide or self-harm, talk to your doctor or counselor or phone your local crisis support line.

Disappointment

Losing a child is a profound disappointment and many parents often report sentiments such as, "When my son died, I felt as if all my hopes and dreams died too." When your child dies, part of your hopes and dreams for the future also end. Feeling disappointment and a loss of confidence in the future is common. You will face reminders of this disappointment in your daily life and in interactions with others that can cause strong emotional responses. For example, a parent who loses a child early in life could have trouble interacting with families that have children or might avoid certain sections of department stores because of reminders of what could have been.

You may also feel disappointed or betrayed by the systems and structures you thought you could depend on, such as doctors, hospitals, the legal system, friends, the universe and God.

The disappointment of a future without your child will remain with you, but over time your sensitivity to reminders of what you have lost will diminish. Rituals to remember your child are helpful in maintaining the presence of your child in your life and can bring peace to disappointments. (For suggestions of ways to create rituals, see chapter 14: *Creating Personal Rituals and Memorials.*)

Epiphany

Have you ever experienced a sudden manifestation or perception of the essential nature or meaning of a situation or an illuminating discovery about your life? This is sometimes called an epiphany. After losing her son, Dana, one parent, described it this way:

> *Everything I thought and believed has changed since my son*
> *was killed. What I once thought was unimportant is now*
> *important—and what I thought was so important is just small*
> *stuff. I realized how precious and temporary each moment of*
> *life and each relationship truly is.*

Losing a child is a shock to one's spiritual, cognitive and emotional systems. The emotional and spiritual vulnerability that comes with this loss makes feelings very raw and intense. Epiphanies have been described as awakening to a new perception of the world. During epiphanies, people have new realizations which lead them to sudden transformations in their worldviews and life choices.

Fear

If you are experiencing fear following your child's death, it may be connected to the circumstances of the death, particularly if they were violent. In one instant, the world no longer feels safe and predictable; bad things happen to good people. After experiencing a traumatic event, you may become uncertain about your safety, isolate yourself or fear to leave your home. Fear is a natural protective response following a trauma, although sometimes it can become uncontrollable or unpredictable. Some parents who have lost their children report, "All of a sudden, out of nowhere, I suddenly become paralyzed by inexplicable fear."

Talk about your fears with someone you trust who can support you as you sort through what is real and what is imagined. Fear can become debilitating. If you find that your feelings of isolation and fear are chronic, it is essential that you speak to a professional about what is happening. (For more information about these feelings, refer to chapter 1: *When Trauma and Grief Combine*. For information on finding a counselor and techniques to manage anxiety, see chapter 13: *Tools for Healing*.)

Flooding/Dissociation

Flooding is the sensation that your emotions are too much to contain. The ability to regulate thoughts, feelings and physiological responses is compromised, as with the human stress response (see chapter 1). You may experience an intense flood of thoughts, images and emotions combined with an increased heart rate and shortness of breath. The onset is rapid and can be activated by thoughts, environmental triggers, flashbacks or emotional cues. As Henry, one bereaved parent, put it:

> Suddenly, unexpectedly, I can feel like I'm right back at the first moment I heard she was dead; my emotions and thoughts are so intense I feel blinded by them. I feel like I'm out of my body—everything around me becomes so surreal.

The power of emotions and information inundating you may create a disconnect between mind and body, which is felt as an experience of unreality or a dream-like state. This state is called dissociation.

When flooding occurs, acknowledge what is happening, distance yourself from the situation if possible, remind yourself that this experience is temporary and take deep breaths to calm yourself. The flooding will subside as you allow your body to relax and release the built-up tension. (For an exercise to help you focus and breathe, see chapter 13: *Tools for Healing*.)

Guilt

Guilt is a feeling of self-reproach or culpability, although often people feel guilt for things they haven't done or had no control over. If your child has died, you might think, *It should have been me; why did I survive?* or *I should have . . . I could have . . . I might have . . .*

There are a number of forms of guilt that can be part of the grieving process, including:

- Believing you have failed as a parent
- Survivor guilt
- Guilt about feeling happy or feeling hope again
- Guilt about events from the past, present and future
- Guilt due to unfinished business
- Guilt due to something that happened regarding the circumstances of the death

As a parent you may feel responsible for what has happened, because you were unable to protect your child as you intended. It can feel as though you have done something wrong—that you didn't do enough, try hard enough or care enough—and are being punished.

Working toward resolving the guilt in your heart and mind will open you to possibilities for creating a new relationship with memories of your child. You can prevent guilt from becoming a lifelong burden by finding ways to release this emotion. Some suggestions are to write a letter that expresses your feelings to your child, release physical stress through exercise or talk to a close friend or professional who will help you to reflect on where the feeling of fault comes from: Are there attachments, experiences or beliefs from your past that are playing out in your grief? (For tips on emotional release, refer to chapter 13: *Tools for Healing.*)

Heartbreak

Heartbreak is defined as a crushing grief, anguish or distress. A common description of heartbreak given by grieving parents is, "It feels as though someone has ripped open my chest and cut out my heart." Your heart is understandably broken; let yourself express it through grief bursts, crying, screaming, wailing and sobbing. Your pain can feel inconsolable. The heartbreak that comes from losing a child is lifelong, not something that passes with time, and that's okay.

The degree of heartbreak you feel is a reflection of your love and eventually it will evolve to become less intense, from searing agony to a softened, remembered ache.

Helplessness

Helplessness is the sensation of having no control over the situation. You may be stunned by how you feel unable to change what has happened. When parents feel helpless, they express thoughts such as: "I don't know what to do. There is nothing I can do to change this. I have no power over this. I don't know if I can go on."

In anticipated child loss, the sensation often stems from watching your child come closer to death and not being able to stop it. With sudden loss, helplessness is often tied to the circumstances of the death and how they cannot be changed. Whether your loss was anticipated or sudden, when your child dies you are faced with a daunting challenge as a parent.

The trauma of child loss can feel as though you have been unwillingly stripped of all manner of choice in your life. Helplessness can be tied to feelings of anxiety and fear, because the sense of having lost control over your fate leaves you feeling vulnerable. A sense of helplessness can complicate grief and contribute to depression, anxiety and other more severe responses such as hypersensitivity and hyperarousal. (See chapter 1 for more information.)

Regaining a sense of control and choice in your life begins with small steps. Acknowledge yourself as you make simple choices; take as much time as you need to make decisions that resonate from your true self. Rebuild your sense of choice and control by listening to what feels right for you and following through.

Impatience

As you grieve you may find that despite your predispositions, you are extremely impatient and easily irritated with people or situations. You might identify with many clients in grief counseling who describe their emotional states this way: "I find myself growing irritable and impatient at the smallest things. My nerves are raw. I feel like I'm losing it when I start yelling or crying over simple situations. It seems like everything is driving me nuts."

You may find yourself acting out at random strangers, family and friends. Much of your focus and energy are directed toward the grieving process, which can make everyday tasks and challenges seem more difficult, fueling your impatience. Feelings of anger about your loss can also contribute to lower patience levels.

Try to recognize when you are acting impatient or are feeling agitated. Take time for yourself away from stress and pressures. When it seems like everything is an obstacle, the focused breathing technique in chapter 13 can help you to calm yourself and become more present and grounded. This will help you to cope with your challenges more effectively.

Isolation

Child loss can affect your desire to take part in social situations. You may decide to self-isolate, because you have difficulty coping with the stimulation of people, traffic and noise. The circumstances surrounding your child's death may have you feeling stigmatized or judged. You may feel estranged and alone because of your experience, but if you talked with another grieving parent, you might hear a familiar description of what you are going through: "Sometimes I wouldn't leave my house for days. I just couldn't handle being around anyone, knowing they couldn't possibly understand how I felt. I didn't want anyone to see me so messed up. I felt so alone."

It is important to take time out for yourself in order to heal. It is also important to find balance between alone time and connection with others. Give yourself space and make the choice to surround yourself with loving and supportive people. Maintaining social contact through your grief and feeling support from those who care about you contributes to your healing. If your current social network is not adequately supporting you, seek local support groups and connect with people who have had similar experiences with whom you can feel comfortable talking. (For more information on social contacts, see chapter 10: *Managing Social Relationships*.)

Jealousy

If, since losing your child, you have encountered a family with children and thought something such as *Why does their child get to live when mine died?* then you have experienced jealousy.

The sensation of jealousy is tied to questions such as *Why me?* or *Why do others get the chance to watch their children grow up and I don't?* You may feel jealous of other parents or children and the experiences they are having as you face reminders of what you have lost.

Jealousy can lead to personal judgments; it can also be acute if the person is a family member. Jealousy can manifest as hostility or resentment toward the lives that continue to move forward for others despite what has happened in your life.

In situations where you find yourself feeling jealous or perhaps acting hostile toward someone, it is okay to leave the situation. Try to recognize and acknowledge that jealousy is representing your deeper pain and longing for your child. Take the space you need to work through the emotion.

Libido

Grief is hard work, even for the libido. During grief, some individuals experience a loss of interest in sexual intimacy while others have increased sex drives. Tim, one grieving father, reflected:

> *After my daughter died, sex was the last thing on my mind, but my wife seemed to want even more closeness. I felt like I was letting her down.*

In some cases, individuals will feel the need to over-sexualize their intimate relationships out of a need for comfort and reassurance. The level of openness and honest communication a couple shares regarding sexuality and intimacy prior to their child's death will influence how they find mutual balance in their relationship as they grieve.

Respecting your partner's sexual needs will help as you navigate your grieving process. It is important to speak openly and work to find a healthy balance that helps you to maintain your loving connection with each other. Working with a professional couple's therapist can be beneficial if issues have arisen that are causing discord between you. (To further explore your relationship with your partner, including sexuality, see chapter 8: *Surviving with Your Partner.*)

Loneliness

Even if family and friends are close by, grief is a deeply personal and some-times lonely journey. You will grieve differently from those around you and you may feel that no one understands you or cares. Gina, one client in grief counseling, stated:

> *People ask me how I am and I don't know what to say. Even if I do try to answer, I know my words can never explain what I feel. Sometimes I just want to give a fake answer, because I can't bear watching them struggle with trying to understand.*

Because of the social discomfort surrounding child death, many peo-ple may be uncertain or uncomfortable about approaching you. You may feel abandoned, alone or further isolated if your child died by suicide or homicide. A few parents comment that their children's deaths rearranged their address books, an example of how death and grief can have an effect on social relationships.

Being open and honest about your needs, feelings and experience can help to guide others in how they choose to respond to you. People are thinking about you and want to help you, but they just might not know how to say it or broach the subject.

It is also very helpful to connect with circles of people who better understand your loss so you do not feel so alone. Grief support groups and writing anthologies, such as *A Broken Heart Still Beats*, are excellent sources of comfort and healing. Through hearing and reading shared expe-riences, you may find you do not feel as alone. For information on support groups and suggested readings, see the appendix and bibliography.

Longing

After a child's death there is a strong sense of longing for the physical pres-ence and life force of your child. Clients have often expressed: "All I want is to hold my son in my arms, to see his face, hear the sound of his voice and look in his eyes just one more time."

You may also long for your daily life to return to how it once was. Longing can give way to frustration, because your desire is unattainable. In response to the need to create a sense of your child's presence, you may create an altar, plant a tree, put up pictures or develop a strong connection with certain be-longings. These practices can help you to build a new sense of connection and relationship with your child and comfort your longing. (For ideas on healthy rituals, see chapter 14: *Creating Personal Rituals and Memorials*.)

Numbness

At the beginning of your grieving it may seem as though you feel nothing at all, not even anger or sadness. You may find yourself telling people, "I'm fine" or "Everything is okay." Similar to denial, emotional numbness is a natural defense mechanism of the human body and mind. Parents attending grief counseling have described it this way: "I remember days where I felt like I was watching a movie. Nothing seemed to affect me. I was empty inside. It was like I was on the other side of the screen looking out."

Following the prolonged emotional endurance of anticipated loss or the shock of a sudden loss, your body may "lock down" your response mechanisms as a protective measure. As with your emotions, your body may feel cut off, closed down, physically numb or frozen.

As you regain your ability to cope, your mind will begin to process all that has happened and gradually the numbness will dissipate. You may be surprised by the intensity of emotions as they start to arise. There is no timeline for experiencing the emotions and sensations associated with your loss and some may take a while to manifest.

If you are still feeling numb after a month or more, it is appropriate to discuss this with your physician and/or therapist. (For more about symptoms such as numbness lasting more than one month following a trauma, see chapter 1.)

Obsession

In an effort to understand what has happened, your mind might continually replay the events surrounding your child's death; you may also find that you cannot stop questioning a detail or a decision you made. This is a function of the mind common to those who have experienced a trauma. Your mind is trying to answer the questions, *What went wrong? How did this happen?*

You, like other grieving parents, might experience obsessive thinking. Judy described her experience:

> *For the first while I couldn't stop thinking about what happened and how it happened. Every little detail kept running through my head. I wondered what I could have done differently.*

It may be important to you to gather information, request copies of records or interview people who may have additional information. Other parents choose to avoid any information that might create more questions. Whichever your process, be patient with yourself. Know that making sense out of the loss can be frustrating. Over time, your obsessive rethinking of the event will decrease as your mind integrates the information cognitively and emotionally, which will lead to an acknowledgement of your loss.

Pain

Losing a child is a profoundly painful experience. You may find yourself agreeing with other grieving parents who have said, "I never knew it was possible to feel so much pain." Grief is pain; it is the acute emotional and mental distress that comes with loss. The pain can come in intense waves or feel constant. Though there is no visible wound, parents have described feeling both an emotional and physical agony. Attending to your pain can be a tool to guide healing. Treat yourself as if you have been stricken with a terrible flu or a serious physical injury. Your body and broken heart need nurturing and rest. Taking care of yourself in healthy ways, releasing your emotions and nurturing the emotional wound you have suffered will help you heal and move forward through your grief as the pain lessens in frequency and intensity.

Panic

Because of the nature of the human stress response following exposure to a trauma, the body's ability to self-regulate may be compromised (see chapter 1). This can lead to panic attacks, which Liz, one of our grieving parents, described to us:

> *The first time I was hit with the panic I was at the grocery store. My heart started racing, I saw stars, I couldn't breathe and I felt like I was having a heart attack.*

Panic attacks may also include freezing (being unable to move or think), heart palpitations, shortness of breath, dizziness, sweating, difficulty concentrating and distortion of time and space.

Recognize that this is your body's reaction to a real or perceived threat and that the panic attack will pass in moments. Take deep breaths (see the focused breathing exercise in chapter 13), sit down or move to a different environment and ground yourself. If you are with family or friends, let them know what is happening so they can help you.

Physical Responses

A myriad of physical symptoms and responses can manifest as a result of grief and trauma; your body experiences loss as much as your heart and mind do. Jennifer, a grieving mother, related her experience:

I couldn't sleep; I couldn't eat. My body was like a stranger to me. I could not figure out what was happening to me.

Here are common responses you may be feeling:

- Oversensitivity to noise
- High energy, need to exercise
- Lethargy
- Energy loss
- Weight loss or gain
- Feelings of weakness
- Nausea
- Diarrhea
- Loss of appetite
- Disorientation
- Sleep pattern disruption
- Adrenaline surges
- Tightness or lump in throat
- Heaviness or tightness in the chest
- Empty feeling in the stomach
- Dry mouth
- Sighing
- Breathlessness
- Nervous energy or restlessness
- Forgetfulness
- Loss of time perception
- Teeth grinding during sleep
- Palpitations
- Feeling "on edge"

Your immune system can also become vulnerable because of the shock to your system. Practice self-care: rest when you can, exercise, eat well, check in with your family doctor and explore alternative therapies such as naturopathy, acupuncture and massage. Remember, you have experienced a wound and need gentle care to help you heal.

Regret

A sudden death leaves no chance to say goodbye and you may be left with unresolved issues and regrets. You may find yourself thinking something like, *We hadn't spoken in over a month. I wish I had apologized after our last argument.* Your regret over unresolved issues may haunt your thoughts and interfere with your grief. This can be very challenging.

You may also experience lingering regrets about how you spent your time before your child died or what you said and how you reacted to your child.

Holding on to regrets can keep you trapped in the unchangeable past, cause further emotional wounding and slow your journey of grief. It is never too late to say what you need to say and it is healthy to express your regrets. There are many ways to help move beyond the past and release your burden. You can write a poem, letter or song to your child or you can talk with someone (e.g., a friend, counselor or minister) about your feelings. (For ideas on expressing regret, see chapter 13: *Tools for Healing*.)

Relief

When a child's death is anticipated, some parents describe feeling relief as they grieve, because their child's suffering is over. As Sharon, one parent, conveyed:

> *It was so hard to watch my son as he lost his battle with the cancer and got weaker and sicker. When he died, I felt such a surge of relief mixed with incredible sadness. Though I miss him with every cell in my body, I'm glad he is no longer in pain.*

A parent may also experience a sense of relief when a child has had issues with mental illness, addictions or criminal behaviors or if the parent-child relationship has been painful and conflicted. This can arouse feelings of guilt, because while the death stopped the suffering, the parent did not truly want the child to die.

It is important to remind yourself that your sense of relief does not derive from the death itself but from the end of your child's suffering. The source of this emotion is love and the recognition that your child is no longer in pain.

Resignation

In a moment when you are feeling miserable and alone you may think: *I guess this is the way it is going to be—I may as well get used to it.* You may feel resigned to your sadness and want to avoid healing, because you believe that would mean leaving your love for your child behind. But that is not the case.

To honor your child, commit to moving through your grief and look toward living life with cherished memories and the loving relationship with your child always in your heart.

Sadness

Some parents have reported feeling sad all the time; others have described their feelings as empty or numb. It is appropriate to feel sad when a cherished loved one dies, even for a long time. As Alicia, one grieving parent, reported:

> *It seems like I have forgotten how to feel anything but sad, even when people around me are enjoying themselves or I'm doing something that once was fun . . . I just feel so sad all the time.*

Sadness is a natural emotion that is part of being human. The depth of sadness you feel reflects the love for and loss of your child. Give yourself permission to feel sad; let the tears flow. They have incredible healing capability.

You may not feel sad right away. Feeling numb may be your way of coping with the intensity of your emotions. Remember, there is no correct way to respond. It may take a while for you to acknowledge the depth of your grief. Over time the numbness will "thaw" to acknowledge your sadness as you are more able to cope.

Seek the company of others who allow you to express your sadness without judging or "cheerleading" you. Explore activities that bring you pleasure. (For ideas, see chapter 13: *Tools for Healing*.)

If your sadness becomes a long-term emotional flatness, you may be experiencing depression. Discuss this with your physician and seek appropriate treatment to recover your emotional health. (For more information, see chapter 1: *When Trauma and Grief Combine*.)

Allowing your emotions to arise naturally and at their own pace will help you to move through your grief with grace and learn the best ways to cope with this life-changing event.

Searching

After losing your child, you may find yourself jumping to attention when you hear a familiar sound or phrase or see a person with a build similar to your child's. You may answer the door or telephone with a hope that can never be fulfilled. As some parents have explained, "Wherever I go, I keep seeing my child in familiar places and in crowds."

Your impulse to search means that your mind is still adjusting to your child's absence as you transition into a life without the physical presence of your son or daughter. Each time you think you see your child and then realize that he or she is gone, you are in the process of incorporating the reality of your child's permanent physical absence. Over time your need to search for your lost child will lessen as you find ways to establish a healthy relationship with the memories of your child.

Secondary Trauma

Because of the reactive period following the initial shock of your child's death, you are emotionally and psychologically vulnerable to additional traumas. Secondary trauma occurs during incidents related to your child's death but is not the loss itself. It can be triggered by a number of influences. In sudden death, particularly homicide, the invasion of privacy and lack of control over external institutions such as the media and the courts can further traumatize. Physical, psychological and environmental events such as thoughtless statements from others or revisiting the environment where the death occurred can also re-traumatize individuals.

Secondary traumas have to be addressed along with your original trauma. One important thing you can do is to recognize your vulnerability and limit your exposure to harmful people, places and things. Choose someone to be a spokesperson who can assume the role of communicating with the public for you. Some crime victims associations will provide an advocate who will take this role and keep you informed of what to expect regarding the criminal investigation and legal process. Working with a professional trauma counselor can help you to sort through your experiences and gain more effective coping skills.

Sense of Failure

The sense of failure that can accompany child loss can have an immense impact on personal levels of self-esteem and self-worth. Common feelings of grieving parents include, "I couldn't stop the thought that I had failed my child; it was my job as his parent to protect him and keep him alive."

Parents are "hardwired" to protect their children. When a child dies, the parent may experience an intrinsic sense that he or she has failed at being a parent. It is important to assess the causal factors outside of your control and acknowledge that if you could have prevented your child's death, you would have.

Many parents judge their grieving processes or feel impatient toward themselves. You may question your own grief and become frustrated and angry with yourself for how long it seems to be taking for you to "get back to normal." Remember that there is no timeline for grief and no right way to grieve. Urging yourself to "get over it" is unrealistic and does not support the grieving process, particularly with a child's death. This misconception can cause disappointment and increase stress, which will inhibit you on your grief journey. Allow yourself the time and space to heal at your own pace and reach out to others who can support you.

Shame

Shame includes feeling you have lost the respect of others, which may be compounded with a sense of fault or blame. A child's death can result in feelings of shame regarding how the child died or the circumstances surrounding the death. "I don't want to tell anyone he committed suicide," some parents who have lost their children in that manner say. You may also feel shame because you believe you have failed in your role as a parent.

Other people's comments about your child's death can trigger shame. These people often do not intend to cause you shame and usually have not consciously considered the impact their words may have on your tender heart. Whether such comments are well-intentioned or not, they still cause pain.

Acknowledging this emotion, working toward resolving your self-doubts and recognizing that you are not responsible for your child's death will help to free you of the feeling of shame.

Shattered Beliefs

The death of a child can turn a parent's perspective about life and the world upside down. You may find yourself struggling to make sense of your existence, future, domestic life, identity and worldview in the aftermath of your loss. Suddenly your life feels entirely out of your control and it can feel like you are no longer the same person. Parents in grief counseling have described rapid changes in the way they viewed their lives: "My world fell apart that day. Everything I knew to be my life ended. There were no rules that applied anymore." Trauma thrusts you into a complex restructuring on existential, spiritual, intellectual and psychological levels.

Individuals react in very different ways to this experience of identity crisis. You may find yourself questioning your values, beliefs or how you choose to spend your time. You may have impulses to make major changes in your life. You may feel lost. You may want to resist the changes and attempt to maintain your life as it was before. Upon realizing your life will never be the same and the future you planned is no longer possible, you may feel an additional need to mourn the life you have lost. (Shattered beliefs are further explored in chapter 11: *Experiencing Identity Loss and a Shattered Worldview*.)

Shock

Shock can be described as sensory and cognitive overload. What has occurred is greater than an individual's capacity to cope, as some parents express when they come to grief counseling: "I couldn't believe it. It was as if everything froze in time, my brain stopped working and nothing made sense. Days later I started to remember little snippets of what was said and done."

The physical sensation of shock feels as if the bottom has dropped out, your energy has been drained, you are walking in a fog or operating on autopilot. Some parents have described seeing their entire lives, past and future, passing before them in an instant.

The physical symptoms of shock are most intense in the immediate hours following a child's death or diagnosis with a terminal illness, as your body and mind react to the traumatic news. The body goes into protection mode and, in essence, you are wrapped in a numbing cushion to shield you from the intensity of what has happened. Emotional and cognitive responses are delayed and will occur over a longer stretch of time as the initial shock and numbness wears off.

There may be multiple events that further deepen your state of shock, such as medical reports informing you of failed medical treatments, police reports of the circumstances surrounding a sudden death or viewing your child's body.

Shock is your body's natural way of protecting itself and the effects will lessen as you learn to cope with the reality of your loss. With time, patience and self-care, the feeling of shock will pass.

Spiritual Change

Death reminds us of our mortality and often raises spiritual questions. In addition to shattering your worldview, the experience of loss can transform your spiritual understanding of the world. You may have mystical experiences, spiritual realizations or a completely new perspective. You may also experience a loss of faith or belief in a higher power. You may say, along with other parents who have lost their children, "I have a sense now that there are things we can't see, but are there." (To explore this further, turn to chapter 12: *Facing Spiritual Emergencies*.)

Storytelling/Need to Talk

When your child dies, you may find yourself wanting to tell your story of what happened, even if it is not related to the topic of conversation. This urge is a natural part of the healing process and talking about the story of your child allows you to incorporate the situation into your life story. Marianne, one client in grief counseling, remembered a strong impulse she had after her daughter died:

> *I was over at a friend's house when all of a sudden I found myself talking about what happened—completely out of nowhere.*

Talking about your child can also help you to feel a closer connection with him or her as you remember the life you shared together. Storytelling is also part of building a new relationship with the child you have lost, one based on memory and your living love.

Vulnerability

When a traumatic death happens, the sense that you have lost control over your life can leave you feeling wounded and vulnerable. It may seem as if nothing in the universe feels as safe or predictable as it once was. Safety and security are violated by the violent nature of sudden death, which can leave you feeling exposed and vulnerable, both physically and emotionally. You may have fears about your family's safety and respond by becoming overly protective. You may feel jumpy and reactive when in a public place. This response is called hypervigilance and can become problematic, limiting your ability to function in your daily activities. (For more information on hypervigilance, see chapter 1.) Greg, one parent who lost his child, conveyed:

> *I feel edgy and fearful when I leave the house now. I don't feel safe, like the world is full of terrible things. The other day I heard a loud noise and jumped.*

It is important to be aware of your vulnerability as you heal. Treat yourself gently, limit exposure to overstimulation, take time to reflect on the basis of your fears and employ the companionship of a trusted friend or family member.

Feeling vulnerable following a tragic loss is a natural response, but if you become disabled by your vulnerability, it is appropriate to reach out to a professional who can help you work through your fears.

Wailing/Keening

In many cultures around the world, wailing and keening are accepted practices for expressing emotional pain. Intense sobbing, wailing, laughter, shouting and screaming all involve deep breathing and exhalation combined with sounds, which stimulate the production of endorphins, the body's natural pain medicine. Loud vocal expressions can have a remarkable ability to give voice to intense emotions and produce a calming effect. Grieving parents talking about their reactions of wailing and keening have described it like this: "When I heard he had been killed the sound that came out of me was involuntary, alien; I screamed and howled for what seemed like hours. It felt like I was turning inside out."

If you are self-conscious about being heard by others, try sitting in a car or going to the beach or a mountaintop. One mother said that when she needed to vent her emotions she got in the shower and wailed, describing it as a cleansing release.

CHAPTER THREE

Exploring the Cause of Your Child's Death

Your grieving process may unfold differently, depending upon the circumstances of your child's death. Though each parent's grief is unique, there are commonalities in the way that specific modes of death shape and define parents' bereavement. In this chapter we outline the distinct challenges and situations associated with different types and causes of death and highlight how the cause of death interacts with the grieving process.

Some of the stories in this chapter express raw feelings and are graphic. If you find that while reading you are experiencing anxiety, flashbacks or discomfort, stop reading or move to another chapter; always practice self-care first.

WAS THE DEATH SUDDEN OR ANTICIPATED?

What if you already knew how your child was going to die? This is called anticipated death and it includes terminal illness, genetic disorders and other medical conditions. The parents are aware that their child will die sometime in the future. Grieving often begins at the time of prognosis and continues through and beyond the death.

In cases of sudden death, parents receive the news of death unexpectedly, without any forewarning or time to prepare. Causes of sudden death include: accident, homicide, suicide, overdose, acute medical crisis, military action or unspecified causes. Parents must cope with the often horrifying circumstances surrounding the death while being plunged into their emotional pain and grief. There is no opportunity to say goodbye, make amends or come to terms with the finality of the child's absence prior to death.

Parents' grieving processes have different characteristics depending on whether the death was sudden or anticipated. The next chart outlines some of the potential differences in a parent's experience.

Sudden Versus Anticipated Death

Sudden Death	Anticipated Death
The news comes unexpectedly, causing immediate and acute emotional and psychological disorientation and confusion.	Parents have had opportunity to build an understanding of the cause of death and the news is expected. Shock and confusion are not as acute.
Trauma response may be stronger in the early stages of grief.	Parents have endured cycles of hope and hopelessness for their child's survival. As a result, the trauma is subtler and trauma injury may occur over a longer time frame.
Emotional responses may be postponed in order to absorb the shock of the death.	Grief often begins with diagnosis. Throughout the course of the illness or disorder, parents have already begun to grieve and experience related emotions (also known as anticipatory grief).
The shock and manner of death challenge the parents' capacity to cope.	Parents absorb the reality and context of the death over a longer period of time and as a result the capacity to cope is higher.
There is no opportunity to say goodbye or resolve conflicts in the relationship.	Opportunities exist to spend quality time, say goodbye and perhaps find resolution to any conflicts in the relationship.
The onset of grief is sudden and intense.	Time spent with the child throughout the dying process has an effect on the grief process.
Parents may feel overwhelmed by unanticipated decisions and obligations regarding final rites.	Parents have the opportunity to plan and prepare for final rites.

Depending on the nature of a child's death, parents feel different levels of confusion and have different capacities to cope. According to Judith Bernstein in *When the Bough Breaks*, "while mourning following sudden death may be more complicated, often taking longer to integrate and sometimes following a more turbulent up and down course, research evidence suggests long-term adaptation is not different from that of mourners following anticipated death." In other words, although the beginning stages of grief are quite different, parents find ways to cope over the long term and are equally able to incorporate the death into their lives regardless of the circumstances.

Sudden Death

Sudden death comes without preparation or warning and in many forms. Though the breadth of this book cannot possibly touch on each form of sudden loss, it is important for parents to recognize how the circumstances surrounding their child's death will impact their bereavement. The examples of sudden and traumatic death that we discuss in this chapter highlight how circumstances can interact with parents' grieving processes.

Sudden deaths have a quality of randomness. Parents may think, *Why couldn't this have been prevented*? and may have a hard time reconciling themselves to the chance nature of the death. Some features of sudden death that may complicate parents' grief are:

- The death may have been caused by negligence on the part of the child or another person (e.g., drunk driver, poor safety or maintenance, unsafe driving).
- Parents may have to travel away from home or arrange transportation of the body.
- A criminal investigation and/or trial may be initiated.
- The person responsible for the death may not be held accountable.
- Parents may question medical services, practices or diagnoses.
- The child's body may have suffered severe injuries or may never be found.
- The media may become interested in the story.
- The sudden and sometimes violent nature of the death increases the risk of trauma responses developing into PTSD.
- The cause of death may not be explained or may remain undetermined.

You may struggle with feelings of guilt, helplessness and self-blame as you try to accommodate the chance nature of your child's sudden death and think about how it might have been prevented. Questions and imaginings about your child's last moments may haunt you. In an attempt to understand what happened, you might reconstruct events and revisit your child's actions in the height of the crisis. Finding resolution with what cannot be controlled or changed is a difficult and agonizing process. Parents confront a dramatic shift to their lives within a very short period of time.

Connect with parents who have had similar experiences. Comfort and guidance can be found by sharing your indefinable and painful grief with others who know intimately the emotional impact of a sudden death. Practice self-care and be attentive to how the circumstances of the death may be influencing your grieving process.

THE AGE OF THE CHILD

How young was your child? How much was your child dependent on you? These are important factors that will influence the kind of grieving you will experience.

The relationship between parents and children who die before or at birth is one of hopes and dreams. Parents imagine changes to their lives and characteristics of the child, but do not get to see the imagined future come to fruition. Because there is no history with the child outside of the womb, the child must be made real by the parents in their grief. Losing a child during gestation is painful and disappointing. Friends and family may not recognize the child as a "real person" or are unable to grasp the magnitude of the parents' loss. Parents can feel isolated; they may feel that their grief is not recognized.

In the life of a young child, parents are actively engaged in the caretaker role. Young children depend on parents to teach them skills and keep them safe and healthy. When a young child dies, parents often struggle with a sense of responsibility or failure in their roles as the primary caretakers. This can result in feelings of guilt, self-blame or helplessness. Changes in day-to-day routines and family roles following the child's death can also contribute to an increased sense of uncertainty and an identity crisis for bereaved parents.

During adolescence, children start to assert their independence from the family system and parents slowly wean themselves from their caretaker roles. This period can be a challenging one for parent-child relationships. Teenagers test boundaries within the family system and may express ambivalence toward their parents. There may be conflicts within the relationship or the adolescent may be troubled or experimenting with alcohol and drugs. If the child dies during the teenage years, parents' grieving processes may be complicated with unresolved conflicts or feelings. Parents may question their parenting skills and struggle to reconcile their feelings about the relationship. Adding to the sadness of the loss is that teenagers are ripe with potential and ready to make their marks upon the world; they represent years of dedication from the parents. When that potential is stolen by death, parents struggle with frustration at the futility of their efforts and the senselessness of the death.

Parents are not as actively engaged in the day-to-day activities of an adult child, but the bond between parent and child has deepened with time. The relationship has developed into one of adult to adult, with some parents defining their adult children as their best friends. Often after the death of an adult child, the focus of support goes to the spouse and children of the deceased, not to the surviving parents. Parents may struggle to assert their needs and have their grief acknowledged in social and family circles. It can be frightening and heartbreaking to let go of the expectation or hope that the adult child will be present to care for parents as they age. Loss of antici-pated milestones, such as an adult child's marriage or grandchildren, may be deeply mourned. In certain circumstances, some parents must shift back to a parenting role for their grandchildren after the death of an adult child. If the child was engaged in self-destructive behaviors or estranged from the parent, it can cause parents to question their parenting in retrospect.

No matter what age at which your child may have died, grief is pain-ful, though you may process the loss differently depending on the circum-stances. The rest of this chapter is a guide through the different kinds of grief that you might experience, depending on the circumstances of your child's death.

CAUSES OF DEATH

These sections include stories from parents who have lost children in cir-cumstances that might be similar to the ones you have experienced.

Miscarriage

At the discovery of pregnancy, parents psychologically prepare themselves for the arrival of their child and plan for associated changes in their lives. As they move through the pregnancy, they imagine what the physical and personal characteristics of their child will be and what it will be like to par-ent this new person in their lives.

Sometimes this process is cut short by miscarriage, which is defined as the loss of a fetus that occurs within the first twenty weeks of a preg-nancy. Norman Brier states in his article "Grief following Miscarriage" in *The Journal for Women's Health*:

> Unlike the loss of other family members, the grieving individ-ual has had few direct life experiences or actual times with the deceased to review, remember, and cherish. There is no publicly acknowledged person to bury or established rituals to structure mourning and gain support, and, often, relatively few oppor-tunities are present to express thoughts and feelings about the loss due to the secrecy that often accompanies the early stages of pregnancy.

When a miscarriage occurs, the woman usually is not visibly preg-nant and the expectant parents may be the only ones aware of the loss. Often, family or friends have not been informed about the pregnancy.

Cecilia, a young mother, told us about her miscarriage:

I [got pregnant] in the first month that we started trying to have a second child . . . I was six weeks along. I was at work one morning and saw blood and I knew it was a miscarriage. I went outside and sat in my car and called my husband and then my friend, who is a doctor. I was panicking about what I should do . . .

I went to the hospital, because I was really anxious to know for sure whether there was still hope. The ultrasound [showed] there were very little remains. I was in shock and felt a huge amount of loss. I cried for days. I was actually really surprised by how much it affected me. When you find out you're pregnant, you're so excited and there are so many things you think about and your life is changing. Then all that is suddenly gone . . . You wonder, Did I contribute to this? It was a process of accepting that it wasn't my fault and was something that just happened.

The cause of a miscarriage is rarely known. A woman may question her body's ability to carry children or over-think actions she performed in the early stages of pregnancy. Expectant mothers often struggle with feelings of self-blame as they try to find reasons for why this happened. Men may focus primarily on the well-being of their partners.

Miscarriages are often private and are commonly acknowledged as the loss of a pregnancy, not a child. If you experience a miscarriage, you may feel isolated in your grief and shy away from your feelings of loss. Family and friends may not know how to approach the subject. Find people to talk with who have gone through similar circumstances in order to build supports for yourself.

Stillbirth and Neonatal Death

Stillbirth occurs when a child dies within the womb between the twentieth and fortieth week of the pregnancy. Parents may or may not be aware that their child has died when the labor begins. Neonatal death occurs within the first twenty-eight days of life. The child is born living but does not survive. This small amount of time with a living child distinguishes neonatal loss from other forms of loss.

In stillbirth and neonatal death, the pregnancy has passed the first trimester, which is considered higher risk. Psychological preparation for parenthood and emotional bonding with the child has progressed. When something goes wrong, presumed guarantees about the child's safety have been shattered and parents are faced with disorienting shock. In some cases, caretakers such as medical staff or midwives are also in a state of shock, which creates additional confusion for the parents.

Ellen lost her daughter two days after giving birth:

The birth was overdue and then I went right into hard labor, but I wasn't dilating past one and a half centimeters. I had an emergency caesarian. I only saw my baby once after that. My daughter died due to severe meconium aspiration in the womb when I was in labor. She was two days old. Medical examiners didn't find anything wrong with her when they performed an autopsy. I wish, in retrospect, that I had seen her more, but I had to have a blood transfusion and was physically and emotionally wrecked.

Rachel had a similar experience due to possible complications from a birth control device:

After [my first child] was born, I had an intrauterine device (IUD) inserted, because we didn't want another baby for a while. The IUD must have moved and I got pregnant. When I first got pregnant I was very anxious, because I was told that if physicians couldn't remove the IUD, you had a high risk of miscarriage in the first trimester of pregnancy. I was told the risk of losing the baby was no more than anyone else [after the first trimester]. I chose to believe that because I didn't want to spend the pregnancy feeling anxious . . .

When I was twenty-three weeks pregnant, we were on a vacation. In the middle of dinner at a beautiful restaurant, all of a sudden I began to leak amniotic fluid. I started panicking and I said to my husband, "I need to go to the hospital now." I was very upset.

When we got to the hospital I went to the front desk and said, "I think I'm losing my baby; I need to see a physician now." The staff rushed us in. We were in a hospital in a different country and it was very unfamiliar . . . Doctors did an ultrasound and said that the amniotic sac had broken. They could try to keep pushing fluid into me and try to keep the baby inside as long as possible, but there was no guarantee. There was a strong chance that I was going to go into labor. They said the baby was too little to survive or he may survive but be severely disabled. It was a complicated mix of explanations. I went into labor a couple of hours later. As awful as the experience was, that is what needed to happen. And then my son was born and he was tiny and his heart was still beating and his legs were still moving and I held him until his heart stopped beating and his legs stopped moving.

Marlee lost her son, Bobby, although she got to spend three weeks with him:

I gave birth to Bobby . . . on his dad's birthday. At the time we wanted him to have his own birthday, but now we're glad they both have the same birthday. I was so overjoyed, because we had our daughter and [now] our son had arrived. I just thought, I'm so lucky. We had three weeks of bliss. Then Bobby couldn't settle down and wasn't sleeping. I was trying to nurse him and it wasn't working really well and he let out this strange cry . . . At about ten o'clock, he became blue around the mouth. We called for an ambulance. When we got to the hospital there was a lot of fussing . . . It turned out he had had a seizure. One doctor said, "I think he has meningitis." I knew enough about meningitis to know most of the time it was fatal. Later the specialist came in and he was lovely . . . I think I knew in my heart it was not going to be the outcome that I wanted. That evening we had Bobby baptized.

From three o'clock in the morning to two o'clock the next afternoon Bobby [suffered] severe brain damage. We waited the night and in the morning the doctor said, "There's really nothing we can do." I said, "I don't want him to suffer any more. How do we do this?" The doctor replied, "We're going to take him off life support." They wrapped him in a beautiful blanket and passed him to me. It was so nice to hold him; I had had to refrain because doctors had said it wouldn't be good for his brain. So I held him. I kept checking his heart and it kept beating. I took it as a message that he didn't want to leave and that was comforting in that moment. I held him and after a while he stopped breathing. I could have stayed there for the rest of the day and probably weeks after. We went from happiness to trauma in less than two days and we had to let him go. He was only six pounds, but he was very strong and very gentle. I think he would have been a very gentle man.

Returning from the hospital without a baby after months of preparation leaves the house and the future feeling vacant. The child who was meant to mark a transformation in your life and future did not survive. Where there was hope and planning there is now an empty crib. It is distressing to readjust your expectations and release the future for which you hoped.

Because you had limited time with your child in and outside of the womb, it can be hard to know how to mark the death. Some parents hold funerals or memorial services, others choose to do nothing. The death of a baby does not fall into the "normal" range of funeral rites within our society. Do what feels natural to you. There are many meaningful ways to mark the death of a child.

You may have an ideal vision of who your child could have been in an imagined future, but recognizing your child as the person he or she was in his or her short lifetime allows you to connect with your child in an authentic manner. Mothers and fathers who lose children in the neonatal period have brief opportunities to get a sense of the personality and character of their children, but much is left undiscovered. Part of your work is to build a realistic vision of your child in your heart and mind.

The death of a child in the womb or closely following birth often is not fully understood or even acknowledged within society. Family and friends are probably unsure of how to support you or how to react. They may consider the grief as less painful than when losing an older child. Family and friends did not have an opportunity to develop a relationship with your child and, as a result, may feel sorrow but are unsure how to convey it. Challenges and feelings you may face with stillbirth or neonatal loss include:

- Loss of expectations and dreams
- Grief that is disenfranchised or unacknowledged
- Feelings of inadequacy as a parent
- Uncertainty about appropriate ways to mourn or honor your child
- Trauma from the medical crisis
- Self-blame
- Changes in sexual intimacy
- Fear of becoming pregnant
- Stress and fear in subsequent pregnancies
- Risk of transposing unhealthy expectations and fears on subsequent children

Mothers may question their actions during their pregnancies or their capacity for childbearing. They also may have to face the physical "ghosts" of the pregnancy such as uterine cramping, weight gain, bleeding or the arrival of breast milk without a child to suckle. The grief of fathers is commonly under-acknowledged in stillbirth and neonatal loss. Men can sometimes focus on the well-being of their partners and neglect their own grief.

Terminal Illness

Sometimes parents may see their children taken away by terminal illness. Terminal illness can unfold over years, with cycles of illness and good physical health.

The moment of diagnosis may be more shocking than the death itself. As the illness progresses, parents prepare mentally for the anticipated death, often imagining the death and its outcomes in an effort to deal with their grief. This may happen in stages, progressively. When parents adapt to the reality of the impending death, they often experience anticipatory grief (grief emotions in advance of the death) as the inevitability of the demise becomes clear.

Dania recounted losing her daughter:

Genevieve was twenty-nine. I had been through breast cancer five years before. We were talking on the phone and she told me she had a little lump on the top of her breast. I said, "I think you better go and see a physician as soon as possible, so you'll find out it's okay." She went the next day to the doctor. They were amazingly quick at getting the biopsy done and after the biopsy getting her to an oncologist . . . It was stage three [cancer]. She quickly elected to get a double mastectomy. Everything seemed to be fine.

[A few months later] she had been having really bad headaches and they discovered that the cancer had moved into her central nervous system: her spinal cord as well as her brain. I was also re-diagnosed with stage four cancer during the same week. It was so hard to be worried for us both and also going through chemotherapy, while she was going through chemo and failing quickly. She lived fifteen months from her first diagnosis.

It was really hard for fifteen months to watch my child keep her head up and be so strong and brave even when she knew she didn't have a chance. It seems so unfair. We had to see her through epileptic seizures and other horrible things and yet she still kept so much grace about her and all kinds of beautiful people rallied around us.

Alex told a similarly painful story:

My daughter Shaughnessy was diagnosed in February with t-cell lymphoblastic lymphoma. The next eight months we went through hell . . .

The tumor was in the center of her chest and it was pushing on her lungs . . . She underwent heavy full-body chemotherapy [and] a bone marrow transplant. I lived with her the whole time and we moved to [a new city] to take care of her. I walked away from my job . . . because she had an 80 percent chance of survival and it would take about a year before she got well. Early August she had another CT scan; it looked as if everything was good. We went to see the oncologist and everybody shook hands, although Shaughnessy didn't seem quite convinced . . .

At the end of August we had a "Live Strong Shaughnessy" party with the people who had helped us. She didn't want to get up that morning; she was really tired. The next day she wanted to go for a walk, but it was painful from the start . . . She had another CT scan which found a tumor. A few days later they identified that the cancer had spread into her blood.

> *Mid-October she was admitted to the cancer agency. The*
> *oncologist saw us the first day, but he never came back. He*
> *sent another fellow to say, "There is nothing more we can do,*
> *Shaughnessy." He talked with her in private and when I came*
> *back I asked what he said. Shaughnessy said, "I have maybe two*
> *weeks . . . Mom, you have to understand that this is my decision.*
> *The pain is too great. I just need to let go; I'm not going to go on*
> *any more chemo." I said, "Whatever you need to do, Shaughnessy.*
> *I'll go with it." She died shortly after. She was twenty-nine when*
> *she died. Eight months of hell she went through for really nothing.*
> *Before that she was a healthy young woman.*

Caretaking is a demanding process, wearing on a parent emotionally, physically and mentally. If you have witnessed your child suffer and die from a terminal illness, you may have:

- Faced cycles of hope and uncertainty regarding your child's survival
- Witnessed the physical transformation and decline of your child
- Endured a rollercoaster of temporary recovery and return to illness, sometimes on a day-to-day basis
- Made treatment decisions on behalf of your child
- Discussed final rites and potentially resolved unfinished business with your child
- Managed shifting roles and disruption in the family system
- Coordinated supports to meet the requirements of the treatments, doctors and post-surgery recovery
- Said goodbye before the death or been with your child at the time of death
- Experienced a series of losses in advance of the death, such as a loss of lifestyle, loss of dreams for your child or loss of a job
- Balanced the ongoing needs of your family with the needs of your sick child
- Undergone financial stress and strain
- Experienced emotional or physical burnout and fatigue
- Managed positive and negative interactions with the medical system
- Faced geographic displacement or a need to travel in order to take care of your child
- Struggled with unanswerable questions such as "Why not me?" or "Why my child?"
- Felt helpless to stop your child's physical pain
- Witnessed your child's struggle with the challenges and emotions of facing illness and death

During the time of caring for a terminally ill child, many parents express a sense of gratitude for the service they received in the hospital and in palliative care. But for others, medical systems can be a source of anger, misunderstanding, frustration or hurt. The medical system is bound by the confines of policy, science and everyday duties. While you are in a hyper-sensitive state and in the midst of a very personal experience, medical personnel go about their routines, trying to serve many people at once. After the death, you may seek resolution to unanswered questions regarding the diagnosis and treatment approaches. Although knowledge about treatments can bring comfort and understanding, there is risk that grief will be postponed if you invest too much energy in legal or technical matters. Take note if searching for answers is dominating your focus.

The time that passes from prognosis to death allows parents to address unfinished emotional concerns with their child. You may have spent quality time with your child or have taken the opportunity to tell your child what she or he means to you. Fulfilling these opportunities can help parents cope after the death. If the opportunity to share feelings or be present was missed, you may be feeling some guilt or regret.

Parents have described feeling a sense of relief and peace mixed with a deep sadness at the time of death. The nightmare has ended; your child no longer suffers and can finally rest. Your recovery from the ordeal requires healing from the exhaustion and restoring your reserves. Practice extreme self-care as you move forward.

Genetic Disorders

There is a wide range of genetic disorders that can have different impacts upon the healthy functioning of a child. Hence, the experience of parents is unique depending on the condition of the child. Certain genetic disorders affect the course of pregnancy, which leaves parents with heartbreak—and sometimes tough decisions. Some genetic disorders limit life expectancy to less than three months, while others require ongoing medical treatment to extend life. Some children are born with a shortened life expectancy but can live into adulthood.

Genetic testing is available to parents during pregnancy. When the tests come back positive, parents are faced with the difficult decision of whether or not to terminate the pregnancy; they must weigh a series of questions about the quality of life for their child and family. Terminating the pregnancy may also conflict with ethical and religious beliefs. If you made the decision to terminate a pregnancy, it can add complexity to your grief. Because of the distinct role you had in your child's death, you may be feeling a sense of guilt, shame and responsibility. You may also be faced with disagreement from family or friends who have opposing opinions on the best course of action. As a result, your support system may be compromised. Seek support through medical professionals and support groups.

Kristeen told her story:

We were debating, researching and questioning why and how we needed to do genetic testing and if it was necessary . . . The midwife made us an appointment for a nuchal translucency screening which is lower risk than an amniocentesis test, 95 percent accurate and noninvasive. They do a measurement of the fluid behind the baby's neck and measure the nose. Everything was fine and it was exciting to see the baby. It was our first child so it was new and exciting. They did a blood test and we waited for a long time. Finally they asked us to come back in an hour. They gave us the results: There was a 90 percent chance that our baby had Trisomy 18. Later I learned that this is a genetic disorder caused by the presence of all or part of an extra eighteenth chromosome.

I just lost it. It was really sad and unfair. But it was a screening and I still had faith that it could be okay. So we had a [diagnostic] test done. We weren't going to do anything until it was a 100 percent diagnosis . . . It was confirmed that the baby had Trisomy 18. My husband and I went through [the] process of weighing the pros and cons. It almost felt like it wasn't much of a discussion. We were both on the same page of "This means he's going to die." I wasn't willing to go through having a baby die at birth. We just were very reclusive and kept it private. It was about me and my husband. We had a week to make a decision; otherwise I would have no choice but to deliver the baby . . . We terminated the pregnancy when the baby was still thriving with a heartbeat and doing fine. Everything was good except the genetic test. Originally we weren't going to find out the sex, but because he was going to die we did; we felt that was a connection to him. We tried to name him [but couldn't]. For us, it was a memory or a feeling that was more powerful than anything else.

Genetic disorders that require ongoing medical treatment or long-term caretaking demand that parents change their family routines to focus on the needs of the child. The constant fear of a worsening condition or death can also increase the stress and fear that parents feel while the child is living. Parents carry the burden of ongoing worry that the child will succumb to the physical challenges of the disorder. If you have lost a child due to a genetic disorder, you may be struggling with the loss of your caretaker role and find it difficult to establish new routines. Parents whose children have died from genetic disorders experience a myriad of emotions, including:

- Guilt or a sense of responsibility regarding the death because of the connection to genetics and ancestry
- Guilt or shame because of a terminated pregnancy
- Anticipatory grief
- Loss of identity or uncertainty due to loss of caretaker roles and routines
- Relief that the child's suffering has ended
- Stress due to financial strain
- Exclusion due to social stigma or assumptions regarding the disorder

When children are born with genetic disorders, they often have a special place in the hearts of parents and strengthen family units; family and friends often rally around these special children, who often exude a unique strength in spite of challenges. The depth of these exceptional relationships can add to the intensity of the loss.

Homicide

Sometimes the unimaginable happens when parents discover that a child has been targeted by violence. Violent deaths are particularly traumatic because of the frightening feelings they create. The event overpowers coping mechanisms, activating the fight or flight response which shuts down cognitive functions. (For more information on the human stress response, see chapter 1.)

Kate shared a story that was unusual and chilling because of the mysterious circumstances in which her daughter died:

> My daughter Stephanie was murdered in Indonesia. She was twenty-two years old. She was wonderful; she was the youngest of my three children. When she came home to her apartment she discovered a burglar inside. There was a struggle. She was stabbed and she ended up bleeding to death on the stairway; she was trying to get away. I still don't believe it and there is this unknown aspect. I know how she died, but I don't know how long it took her to die.
>
> I went to Indonesia to get her . . . I got to see the crime scene, which they hadn't cleaned, and the autopsy pictures . . . We saw her body [at the morgue] . . . We tried to piece it together. I went with her stepfather. We were exhausted; we didn't even eat . . . we were so tired. It was a whirlwind and that was good, because we didn't have much time to think about anything. When we did have time, we ran thoughts by each other.

There was a lot of media . . . and we felt a lot of skepticism about whether we were actually going to be told the truth . . . like maybe it was a cover-up. So it was really difficult to see what we were seeing and believe what we were believing and then read what was being said in the media.

I had to keep it together. I have no family except my husband. No brothers or sisters; I've lost both my parents. I had to keep going for my surviving children as their only support person . . .

I had to go back to Indonesia for the trial. I was operating on some other energy. I didn't come down from that for a while. I went, I asked questions, I was . . . removed from my feelings, I couldn't break down. I felt I had only one chance, right then. I had to go back and forth to Indonesia for the trial; the whole process took a year.

My husband couldn't deal with it and he was actively not taking care of himself . . . he just died six months ago. I was with him when he died. Because we originally went to Indonesia together, he was the only person [I had] to talk to about it. The day after he died I started having panic attacks . . . my body took over. These last few months have been even harder, because [my] compartmentalizing [is breaking apart]. It's this rollercoaster that I'm so sick of being on.

Bereavement following a homicide brings unique elements to parents' experience. Parents must face the reality that someone purposefully or negligently killed their son or daughter, often in violent ways. Grief responses are compounded with layers of intense emotional, physical and psychological reactions that overwhelm parents' abilities to cope. Victims of homicide also endure outside intrusions, practical challenges and social stigma that complicate the grieving process. Murder is profoundly senseless. Parents speak of the futility and the frustrating sense that their child's death was preventable. There is no rationale and no part of it is acceptable.

Knowing someone caused undue harm to your child can be horrifying. You must grapple with the incomprehensible, with the seeming impossibility that someone could harm your child with intention and malice, wondering if your child experienced terror or was made to suffer intentionally. You may be compelled to work through an internalized fantasy of your child's last moments of life. You subjectively feel your child's death happen, which creates a resounding sense of helplessness.

Parents describe the first thoughts in their minds as, *There must be a mistake; this can't be true.* The death may have been at the hand of a stranger, acquaintance or family member, which shatters your assumptions of safety and continuity in the world. Nothing has prepared you for this intensity of psychological trauma. You may search for more information, leading you to ask questions in an attempt change the story of what has happened. As time passes, you will ask questions that will help you to construct the timeline and elements of your child's death. Though you may not come to a place of resolution, you will gain answers that help you to comprehend what has happened. You will begin to process the reality through creating a story you can incorporate into your worldview.

Kathy related her story about her adult child:

> *My daughter Tammy was thirty-three when she died. Her second husband was a very strange guy. We think she thought a husband would help her with her three children; she also had a chronic illness, so she was tired a lot. Her husband threatened her and she went to the police and got a restraining order. They had been married for only four months. I don't know what happened after that but he came back . . .*
>
> *Tammy's oldest child was in school. Her husband brought the other two over to my house and then went back to their house and murdered her . . . He drugged her and the autopsy report said there were seven blows from a pickaxe. He obliterated her face. I hear that kind of violence is common with somebody who's jealous . . . He could never get to her level, because she was very bright, very accomplished and the three kids were just great. The police arrested him and he was put on trial.*
>
> *You're expected to be a witness and get up on the stand and talk about what happened. And all the time this crazy man is sitting there looking at you. When I got on the stand I thought, You're not getting away with this. I was very good actually. My other daughter was looking in the window; she couldn't come in [the courtroom], because she may have had to testify. He was convicted of first-degree murder, but he's in [a mental health prison], a sort of fun place where he's serving out his last years. We feel there was no justice for what he did; it's just crazy. Tammy was a wonderful mother and she really loved her children. I've always thought, If I'd helped her more with the kids, she wouldn't have married this guy.*

It is common for parents to have murderous impulses and rage toward the killer. They may have elaborate fantasies of revengeful acts that they consider carrying out if given the chance. Parents are often shocked and frightened by these impulses, which are in conflict with their values and beliefs. They may withdraw in shame, thinking, *Am I as hateful as the murderer?* It is important to release these fantasies and impulses in healthy ways with the support of a trained professional. Shifting the destructive energies toward effective and constructive activities can enable a sense of empowerment. Explore what you *can* do within the limitations of your circumstances. Part of your internal struggle is to overcome helplessness and regain your sense of personal power.

Circumstances surrounding the death and the aftermath can keep parents in an aroused state that renders them more vulnerable to long-term trauma injury. Trauma response interferes with one's ability to function and complete normal tasks such as to problem solve, retain information, make decisions or plan. The intensity and duration of initial trauma responses can provoke post-traumatic stress responses such as repeated intrusive traumatic memories, nightmares, hypervigilance, hyperarousal and fear of being in public places. Trauma response takes precedence over grief and can prolong and complicate your recovery. (For more information, see chapter 1.)

Common emotional, cognitive and psychological reactions that you may experience include:

- Frustration due to the preventability of the death, your inability to reverse what has happened or the ineffectiveness of the justice system
- Fear and vulnerability due to losing your sense of safety
- Perception that life is meaningless or pointless
- Helplessness and powerlessness
- Feeling of failure as the parental guardian, nurturer and protector for your child
- Deep sense of shame
- Self-blame and guilt
- Pervasive fear for the safety of surviving children and family members
- Terror and shock
- Emotional and psychological overwhelm
- Violation
- Physical and emotional paralysis
- Denial and numbness
- Confusion
- Anger toward:
  ▷ Oneself for not preventing the death
  ▷ One's child for putting himself in the situation or for dying
  ▷ One's partner for not foreseeing or preventing the death
  ▷ The perpetrator
  ▷ God/the universe
  ▷ The media
  ▷ The criminal justice system

In addition to the emotional and psychological shocks of your loss, you will be confronted with numerous external factors related to homicide investigations and criminal trials. When your child has been murdered, you may have to undergo:

- Criminal investigations and trial processes
- Intrusion by the media
- Re-traumatization through exposure to details of the murder in the media and trials
- Restricted access to your child's body and delayed funeral rites
- Upheaval of your personal life
- Financial stressors
- Social stigma about the murder or your child's involvement in a crime

If your child was murdered, it is important to recognize that the circumstances of your child's death were out of your control and if you had any chance to alter the outcome, you would have. Gathering information, sorting through your feelings and reconstructing your emotional resiliency forms a foundation upon which you can make meaning from your loss. Little by little, as your mind is able to grasp and adapt to more information, you will feel less overwhelmed. The key words are time and patience. Acknowledge that some things are out of your control. Focus on what you can accomplish and influence. You cannot change what has happened, but you can make everyday choices about how you cope with this experience.

The path to regaining a sense of safety, control and power in your world begins with the first step. Explore what you can do, express what choices you can make and build one upon the other. Your choices may be as simple as deciding to take a walk or as profound as deciding to prevail through your ordeal.

Suicide

What if your child took his or her own life? In his book, *Why Suicide?*, Eric Marcus describes the literal definition of suicide as "deceptively simple" and comments that it has many different meanings for the loved ones of suicide victims. He broadens the definition by adding the many words people have used to characterize it, such as:

> tragic, shocking, horrifying, enraging, mysterious, a relief, a shame, a stigma, a shattering legacy, a cry for help, a release from pain, selfish, heroic, insane, a way out, the right choice, the last word, punishment, revenge, a protest, a weapon, a political statement, tempting, desperate, upsetting, unsettling, a mistake, angry, hurtful, dramatic, a cop-out, devastating, and unforgivable.

Suicide can result from an outright action that abruptly ends life or from less direct behaviors and choices that are equally fatal, such as substance addiction. Parents must grapple with the reality that their child's choice to end his or her life was deliberate. Parents' grief is interwoven with feelings of guilt, shame, self-blame, anger, rejection, confusion, helplessness, denial and crushing hurt. The complexity of these emotions is a stark reminder that bereaved parents are particularly victimized by this type of death and are susceptible to intensified and conflicted grief.

We spoke with Judith and Phil who shared their story of their son's suicide. Judith spoke first:

> *Kevin was thirty-seven when he died. He was in a complicated situation. His wife had died four years before and he was threatening to take his life then . . . He was hospitalized for six weeks and put on antidepressants. He came out of there in the best condition he had been in many years. Initially the medications helped him. He was doing well for about a year . . . Then he began calling me and it was one bad day a week, then two . . . It came to the point that he wasn't having one good day out of seven. His doctor suggested that since he had done so well on the medications initially, he should just keep taking them.*
>
> *On Valentine's Day he came into my room, but he wouldn't come near me, hug me or touch me, which was pretty unusual. He was in a strange mood. I was doing a lot of listening and he kept gazing away, which reminded me of people who are dying and they're already looking out and beyond. Something was strange about that whole time and I don't know why I didn't catch it . . . He told me that his life amounted to nothing, he left a good job, he was destitute and he had no place to go. He said, "There's nothing left." I should have realized at that point something was very wrong, but we had been with him in so many situations in which he struggled that I think we got to the point where we felt he had to take responsibility for his own life. I should have recognized how serious it was, but I didn't.*
>
> *Late in the afternoon the police came to the door and said they had officers in helicopters looking for Kevin, because [his girlfriend] received a phone message from him saying, "I have a box in your garage that is for my mom that has the last twenty years of my life in it. Would you give that to her? I love you and goodbye." She went over to his place and found a whole bunch of notes . . . full of anger and everything else crunched up. In the last one was a message to me that read, "Mom, forgive me." The*

authorities told me, "We have a suicide note from your son" and
I looked at my husband and said, "He's dead."

 The authorities looked for him. We looked; everyone
looked. His car was white and it had snowed that night. For
over a month we waited and watched.

 In March, we got a phone call and the police asked us if we
could come down to the station. When we got there I could tell
by their faces. When I saw his girlfriend crying, I knew he was
dead . . . At the time our house was on a lake and right across
the lake there was a high peak and a steep embankment. He had
driven between two poles and gone over this embankment with-
out a seatbelt and without any drugs or alcohol in his system.

 I was reeling . . . It felt to me like when you have a baby
and you go through the labor pains to bring that baby into life;
well, it felt like the labor pains were worse than that, but I was
letting go . . . it was like the labor pains were so intense and
with time they would loosen . . . it was labor pains in reverse.
It was the epitome of that anger and denial, that screaming. I
wanted to deny that he was actually dead.

After Judith finished telling her version, Phil talked about his experience of losing their son:

My emotions right after I found out: I was a bit confused, but
I was trying to be present for Judith. There was no comfort-
ing her at first; she just had to get out what she had to get out.
The sounds that I heard come out of her were unlike any I had
heard, almost like animal sounds, coming from her insides . . .
I knew it wasn't just screaming; it was an expression coming
from a place inside her where you don't touch very often. I
didn't discard it or diminish it. I guess that we were waiting for
this sudden message to . . . register . . . absorb. After about ten
minutes the officers asked, "Are you ready to listen?" and we sat
at the table and they told us they had found Kevin's car at this
location and he had been identified and that was it. We just left.

 Afterwards I asked our son's doctor about the antidepres-
sants and he blamed us for Kevin's death. I couldn't believe this
man and his total absence of medical ministering skill at a time
like that. I didn't hold the pen to the paper of the prescription
pad; it was almost a complete divestiture of responsibility . . . I
was hurt by it because I thought this person . . . doesn't under-
stand . . . doesn't get it. I just left his office.

The vast majority of society looks upon suicide with fear and a lack of understanding. When confronted with a suicide death, the first questions are often: Why? What was wrong? Friends and acquaintances may seem uncomfortable talking about your child's death. Parents can interpret stigma and social recoil as a judgment that they failed to help, have done something wrong or didn't care enough. Fear of judgment can motivate families to hide the cause of death, which promotes isolation and self-contempt. Shame cripples emotional movement and can freeze bereaved parents in a holding pattern that prevents healthy grieving.

Survivors see suicide as the ultimate rejection of life, family, the future and hope. You may feel tormented, wondering if the act was intended to punish your actions or if it was a statement that your love and parenting were insufficient. It may take a long time to come to terms with your feelings. Recognize that the actions of your child were self-directed and formed from her or his own inner experience.

If your child died by suicide, you may experience some of these situations, reactions and issues:

- Thoughts about what you could have done differently
- Trauma injury caused by discovery of the body, witnessing the suicide or cleaning the death scene
- Criminal investigation, including invasion of privacy and potential treatment as a suspect
- Erosion of self-esteem due to feelings of self-blame, guilt or shame
- Unshakable sense of failure for not being able to prevent the death
- Relief due to the end of a long struggle with mental illness, addiction, chronic pain, illness or relationship conflicts that have exhausted your emotional resources
- Fear that surviving children and family members may also commit suicide
- Rifts between members of the family system due to judgments, fears or lack of communication
- Anger
  - ▷ At yourself for failing to prevent the death
  - ▷ At your child for abandoning life and leaving unanswered questions
  - ▷ At the systems that failed to help (e.g., doctors, clinics, therapists)
  - ▷ At God/the universe

Suicide can exert stressors on a fragile family system and create destabilizing ripples of blame or silence that estrange relationships. For some families, losing someone to suicide may introduce issues such as:

- Adults may decide to hide the truth about the death from surviving children.
- Exposure to the concept of suicide as a solution to suffering can increase the risk of suicide for surviving family members.
- Survivor guilt or self-blame can be prevalent among surviving children.

Being open to each other's individual grieving styles, avoiding hurtful actions such as placing blame upon one another and talking about the suicide honestly will help a family to survive this painful experience. As a parent, is important to remain alert and dispel any misconceptions or untruths that arise within your family.

The death of a child by suicide is not easy to grieve; you may have to work through a maze of emotions, questions and reactions. The more direct and truthful you are about how your child died, the more you will foster your own capacity to cope with and come to terms with the cause of death. This is not a journey parents need to travel alone. It is important to reach out to a trusted advisor who can guide you to a more honest and balanced view about your child's suicide. This will help you make peace with your child. There are many sources of support available to you, such as survivors of suicide support groups and suicide hotlines.

Military Death

Many military families have lost their sons or daughters to war. People who serve in the military know the level of risk that comes with their tours of duty. It is a conscious choice to join the military and they want to serve. Parents are keenly aware of the risks their children face and listen anxiously to any reports of military actions, wondering if their children have been injured or killed. Enlisting is a choice that their children have made and though they have chosen to risk their lives on behalf of their countries, they ultimately did not choose to die. Maureen told the story of the death of her son, Andrew:

> Andrew was in the back of a G-wagon in Afghanistan coming back from a supply delivery . . . He had volunteered to go back out that day. It was a routine run that was only going to take a day, out to Spin Buldak and back . . . On the way back their G-wagon was rammed by a truck with a suicide bomber. We believe the suicide bomber was a seventeen-year-old . . . The G-wagon was pushed over onto its side. The two soldiers in the front were able to get out and they were basically uninjured. They tried to get Andrew out and they couldn't and the G-wagon went up in flames. The suicide bomber was killed and Andrew was killed. All the soldiers had to stand around while [the vehicle] burned

with my son in it. I believe that Andrew was killed on impact; I
have to. And I believe that before the fire hit the G-wagon, he had
already heard the words, "Well done, my good and faithful son."

The first few days after his death were frantic, especially
because the military was involved. The phone rings all the time. The
media is on you too, wanting to know your reaction and what you're
doing. You're in this state of shock. And you're being told what to
do . . . you become almost puppet-like. All the plans for ceremonies
are set for a date depending on when they can get the body home.

When it was time for the funeral I was asked what I
wanted Andrew dressed in. Because of this I thought there was
a body . . . a burnt body. For months I woke up with nightmares
of how badly burnt his body was. All I wanted to do was hold
his hand and they told me I couldn't. They didn't tell me he had
literally been cremated in the explosion. When I found out there
was no body it was almost a relief, because I could stop having
the nightmares . . . it was easier to deal with . . . He was gone.

When you're killed in service to your country, you don't
just belong to your family anymore; you belong to the country.
You have to understand that. It's hard . . . and you can close
out a lot, but you can't close it all out . . . because it's not just
you who's grieving. It's all his buddies, his unit, his comrades
who may have never even known him . . . There's a brother-
hood that's bigger than family . . . it's bigger than you are . . .
it's respectful to his buddies to allow them the opportunity to
grieve . . . There is huge military protocol and it's very respect-
ful. I don't think you can deny your [loved one] that respect.

Military death is not always a result of direct hostile action. Soldiers can die in random accidents during training exercises, while on leave, as a result of friendly fire, from illness and also by suicide.

Parents are pulled in many directions when a child dies in service to her or his country. The shockwaves of a military death send ripples of grief into the hearts of family, comrades, commanders, communities and nations. When the news comes, parents are suddenly caught up in a whirlwind of military protocol and public reaction. As a result, parents may put aside their grieving until the public reaction fades. It is then that the intensity of personal grief overtakes parents, potentially leaving them feeling isolated and alone. You may have to endure these challenges:

- Your family's grief is exposed in public memorials and funerals.
- Information about the death may be inaccessible due to classified investigation.

- Bureaucratic processes may delay information about actual events.
- The media intrudes on your family.
- You are subjected to ongoing, assumptive or incorrect media reports that re-traumatize.
- Your child's body may not be found.
- Due to extent of injury, you may not be permitted to view the body.
- You endure private and public exposure to conflicting or judgmental political views regarding the value of your child's involvement in the military.
- The perpetrator may not be identified.
- You attend military functions and memorials in a state of shock and disbelief.
- Emotional overload occurs as you are drawn into the responses and needs of military personnel.
- There is an interplay of pride and pain, guilt and anger, resolve and distress.

Parents have found tremendous healing through connecting with others who have experienced a military loss. There are resources for supportive networks available through your military liaison as well as international nonprofit organizations.

Eventually you will be able to move away from the broader aspects of your child's involvement in the military. It may be important when that time comes, after the military ceremony and public reaction has settled, to hold a private ritual or memorial that allows you to express and honor your own intimate relationship with and grief for your child. Seek balance in your grief between honoring your child as a fallen soldier and as the unique person with whom you shared life.

Accidental Death

Lynn told us of losing her daughter to a car accident:

> [My twenty-six-year-old daughter] Ada had a traumatic head injury . . . It happened on the way back from a concert . . . She was thrown out of the back of an SUV that hit a guard rail. The two girls were sleeping in the backseat and were not wearing seatbelts and were thrown out the back window; one girl was injured and survived, but Ada's head must have hit something very hard. I got the call at three-thirty in the morning. We left right away and got to her . . . she was being well looked after . . . We never got to see her face . . . They had it covered . . . but I had her warm hand to hold. She was gone.

Annette shared the story of how she lost her daughter:

I lost my daughter Marie. She was in a single-vehicle car accident. Her car went off the road just one street over from where she lived, hit a tree and toppled over . . . She hit her neck and she suffocated instantly. We have no evidence of hard braking in the car, so we figure her foot hit the gas pedal instead of the brake. My son-in-law called me at six in the morning and told me. She was forty-three years old.

Joanna's story revealed her daughter's death in an accident that happened on the job:

Jane was an instructor in England for an outdoors program. She went out one cold winter morning and was waiting for her coworker to arrive. She prepared the zip line for her first client, a paraplegic boy sent by the local government. These kids are given outdoor experiences with trainers in the forest on a regular basis to keep their spirits up. Jane was phenomenal at this work. She went up onto her zip line and she put her harness on wrong. By the time the client and the coworker arrived, she was hanging up in the trees, caught by her harness, dead. She had been strangled by her own harness. She was so selfless and worked so very hard. I think she was just very tired and she made a mistake. She was always phenomenal on safety . . . it was just one of those human errors that can kill you.

Sudden Unexplained Infant Death Syndrome (SUIDS/SIDS)

Angela, a young mother, recounted to us how she lost her son unexpectedly:

My son Aaron died when he was two years and two months old; doctors never [determined] the cause of death, so I was left with not knowing what happened. The hardest thing was that it was unexplainable and I felt helpless . . . After I had my daughter I remember looking [at her] the first day and thinking, Do I have to go through this again? I waited for the anniversary of her turning two years old and just prayed that she would get beyond the lifespan of my firstborn.

Acute Medical Crisis

Brea lost her son due to a different sort of medical crisis:

My son Sean died on Easter Sunday. We spoke with him that night and he went to bed and never woke up. He had silent

*pneumonia [that] he didn't know he had . . . He was an actor
and his rhythm of sleep was always off, because he had to work
such strange hours. So he took a sleeping pill to stabilize it and
the effects of the sleeping pill combined with a pain medication
he took reduced his respiration even more and he just stopped
breathing. He was thirty-nine and we were very close.*

MULTIPLE DEATHS

Experiencing grief when you have undergone multiple losses is especially
difficult. When more than one child or family member dies at the same
time, parents are barraged by emotions and may be overwhelmed with
grief. It can be difficult to determine the source of emotions or identify
for whom you are grieving. Multiple losses increase the risk of extended
or complicated grief. The potential for post-traumatic stress disorder and
survivor guilt intensifies if the parent witnessed the deaths or was involved
in the circumstances. Mia lost both of her children:

*The children were premature girl twins, extremely underweight
but with no immediate signs of deformities. That they were
twins was also unexpected. I gave birth to one daughter and everyone left the operating room other than one nurse. The second
daughter was a breach birth and a total surprise.*

*I only saw my daughters one time. Then I sat in my hos-
pital room and waited for news. I don't know if doctors did any
emergency surgery to try to keep them alive or maybe they just
let it happen. In those days two-pound children didn't generally
survive although less than three months later a little girl born at
one and a half pounds survived in Montreal. The hospital chose
not to inform us of their deaths until both were gone. I know
they were alive the first few hours after birth. The second died
around twelve hours after birth.*

I gave them beautiful names and dreamed about them.

Some parents have to face the death of more than one child but not
at the same time. If another of your children dies, you may experience a
resurgence of the trauma, grief and feelings that you felt for your first loss.
How well you are able to cope with the second loss will be affected by the
experience and degree of grief work you have done in relation to the first.
If unresolved emotions exist, the grief for the two children can combine.

The complexities and layers of multiple loss can cause emotional and psychological overwhelm.

Overwhelm from the loss may block a parent's ability to cope. Aspects of multiple losses that can complicate bereavement are:

- Multifaceted emotions and grief reactions that are difficult to sort through
- Feelings of a loss of control
- Ongoing numbness and confusion
- Substantial risk of emotional burnout or overwhelm
- Potential for PTSD or complicated grief (see chapter 1)

To cope with multiple deaths, you will need guidance and support to separate out each loss and address the emotions, reactions and feelings related to each individual. You may need to seek counseling support to incorporate the deaths into your life in healthy ways.

CHAPTER FOUR

Taking Your Child Off Life Support

Facing the decision to take your child off life support is profoundly counterintuitive. Parents are hardwired to protect and nurture their children. After all the hopes, dreams and good intentions directed toward bringing a child into the world, this experience is devastating and life-altering. Sarah related:

> *When presented with the reality that my child's body could not function without support from machines, my whole body and instinct screamed out. I was supposed to be bringing life into the world; how could I suddenly be faced with a decision to take it away?*

Life support is employed in a variety of situations to maintain certain functions of the body, such as respiration or food intake. Life support is used most often in the course of an emergency situation due to illness, injury, genetic flaws, chronic disease or organ failure. When the crisis arises and the purpose of life support is to sustain your child's life, there is no time to consider the long-term outcomes, only the hope that the crisis will pass and your child will recover.

Most medical professionals present a patient's condition in a detached, scientific manner. While offering support to parents within the confines of policy, they must provide the parents with a rational explanation for the need to terminate life support due to the outcome of test results or failure of internal organs. Such rational explanations can clash with the feelings of the parents, who love their child and cannot see the issue in a purely scientific light.

When first presented with the need to make a decision regarding the cessation of life support, parents are flooded with a number of intensely painful and conflicting emotions. They are forced to weigh the question of their child's quality of life while struggling with the faint glimmer of hope that remains for survival. Cultural and religious beliefs and traditions can also play a role in the emotional struggle to make decisions about a child's life.

Parents who have had to face the agonizing decision to take a child off life support are affected in unique ways and trauma can occur from a number of sources. However the decision-making process unfolds, parents face different kinds of emotional trauma in the aftermath of the death, depending upon what manner of preparation and support was available to them during the child's time on life support.

RECOVERY AND RELAPSE

Whether your child endured a brief or prolonged bout of illness, you may find you're feeling raw and agonized because of the fluctuations in your child's health, which alternately give you reason to hope and then take it away. As Joyce, one mother, said:

> One day Josie was feeling really good. We had a few laughs, watched movies and played board games. Things felt normal for a day. I felt such hope that she would make it. Then she slipped into a coma. I watched her every movement, hoping she would wake again. I just couldn't give up on her. It was exhausting torture. Looking back on it all, I'm so glad I had that day with her.

Changes in the condition of a human body can happen both gradually and abruptly. One moment your child may have been alert and active and the next, gone into a relapse or worsening condition. There may have been many waves of recovery and relapse before parents were advised to take a child off life support.

In the times when the child rallies, it is possible for parents to express their love and support for their child. These moments can be cornerstones during grief work, providing memories of moments that parents can hold on to and treasure.

While a child is on life support, this rollercoaster of hope and despair is exhausting and draining for parents. Once the cycle is over, parents may have a number of emotional responses linked to the experience. These include:

- Spiritual questioning or religious crisis
- Relief
- Anger at the medical system for not saving their child

- Anger at having gone through the experience only to have it end in death
- Guilt for having been the one to decide to end life support
- Frustration, helplessness, hopelessness
- Reliving the moments when the child rallied and there was hope
- Longing and sadness
- Questioning such as "What went wrong?" and "Why didn't s/he survive?"
- Anger toward the child for "giving up"

THE PHYSICAL CONDITION OF YOUR CHILD

Witnessing drastic changes in your child's physical abilities and functions due to illness or injury is jarring and heartbreaking. If death was caused by physical trauma, there may have been areas of your child's body that were severely damaged. If your child suffered brain damage or fell into a coma, you may have felt your child was gone before physical life ceased. If your child was ill with a chronic, disabling disease or born with a genetic condition that led to a challenged and shortened life, you likely struggled with watching your child's life slip away. All of these situations can evoke a trauma response as parents are forced to witness an unimaginable transformation.

Because of the traumatic nature of these experiences, images connected with your child's death might haunt you. Working through the images and reframing your experience in a supportive and safe environment will help you to move toward healing from the trauma and will allow gentler and happier emotions and memories to surface.

MIXED EXPERIENCES WITH THE MEDICAL SYSTEM

Despite the amazing efforts of nurses and doctors, the many variables of your child's treatment in the hospital can leave you feeling disappointed or confused. Your experience of the medical system can be a source of anger, misunderstanding, frustration or hurt. Or you may have felt deeply supported by the medical staff and guided gently through your difficult task. Each experience within the medical system is unique. Working through how things happened and what happened is part of your healing process. You may find that you need more closure relating to your experience in the hospital.

HOPE FOR SURVIVAL

Until the final moment, you may have hoped for your child's survival. Despite any discouraging words spoken by the medical staff, even as the machines are turned off parents hope for a miracle recovery. This is a reflection of your love for your child. Hope persists, especially in crisis, which emphasizes the difficulty of reconciling your dreams as a parent to see your child live a long and healthy life with the reality that your child is dying. The loss of hope that comes as your child's life ends has a profound emotional and psychological impact. Reconciling lost dreams for your child is an important piece of grief work.

REDEFINE HOPE

The purpose of this exercise is to redefine the hopes and dreams you held for your child and to help you recognize the hopes that were fulfilled in your child's lifetime.

Find a private, quiet place where you feel safe. Using a journal or notepad, brainstorm hopes and dreams you had for your child. Some examples are happy, loved or creative. Once you have a list, take one hope and write or reflect on a memory or time when that hope was satisfied. For example, when thinking of the hope you held for your child to be loved, reflect upon the endless love you and others were able to share with your child. Repeat the process with each hope you have identified as many times as you need. This exercise is a realistic way to balance lost hopes with ones that actually manifested in your child's life and in your own.

DENIAL AND SHOCK

Hearing the doctor's explanation of your child's condition and the need to stop life support is stunning and painful news. Kara, one parent, expressed:

> When I heard those words it sounded like a foreign language;
> I could not translate what was being said to me into anything
> understandable. I couldn't believe it was happening; it couldn't
> be true. Sometimes it feels as though I didn't really know what
> was happening until it was over.

Even as parents nod their heads and mechanically go through the motions, they are emotionally in shock and not fully present to the situation. These sensations are common in all forms of child loss, but in the case of taking a child off life support, parents may experience two phases of denial and shock: one upon first learning the child will die and the other after the death. (For more on denial and shock see chapter 2: *A Dictionary of Emotions for the Grieving Parent*.)

SAYING GOODBYE

Having a child on life support allows time for parents, family and friends to say goodbye. Parents and families say goodbye in many unique ways. Some invite only close friends, others allow the opportunity to anyone who wishes to come. Some families host gatherings in cramped hospital rooms. Others sing songs or tell stories. Some individuals perform small acts to say goodbye in their own ways. Some parents may not choose to say goodbye and instead leave before the final moment. How individuals choose to say goodbye is defined by their needs, their relationship with the child and family dynamics.

The time to say goodbye allows parents to express gratitude and regrets with a child, make amends for past or present actions, perform religious rites or rituals if desired, hold the child and express love for the child in bodily form. Though it does not resolve the pain of losing a child, the opportunity to perform these activities can bring a sense of peace to mind and heart.

The medical apparatus and beeping machines surrounding and connected to your child may have interfered with the level of intimacy you desired. The equipment and environment is invasive and can provide barriers to touching or embracing a child the way a parent would like. The limited privacy in a hospital setting may be a reason for holding back emotions or expressing regrets to a child. (For suggestions and activities to help you to resolve feelings and thoughts that you were unable to express to your child during his or her lifetime, see chapter 13: *Tools for Healing*.)

THE MOMENT OF DEATH

When the machines are turned off, the moment of death is unpredictable. It may happen quickly or it may be a slow progression. Witnessing your child's death may have brought forth an overwhelming surge of emotion and pain. As Carla, one grieving parent, explained:

> *I suddenly found myself frantic with the need to hold my son. My body was overtaken and I began to wail uncontrollably, an otherworldly sound emanating from my heart and soul. This moment still marks an irreversible shift in my being and life; my heart, in this moment, shattered. Even today, replaying this moment in my mind brings a feeling of indefinable heartbreak.*

Parents have also described feeling a sense of profound love and peacefulness upon witnessing their child's death. However you define the experience of your child's last moments—no matter how it unfolded—you need to approach it with compassion and love toward yourself. You did the best you could with what you had at the time. Emotions and insights from the experience will evolve over time.

EXPRESS EMOTIONS REGARDING THE MOMENT OF DEATH

Find a quiet and safe space. Choose a creative medium that you are drawn to—pen, paint, pastels, clay or a musical instrument. Think back to the moments surrounding your child's death. Allow your feelings to emerge and bring forward the memories. Take up your chosen medium and start expressing those emotions through drawing, making music or writing. Keep with the emotion and lay it out on the paper or in the music until you feel done. If other emotions arise, repeat this process. This exercise allows you to release the emotion slowly in a safe and contained way. Release it from inside you so the emotional burden gradually lightens.

Helplessness

Parents may have felt helplessly swept along by a wave of medical procedures and decisions. They may feel powerless due to additional factors, such as having difficulty understanding medical terminology and diagnoses. Because of the gravity of the decision to stop life support for their child, they may have other feelings of bewilderment and helplessness about the choice they had to make and the fact they could not save their child's life.

In order to understand what has happened and regain a sense of control, parents may want to better understand the medical condition or circumstances that led to the child's death. Engaging in research and questioning medical professionals are ways that parents can pursue additional answers.

Replaying Images or Experiences

In an effort to make sense of the experience, parents may find themselves replaying images and events leading to the death of their child. These flashbacks are a signal of the traumatic and impactful nature of the experience. After a time, the intensity of these images or flashbacks typically dissipates. In some cases flashbacks persist, accompanied with heightened anxiety or emotional intensity that does not resolve. This may signal the onset of PTSD, which can be resolved with appropriate intervention. In these cases it is recommended to seek help from a physician or mental health professional. (If flashbacks persist beyond one month, see chapter 1: *When Trauma and Grief Combine*.)

Relief

Seeing a child suffering or in pain is very difficult. It is only natural that once the suffering stops, a parent feels some sense of relief. Some parents can misinterpret this sense of relief and subsequently feel guilt or shame. But the kind of relief you may feel can be an expression of the love you have for your child and your desire for him or her to be free of pain and suffering. Sometimes the relief comes with recognizing that the death was appropriate. If you find yourself feeling relief, reflect upon the source of relief before you judge yourself or your emotions.

Questioning

As shock and numbness lift and memories of the experience begin to surface, many parents begin questioning what took place, the advice they were given and how it all happened. After a child has been taken off life support, parents may ask questions such as:

- What if I had chosen to keep my child on life support?
- Should I have waited for a miracle?
- Was the medical advice I received correct?
- Did I give up too soon/too late?
- Were my decisions fully informed?
- What if my child had different doctors?
- What if my child had been treated in a different hospital?

In an effort to analyze and understand why your child could not live, the process of asking "what if" questions is a natural part of trying to make sense of your loss. Having to make the decision to cease life support raises questions that can influence how you feel about yourself, potentially imposing negative self-judgments such as guilt, shame and disappointment.

Guilt

As the primary decision makers, parents potentially burden themselves with feelings of guilt. Struggling with this guilt can be difficult and can complicate the grieving process, extending it beyond a healthy range.

As a parent, it is hard to separate the rational or scientific knowledge from the emotional experience. Your heart's desire and your understanding of your role as a parent do not necessarily reconcile you with your decision to cease life support, although it was the humane thing to do for your child. Instead of judging yourself, consider what motivated your decision. Something informed you that it was the right choice, be it science or intuition. Have faith in your decision and work to release any blame you direct toward yourself. (For more information on guilt, see chapter 2: *A Dictionary of Emotions for the Grieving Parent.*)

Self-Loathing

In extreme cases of guilt and self-blame, parents may experience self-loathing. Self-loathing is the process of constantly blaming oneself and/ or feeling contempt toward oneself and can also include suicidal thoughts. All of this can foster a state of depression and self-destructive behaviors.

If you are experiencing self-loathing, depressed moods or suicidal thoughts, it is crucial to your healing that you break this cycle. Find a professional you trust and begin to work through the emotions and thoughts with which you are struggling. (For advice on finding the right counselor, see chapter 13: *Tools for Healing.*)

IMPACT ON COUPLES

Being faced with the decision to cease life support is an emotional and challenging situation for couples. It can impact both the individual and shared grieving process. Parents may lay blame on the other parent or initially disagree on the decision. Or, if one parent assumes responsibility for talking with the doctors, the other parent may have to resolve feelings of being excluded from the discussions. The experience of child loss can bring couples closer together or spotlight preexisting issues in the relationship. (For more information on the impact of loss on martial relationships see chapter 8: *Surviving with Your Partner.*)

Difficulty Finding Resolution

It can be hard to resolve your decision to take your child off life support because of the conflict between your role as a nurturing parent and the reality of having to participate in the end-of-life decision. If the decision conflicts with religious principles or previously held moral and ethical values, grief can be further complicated.

Finding resolution can be smoother if you are able to disentangle your grief from your feelings about having to take your child off life support. The counsel of a clergy member, grief counselor or mental health professional can support you as you seek resolution. (For further discussion on spiritual experiences related to loss, see chapter 12: *Facing Spiritual Emergencies.* For exercises and ideas to help with sorting emotional responses see chapter 13: *Tools for Healing.*)

CHAPTER FIVE

Seeing Your Child's Body

W hen a child dies, the parents are gravely hurting, yet every parent also feels the press of practical needs and responsibilities which demand decisions regarding the child's body. Whether a child's death was sudden or anticipated, parents' first experience of seeing their child's lifeless body is an overwhelming and painful moment. The stunning reality of the absolute permanence of death can leave a lasting memory, frozen forever in time. Although parents know intuitively that their child is no longer "present" in his or her body, there is still a need to be close to the child, to carry out their final protective act and to touch, care for and honor their child's body.

Parents have shared that final goodbyes are expressed in many ways. Circumstances surrounding a child's death profoundly influence how this experience unfolds. With anticipated death, some plans may already be in place. When death is unexpected, violent or the result of a crime, the right of parents to be with their child's body and express sorrow may be restricted, delayed or prohibited. If death is assumed due to disappearance, loss at sea or a natural or human-made disaster, there may be no body. In other circumstances, parents may be able to spend intimate time with their child's body.

This chapter focuses on factors that affect the end-of-life experience and choices that parents may encounter, including autopsy, organ donation, body preparation, burial or cremation and miscarriage. It is intended to provide parents with information that may help them reflect upon and sort through their experiences.

AUTOPSY

An autopsy is a medical examination of the body after death that focuses on identifying the cause and manner of death. Throughout modern history, the practice of postmortem examination has fostered many medical advances by helping to identify the disease process and discover new ways to save lives.

Highly-trained specialists called pathologists perform autopsies. To become a pathologist, a medical student must complete four years of pathology residency. Forensic (criminal) pathologists must complete an additional one to two years of training. An autopsy is a respectful surgical procedure that includes a thorough examination of organs, tissue and body fluids. Final reports may take several weeks to complete while toxicology tests are run.

Autopsies are only performed in certain situations, unless specifically requested by the parent. If an autopsy is required due to the circumstances surrounding the child's death, parents will be notified in advance if possible. In general, the autopsy does not interfere with the appearance of the child nor prevent an open casket viewing.

When the circumstances surrounding a death require an autopsy by law, it can be a troubling experience for parents. The parents' sense of responsibility to protect, care for and decide what is right and wrong for their child is superseded by a legal requirement in which they have no say. When law requires an autopsy, parents' access to the child's body is restricted, delayed or prevented until the investigation is completed. Not being allowed to see or touch their child adds another layer to the emotional pain of losing a child, making it more difficult for parents to grasp the reality of the child's death.

Anne knew because of the way in which her son died there had to be an autopsy:

> I knew that I would have no choice in the matter of my son's autopsy, but I wanted to see him first. The police were very understanding and allowed me to spend some time with him. They told me I was not allowed to touch him, but just being near to him and seeing him helped me to accept what would come next.

Situations when an autopsy is required and generally investigated under the authority of a medical examiner or coroner include:

- UNNATURAL OR SUDDEN DEATH: Sudden or unexpected death such as an accident, suicide, poisoning, overdose, injury, sudden infant death syndrome or a death that has no clear causal factors.
- SUSPECTED CRIMINAL OR LEGAL INVOLVEMENT: Homicide or any death for which the results of an autopsy are required for a pending legal proceeding. Insurance companies, the Veterans Administration and workman's compensation boards may demand an autopsy in order to determine the appropriateness of survivors receiving compensation.

- PUBLIC HEALTH INTEREST: The cause of death constitutes a potential threat to public health such as suspected death from a communicable disease.

Laws regulating the terms of required autopsies vary within federal, provincial, state and military mandates, with some provisions to honor religious objections. There is no charge to the family if law requires an autopsy. It is also recommended that a forensic examination take place in cases when the body will be unavailable for examination at a later time, such as cremation or burial at sea.

Upon completion of the forensic investigation, the child's body is released to the parents. Parents can then begin to make choices on behalf of their child and reclaim their sense of parental rights such as:

- Preparing the body for the funeral (washing, grooming, dressing)
- Spending private time with the body to say final goodbyes
- Holding a wake with the body in the home or other location
- Releasing the body to a funeral home
- Attending a viewing, funeral or memorial gathering
- Planning and carrying out a burial or cremation ceremony

When an autopsy is not required, parents may still wish to have one performed to better understand the cause of their child's death. In some cases, parents may want a second autopsy performed if they do not accept the results of the first examination. The service may be provided by the hospital where the child died, a private medical services company or another hospital's pathology department. When parents request an autopsy, there may be a charge for the procedure and insurance does not generally cover autopsies. A hospital social worker can guide you through this process.

A requested medical autopsy cannot be performed without signed consent. Consent forms allow parents to limit the extent of the examination and to approve matters such as retention of the organs and tissues for teaching. A frank discussion with the pathologist will help to determine what is required to answer your questions regarding the cause of death.

Even if a parent is eager to further understand the cause of death, consenting to an autopsy is a difficult and emotional experience. Religion, cultural traditions, ethnic background and personal beliefs may influence how parents are guided to their choices. It is important that parents listen to their hearts and, when appropriate, seek counsel with a trusted advisor.

Reading an autopsy report can be a daunting task for parents. Reports contain technical language and medical terms that are often difficult to understand. Information that is potentially shocking or painfully graphic may also be disclosed in the autopsy report. If possible, it is important to choose an appropriate time and place to review the document. When the report is considered evidence in a legal proceeding, parents will hear the report for the first time during the course of a trial. Copies of the report will not be released prior to completion of the legal process except through a lawyer's request.

Kate related her feelings at seeing the autopsy report for her child:

It seems like so much is bittersweet. It's like . . . I had to see the autopsy pictures knowing that I'd be haunted by such a thing. But I had to . . . I'm glad I did . . . but I wish I hadn't sometimes.

Anne also had poignant feelings:

It was extremely important to me to find out exactly what had happened to my son, how he had died, how long it took . . . everything. After the trial was over I went to the medical examiner's office and he sat with me while I read the autopsy report. He explained everything I asked about. I experienced a strange combination of horror and relief. And in some strange way it helped me put another piece of the puzzle of my grief together.

The results of an autopsy are not always conclusive or sufficient in answering parents' questions. Sometimes the death remains unexplained. Learning that the medical cause of death is undetermined and the child was otherwise healthy may intensify the sense of preventability and helplessness felt by the parents. In these situations, parents may feel a need to do research on their own or to pick through every detail of the report to find an answer that may have been missed.

Michael, a father who had to review his son's autopsy reports, told us:

Going through the autopsy reports with the doctors and realizing that there was no proven medical reason for Luke's death was shocking. It took a long time for me to accept that I would never have a concrete answer for why he died.

Processing the information contained in an autopsy report is emotionally and psychologically challenging. Prepare for the experience by recognizing the impactful nature of the information you will receive. Ensure that you have support during and after receiving the autopsy report. You may have many questions. Help and information is available from the medical examiner or coroner, a victim services worker or your family doctor.

DONATING YOUR CHILD'S ORGANS

Organ donation is the process of removing healthy organs and tissues from a person who has died for transplant to a living individual. Organs and tissues are also donated for the purpose of medical research. The kidneys, pancreas, liver, lungs, heart and intestines are the organs that are normally transplanted. Tissues include skin, bone, bone marrow and corneas. Donations from one individual can help up to fifty people. All over the world, in diverse cultures and religions, organ donation is considered a charitable act. Parents often choose to inform others of the organ donation in a child's eulogy or obituary. In most cases, organ donation for transplant is only possible when brain death has occurred. The term *brain death* means that there has been a catastrophic, irreversible brain injury and all brain activity has ceased. Though the person has been pronounced dead, the heart and lungs continue to function with life support apparatus. Parents who are approached by hospital personnel regarding the question of organ donation are faced with making a choice during an intensely painful, traumatic and stressful time. Consenting to organ donation can be a difficult and confusing decision, because parents are being told their child has died yet their child's body seems to have life. They may also be unsure of what their child would have wanted.

Organ donation cannot occur without specific consent. This can be in the form of a living will, participation in an organ donor registry or consent provided by the parents or guardians of a minor child. In most jurisdictions, permission can be granted by surviving spouses or the next of kin of a deceased adult. Consent documents will detail all aspects of the donation, including which organs or tissues are to be donated. Specially trained hospital staff help the family with information and support.

Once the decision to consent to organ donation has been made, family members have time to spend with the child, to hold and touch flesh to flesh and to say goodbye. The entire process of organ donation, from pronouncement of brain death to completion, can take up to thirty hours. The process of organ recovery is a surgical procedure and is performed by a team of surgeons in an operating room. The donor is treated with the same level of respect as any surgical patient. Incisions are normally small and are made with consideration for open casket viewing. Once the surgeons have completed the surgery, the child's body is released to the prearranged funeral director.

Lynn described her experience with organ donation:

When we knew that Ada was gone, her dad and I decided to donate her organs. We knew that was what she would have wanted. They had to keep her stable for three days to run tests

*and so I had her warm hand to hold for those three days. I
couldn't see her; they had a towel over her head. And she never
had any consciousness, not a word. I was grateful to have her
warm to me. The morning they took her, we had to say goodbye and watch her go down the hallway. We knew it was the
right decision . . . I never thought about it at the time . . . when
I realized what was left of her was cremated and parts of her
were being sent all over, I felt again that my girl is in pieces. I
wouldn't take it back, but I didn't expect to feel like that . . .
I want to meet all those people she helped.*

Consenting to organ donation on behalf of your child can have an
unexpected effect on your grieving process. Parents have described a myriad of emotions and thoughts including:

- Discomfort about the child's body no longer being whole
- Resentment or anger toward the recipients, because they got a
  second chance at life when the child did not
- Gratitude, knowing that the child continues to improve the lives
  of others

Some parents choose to make contact or develop a relationship later
with organ recipients. It is important to recognize that your feelings about
your child's organ donation may be mixed and confusing. If you are having
difficulties with your feelings and thoughts, organ donation societies offer
resources for donor family members and may be able to provide the support you need to resolve your emotional conflicts.

VIEWING YOUR CHILD'S BODY

There are many circumstances in which parents will see their child's lifeless
body for the first time. Death transforms the human body. Skin is cold to the
touch; there is no movement, breath or heartbeat. There is an absence where
there once was a child whom the parents loved, sheltered and nurtured. The
realization that your child's life has ceased is a stunning and life-altering
moment. For many, viewing the body begins the process of acknowledging
what has happened. It may awaken their hearts and minds from the cloud of
disbelief that enveloped them when they first heard the news.

Anne spoke of her conflicted feelings at seeing her dead son:

*We had driven all night to get there. The entire time, I could not
believe what I had been told. I wavered between agonizing pain*

and absolute numbness. When we got to the hospital, I was ush-
ered down to a lower floor by a chaplain and a detective. The
chaplain opened the door and the detective unzipped the body
bag as far as my son's collarbone. As I looked at my son lying
there dead, I felt stunned, stupefied and a strangely sacred sense
of awe. I will never forget that moment, how my disbelief and
hope shattered and I finally understood that he was gone.

Circumstances related to the death may influence the location and conditions in which the body is viewed. Viewing the whole body following a violent act or accident may cause undue suffering for a parent and has the potential of forming traumatic images. Often, coroners, funeral directors or hospital staff will cover damaged parts of the child's body. By doing so, they provide a gentler way for parents to have contact and spend time with their child.

Parents may choose not to view the body, preferring to remember their child in a living state. With no viewing or partial viewing of the body, parents may later find themselves imagining what they did not see in an effort to complete the story of their child's death.

Your first contact with your child's body is a moment in your life like no other. Memories, thoughts and images of this moment can arouse intense emotions as you weave this experience into your grieving process. (If you are experiencing ongoing visual flashbacks of your child's body that are unsettling or produce anxiety, see chapter 1: *When Trauma and Grief Combine.*)

PREPARATION OF YOUR CHILD'S BODY

Cultures, religions and traditions around the world have different ways of attending to and preparing the body for burial or cremation. How a family chooses to approach this step depends upon the cultural, religious and personal practices that influence their preferences. For some, preparing the body is a deeply personal activity that is shared by close family members. For others, the preparation is fulfilled by an individual who is sanctified in a religious hierarchy or by a funeral director. Some families will also choose to bring the body into the home for a wake or sitting.

Parents may be surprised by the intensity of their desire to take part in the process. Those who choose to prepare the body themselves or who follow religious traditions describe the act as having a sacred and healing quality. There is no right or wrong approach to this step in acknowledging your loss. It is a deeply personal choice.

Joyce remembered seeing her child after death:

The time I spent with my daughter's body is one of the most pre-
cious memories I have. A group of us washed her body, dressed
her and did her hair. I was reminded of fixing up cuts and tying
her ponytails. It was important for me to take care of her one
last time.

The circumstances of your child's death may have made it difficult
or impossible for you to participate in a way that fulfilled your needs. If
you were unable to carry out preparation of your child's body in the way
you wanted to and have lingering regrets, you may find solace in a ritual
or activity that helps you to release your unexpressed tenderness. (See
chapter 13: *Tools for Healing* and chapter 14: *Creating Personal Rituals and*
Memorials for ideas.)

BURIAL OR CREMATION?

Having to bury a child can feel contradictory to the natural order of life's
cycles. Choosing whether to bury or cremate a child is one of many difficult
steps a parent must take following the death of a child. Parents may have
only vague memories of what happened in the days immediately following
their child's death. They may also have vivid memories of having to make
decisions while in a state of emotional shock, answering questions they
found unreal and confusing.

Burials include a process of embalming, preparing and placing the
body in a coffin. This is followed by interment in a grave where grave mark-
ers are often placed at the site. Family and friends revisit burial sites. Some
individuals feel the gravesite is a special place to visit and be close with
their child, while others might identify a different location where they
honor the memory of their child.

Cremation is a process of incinerating the body, which reduces it to
ash mixed with bone fragments. Ashes are formally called cremains. Prior
to cremation the body can also be embalmed and prepared for viewing.
Families may choose to respect and honor their child's ashes in unique
ways. Some families keep the ashes in a container in their homes; others
select a special place or places to spread the ashes. Cremains can also be
interred in a structure called a columbarium, which has individual niches
with a traditional marker, or buried in a cemetery with a headstone marker.

Joanna treasured her last memories of preparing her daughter's body:

Jane's very dear friend made the coffin and I lined it with silk
and one of her other friends who was an upholsterer provided

*the padding . . . we did it together. Then another friend put the
body in the coffin and we decorated it and wrote our messages
on it . . . all our wishes for her soul . . . and then the very beautiful ceremony . . . the dignity of her . . . and then the awful moment when the coffin goes away to be cremated . . . and then we
divided the ashes, because she was to be scattered in various different parts of England and Canada. All this needs to be done
with grace and care. It was beautiful. We were doing creative
things that helped, but beneath was the absolute pit of despair.*

With anticipated death, parents have some opportunity to consider
their options in advance. In cases of terminal illness, the child may have
expressed his or her preference, which helps to facilitate the parents' choice.
Following a sudden death, when prior arrangements have not been considered, decisions must be faced in a compressed time frame when overwhelmed emotions are in a state of confusion. Religious or cultural beliefs
may help to guide choices. For those who are assisting parents, it is essential to give the parents time to sort through their feelings and needs
without their feeling pressured by outside influences. Respecting privacy
and personal choice will support parents as they determine which decision
is right for them and the child.

Parents will sometimes have difficulty as they imagine cremation or
decomposition of the body. Images of death in movies and popular culture
may affect parents' imaginations. If you are struggling with the physical
aspects of burial or cremation, it helps to consider that there is an intrinsic
human connection to the cycles of our natural world and the transformation of your child's body into a new state is a part of that cycle.

When the funeral director presents the ashes or the first shovel of dirt
lands on the coffin, parents have described a shocking sense of permanence
and despair. There is a desire to undo what cannot be undone. As you move
through your grief, the intensity of these feelings will lessen. Finding ways
to make connections and develop a new relationship with your child after
death is part of your healing journey. (See chapter 13: *Tools for Healing* and
chapter 14: *Creating Personal Rituals and Memorials* for ideas.)

TRANSPORTING A BODY ACROSS BORDERS

When a child dies in another country, in the midst of shock and despair,
parents are compelled to make arrangements to get to their child's side.
Because of the logistics of travel, there is often an extended delay between
receiving the news and finally reaching their destination. In addition,

parents may be arriving in a country with unfamiliar customs, languages and regulations. Coping with these barriers compounded by separation from established support systems at home may leave parents feeling isolated and vulnerable. This can deepen the state of shock and the traumatic nature of their loss.

Each country and jurisdiction has unique procedures and regulations that must be followed in order to transport a body across borders. Depending on the circumstances and location of the body, parents may not be allowed to perform rites or prepare the body in the way they would like. Regulations may require cremation or autopsy prior to transporting the body. Because of the potential impediments related to international transport of the deceased, delays could complicate arrangements for a funeral in the home country.

Navigating these procedures and requirements can be challenging, whether it is bringing home the deceased or transporting the body to another country for burial. Coping with and resolving the unique elements of this experience are difficult. Parents may have to revisit the experience after the fact to understand the effect it has had on their grieving process. Working with a registered counselor in a safe and supportive environment can assist in sorting through the emotional and psychological layers of the experience and help to facilitate healing. (For guidance in finding a counselor, see chapter 13: *Tools for Healing*.)

NO BODY

When the death is of a catastrophic nature and the body is not found or cannot be recovered, it may be more difficult for parents to grasp the reality that their child is dead. Facing loss without a body to view or bury can leave a parent haunted with lingering doubts and disbelief. You may struggle with relentless hopes that your child is actually alive and might still return. Parents have described their experiences as living with a sense of suspension and unreality, as being locked in a holding pattern, not knowing or believing and unwilling to give up hope. Not having confirmation that verifies the death may mean there will be no funeral or ritual, minimal public grieving and an unfilled absence that inhibits movement in the grieving process.

Georgette related the agony she felt, not from her son's death, but because his body was not found:

> My son's body was never recovered. He was lost at sea and for
> the first few years I couldn't help feeling an expectation that he
> would come home. One day I walked along the beach spreading
> rose petals along the shore. Afterwards I sat and watched as
> the tide washed the rose petals away . . . since that day, I have

known in my heart that when I touch the ocean, I am touching
my son.

In some cases such as plane crashes, natural or human-made disasters and military action losses, there is a supportive response from the community: memorials and rituals are performed to honor the dead. This response helps parents to feel that their grief is acknowledged. Parents who must face their loss without this community support often create their own ceremony or memorial, inviting family and friends who share in the loss.

Each act of acknowledgement, whether small and private or shared with a larger community, helps parents fulfill their need to honor their child's life. (For ideas on ways to create acknowledging ceremonies and rituals, see chapter 14: *Creating Personal Rituals and Memorials*.)

Miscarriage

The love that binds a parent to her or his child exists on a deep and instinctive level, whether that child is an adult or a tiny being within its mother's womb. Parents who have lost a child to miscarriage sometimes have difficulty finding acknowledgment and support for their grief. In miscarriage there is often no physical body to grieve. For family and friends, there was no opportunity to meet the child and build a relationship; they sometimes mistakenly presume that the parents feel the same lack of connection to the child. Miscarriage is an abrupt ending to the expectancy of what was to be. Dreams are shattered and hopes washed away, replaced with profound aching for unrealized potential.

Madison discussed with us the intensity of her feelings when she miscarried:

> *I lost my baby when I was eight weeks pregnant. My husband*
> *and I were so excited by the pregnancy. I had just told my*
> *mother the day before. When I miscarried, I felt as if I had lost*
> *a piece of myself. There is so much doubt in the experience:*
> *Did this person exist? Was the child meant to be? The loss is so*
> *unspoken. For me it was a horrible medical process. It is like*
> *a part of me was dying in place of my baby. A poignant thing*
> *about the pain I experienced is how private it was . . . it was not*
> *a raging river; it was so painful under the surface, like a deep*
> *toothache pain that no one can see. Even though my baby was*
> *gone, my internal clock kept tracking the pregnancy. The month*
> *that I would have given birth, my grief changed. It was like a*
> *cloud lifted and my sadness softened.*

Parents may struggle with a desire to have the unmet child acknowledged but uncertain of how to go about it. Creating a ritual to mark the unmet child's existence in parents' lives is an effective way to express the grief and mourn the loss. Some parents choose to name the child, create a marker, plant a garden spot or tree or write a song, poem or letter for the child. Consider including siblings who were anticipating the arrival of a brother or sister. What is most important is to realize that miscarriage grief is real and to allow the feelings without judgment or shame.

COMING TO TERMS WITH YOUR DECISIONS

We have explored the different choices you might have faced concerning your child's body after she or he died and how those choices may affect your grief journey. These are choices parents never wanted to face and yet are compelled to consider in difficult and painful circumstances. Decisions may be made during times of extreme duress or made with gradual consideration. You may be struggling with feelings of regret or confusion for the decisions you made or you may feel accepting of how things unfolded. If you are wondering if you were right in your decisions or are experiencing regrets, guilt or anger about what happened with your child's body, it is helpful to recognize that you were doing the best you could at that time. Your actions were subconsciously attuned to loving your child in the best way you knew. It has been said by many parents that there is never a good time to bury a child. Be gentle with yourself when reflecting upon how you approached this experience. (For information on coping with difficult emotions, see chapter 2: *A Dictionary of Emotions for the Grieving Parent* and chapter 13: *Tools for Healing.* For help with ideas on how to create your own memories, memorials or rituals, see chapter 14: *Creating Personal Rituals and Memorials.*)

CHAPTER SIX

Handling End-of-Life Rituals

The first few weeks following a child's death are often spent notifying friends and family and organizing a celebration of his or her life, memorial or funeral. Parents experience this end-of-life ritual very differently; some characterize it as deeply painful, while others see it as a much-needed and valued event that helped them to cope with their child's death. No matter where your experience falls in the spectrum, end-of-life rituals influence your grieving process. The first part of this chapter outlines different methods of notifying people and presents information about funeral and memorial arrangements. Later in the chapter, we discuss the experience of addressing your child's possessions and the financial stresses that can accompany a loss.

NOTIFYING LOVED ONES

Within our society, we inherit the expectation that we will live long, healthy lives, followed by graceful death in old age. It is expected that our children will outlive us and carry on after our death. However, the death of a child contradicts this common understanding of how the world works. Preconceptions about life and death not only impact parents' abilities to absorb what has happened, but also are a prevalent factor in how friends and family will respond to the news.

Maureen spoke of the difficulty of telling others:

> When Andrew was killed I couldn't bear the thought of telling people; I could not even speak the words to myself—but my husband was able to make all the phone calls. It was his way of feeling as if he could do something about our son dying.

Child loss falls outside of the framework of the usual condolences. When a person learns that your child has died, shock or disbelief may be the first reaction; you may be asked to repeat yourself or explain details. People who hear the news may be overwhelmed and unsure of how to support you; it is common for them to respond by saying, "I don't know what to say." It is important that you decide how you want to be involved in this task. To give yourself support and space in this difficult time, you might ask a friend or loved one to give notice to people in your social network who haven't been informed yet.

However you decide to inform others of your loss, you may find that you will have different experiences using different media. Next we provide a short guide of different ways to notify people and review the benefits and attendant concerns associated with each medium.

Phone Calls

Phoning individuals to give them the news can be an intense experience. The reactions of those you call can be very emotional and often people will ask intimate questions; they may ask for details about your child's death that you are not ready to share. Before you begin making calls, ask yourself: *Am I able to share right now? Am I able to expose myself to another's emotions and reactions?*

Write a list of those you wish to notify and check off each name after making contact. This way you will not forget whom you have already informed. Take your time. Take breaks or stop altogether if it becomes too difficult. If you determine that you aren't able to make the calls yourself, identify someone you trust to make the calls for you. Provide a list with phone numbers.

E-mails

Group or individual e-mails are another method of informing people. The process of sitting down and writing the e-mail can be a cathartic experience, helping you to express in words what has happened. Unlike with a phone call, you may not receive a response immediately or at all, as some individuals may not know how to respond. Providing notification electronically allows some separation from the emotional response of others, which can be a benefit. As a courtesy, identify in the subject line that the content of the message is unhappy news. Provide your contact information for those who would like to send condolences or phone you. If you already have the funeral details arranged, this is a good opportunity to share these specifics as well.

An Obituary in a Newspaper

Like e-mail, the process of writing an obituary for print media can be therapeutic. Announcements in the newspaper often highlight accomplishments and contributions. As a family or individually, brainstorm about the many things your child brought to your lives. Doing this exercise as a family is a way to start the discussion of grief with other children. It also allows siblings to feel as though they are making a contribution to planning. Some parents have commented that submitting the obituary was tied to the desire to maintain historical records for the family.

School Announcements

If your child was attending school, you may want to make an announcement to the school. The school will provide a staff person to support you with this process. The announcement may be made through an assembly, through individual teachers in each classroom or through a school newsletter. Working with the school is an effective way to let classmates and parents know what happened. It is an important act toward healing for the community that surrounded your son or daughter during his or her day-to-day life. If you find this task too difficult, ask someone you trust to help you to perform this task on your behalf.

Social Media

Choosing to post information on social media platforms is becoming a more common practice when someone dies. Before making announcements through this medium, it is important to recognize that the information you post may be reposted and may reach a larger audience. You may get condolences from people you haven't spoken to in twenty years, while your closest friends do not respond to the announcement. This is the least controlled, most open form of electronic communication. Deciding to use this type of communication depends on your comfort level with sharing the information.

In addition to creating your own post, it is possible others may have already started an online memorial or created groups in memorandum, allowing friends to post stories and photos and share feelings about their loss.

ASKING FOR HELP

Notifying people can bring about positive responses from others such as a wave of support and stories of shared experiences. Mark, one parent, commented:

When our son died, I was touched by the number of people,
family members and distant acquaintances who came forward
with similar stories of loss. Even complete strangers who heard
our story through others contacted us to share their experiences.
Knowing that we were not the only ones provided a sense that
others understood and had somehow navigated the unknown
waters we felt ourselves lost in.

This outflow of support and love that comes from family members
and friends may be an important cornerstone of support in the weeks,
months and even years following a child's death. When people come forward saying, "I don't know what to do" or "Let me know if you need anything," it's *okay* to give them a task. They want to help and need to show
their support but may be afraid or uncertain how to do so. When your
energy, emotions and thoughts are consumed by your grief, everyday activities and old routines are a challenge. It is important that you ask for help
with the management of daily tasks. Here is a list of some helpful things
willing family members and friends can do to help:

- Prepare meals
- Make phone calls
- Do laundry
- Listen
- Help with funeral arrangements
- Run errands
- Shop for groceries
- Clean the house
- Walk the dog
- Babysit
- Pick up children from school
- Care for grandparents
- Feed the pets
- Handle the mail
- Mow the lawn
- Do yard work
- Make tea and sit with you

Use this list or make your own, then let family and friends choose
what they would like to do. This will relieve you and your family from
trying to keep up with everyday routines as you make arrangements for the
funeral or memorial.

COPING WITH RANDOM ENCOUNTERS

Running into acquaintances, coworkers or even close friends whom you haven't had a chance to notify yet can be an uncomfortable situation. Having to inform them, unexpectedly, face-to-face, can arouse painful emotions. Gina, one parent, said:

> *Someone asked me if I had children . . . I couldn't think of what to say. I felt like I would either choke or burst into tears.*

Alex confessed her difficulty meeting people who don't know that her child had died:

> *When I run into someone I haven't seen since before my daughter died I feel speechless . . . I'm afraid to tell them what happened, because I know they will react and I feel like I have to protect them from the hurt of finding out.*

Maybe you are out shopping to distract yourself or have even gone away for the weekend to have some time alone and suddenly you feel exposed and vulnerable. Your comfort level with the relationship and the situation will determine if you choose to speak about what has happened or not. Stay within your comfort zone; you can choose to tell whom you want, when and in the way you want. Remember: always take care of yourself first.

Paula, another parent, said that when strangers ask her if she has children she answers:

> *"I have two children; one is twenty-four and the other is deceased." This way I can acknowledge that my son is still a part of me and I will always be his mother.*

FUNERAL ARRANGEMENTS

Funerals are often held within one or two weeks following a death. Often the first few days of grieving are filled with making arrangements and previously unimagined decisions. Organizing a funeral can be an intense and demanding process.

It is important that you keep two priorities in mind: Choose a memorial format that meets the needs of you and your immediate family and ask for help whenever possible. Prioritize by planning those parts of the event that mean the most to you and ask for help with the less important details. If you prefer to do the planning on your own, allow others to make food, shop for groceries or take on other tasks.

Heidi's painful memories of making funeral arrangements were similar to many parents':

> *I remember sitting in the funeral home making arrangements for my daughter's funeral and being in a complete daze; it was like I was watching a movie. I was so confused by the questions I was being asked. If my sister had not been there to help me, I don't know what I might have done.*

When planning a funeral, common complications include conflicting desires of family members, sudden financial strain and pressure from the inappropriate demands of others. Let your immediate family members remain the priority and help them feel involved; you can do this by having discussions as a family before making important decisions. Discuss questions such as: What are your expectations? What is important to you? What do you think your child/brother/sister would have liked? What part would you like to take in the ceremony?

With divorced or blended families there may be some challenges to meeting everyone's needs. If your relationship with the co-parent of your child has been distant or estranged, consider initiating a conversation with your previous partner that allows for an exchange of ideas. You may even consider involving a neutral person in the role of mediator to help assure there is no conflict. It is important to recognize that you are both grieving your child's death and will both desire to have some ownership over the funeral arrangements.

Relatives may visit your hometown and house to attend the funeral. Some individuals may make demands on you or make requests regarding the funeral. You may be barraged with questions from family and friends as they struggle to understand what has happened. This can be overwhelming and may require you to assert boundaries regarding your personal space, what you are willing to discuss and your choices for funeral arrangements. Letting people know what you need to take care of yourself can help you avoid unnecessary stresses. It can be very helpful to appoint a neutral spokesperson to manage this for you.

There are many diverse approaches to creating funeral rites. It is not necessary that you adhere to any particular format but rather you should decide what is right for you and your family. Choosing how to mark the passing of your child's life is a process that is uniquely your own. Take courage and follow through on your heart's desire; your heart is telling you what it needs.

The costs that arise for funeral details as well as potential loss of income from work absence can add even more stress to your grief. Choose a friend or family member who is good with finances to work with the funeral director and help you budget. In some cases you may have to make decisions based on financial constraints. Consider if certain aspects, such as a memorial gathering, can be postponed until a future time or if it is essential for you to do it right away. If you can wait, this is one way to mitigate the financial impact of the funeral.

The Details

You probably never thought you would have to plan your child's funeral. Some parents have described it as the hardest step they had to take, because it made real the finality of the death. Each parent we spoke with had a different story to tell about how he or she chose to arrange the ceremony marking his or her child's life and passing. Some followed traditions that had been passed down through generations; others found entirely new ways to honor and celebrate their children. Some held large gatherings and others arranged intimate private meetings.

Melinda discussed how difficult deciding how to handle her son's funeral was:

> We aren't religious people, so we didn't feel right going into a church for the funeral. Instead, several gatherings happened following my son's death: We had a viewing at the funeral home where I was able to have private time with my son, then his friends had a gathering in a park and over one hundred people attended. Another was at a dear friend's house and all our closest friends and family came. We also held a very intimate gathering in our home for just us.

The funeral or memorial is an opportunity to recognize your child and the things that made her or him unique in the world. This could mean dressing your child's body in a favorite T-shirt instead of the traditional suit, playing rock music or serving hot dogs because they were your child's favorite food. You have the freedom to choose how the ritual is conducted and what you want to do or say to mark your child's passing. Here is a list of things to be determined in this light:

- Style of wake, funeral and/or memorial
- Location of funeral, wake and/or memorial
- Number of attendees
- Method of notification/invitation

- Cremation or burial
- Type of casket or urn
- Date
- Time
- Catering (food, refreshments)
- Clothing for your child's body
- Pallbearers if a burial
- Flowers
- Burial plot, columbarium or place(s) to keep or release your child's ashes
- Displays, videos and/or photographs
- Gathering place following the ceremony
- Obituary notice

Eulogists will often come forward and ask to speak. You can also approach individuals who come to mind and ask them if they would like to speak at the gathering. You may also want to set aside an open time during the funeral and invite people to come forward to speak if they choose.

Whenever necessary, draw on the expertise of the funeral director with whom you choose to work. Funeral directors will assist with the details and often have years of experience supporting individuals through their times of loss and grief.

If you have lost an adult child, your child's partner or children may organize funeral arrangements. As a parent this can be challenging, because decisions or rituals you would like to perform are not yours to control. The level of complication regarding this situation is often determined by the relationship and the quality of communication between you and your grandchildren or child's partner. An approach that acknowledges each of your experiences of loss and respects your unique relationship will foster a sense of partnership in the planning.

If your child's funeral already happened and you feel you did not have the opportunity to mourn or mark your child's life at that time, it is never too late to acknowledge your loss through additional ritual. Ritual is innate to human existence and is a powerful healing tool. (For ideas on healing rituals, see chapter 14: *Creating Personal Rituals and Memorials*.)

MEMORIALS

Memorials are commemorative places, representations or objects that honor the memory of your child. You can create a memorial through a formal institution or do it privately. Examples include planting a tree or creating a special garden space, donating park benches or raising headstones and plaques. Setting up a fund that receives donations for a special cause can also act as a memorial and often the organizing charity will post something in acknowledgement.

Selina related the special place she goes to remember her daughter:

I have a special place in my garden just for my daughter. I planted all her favorite flowers, made a little pond and put in a log to sit on. It's my secret garden. I always have a place to be with just my memories of her beauty and love of nature.

Consider what would hold special meaning for you. Do you want a place to visit that allows you to feel a sense of restfulness and comfort? Was there a place that was special to your child or your family? Is there a program or cause that you would like to fund on behalf of your child's memory? A memorial can be created at any time; there is no timeline. Allow yourself to be creative and open as you ponder how to commemorate your child's life.

In the course of grieving and healing, you might take a cue from some creative ways that other parents have created memorials or rituals for their children. Here are a few things you might try:

- Donating a bench to a local park with a name plaque
- Traveling to places that your child loved to spread ashes
- Designing a special garden space
- Starting a fund that provides support for teens with depression
- Planting a tree overlooking a child's favorite view
- Sewing a quilt using squares cut from the child's clothing
- Assembling a photo collage of your life together
- Creating a special place, basket or box to keep memorabilia
- Lighting a candle on special days
- Having a birthday party with special friends every year
- Writing a poem, song or story and sharing it with others

(For more information about memorials, see chapter 14: *Creating Personal Rituals and Memorials*.)

CONDOLENCES

Condolences come in many forms, such as flowers, cards, letters and phone calls. Marla, one parent, remembered the condolences she received during her time of grieving:

We were flooded with cards from so many people; it was comforting to receive them and know how much people cared. I kept them in a special box. For a long time I was unable to look at them, because they brought back so much sadness. A long time after my son died, I felt ready to look at them again. I cried as I read the words of love and felt comforted all over again.

It is not necessary to respond to condolences, so you need not feel obliged to do so. You may want to send special thank-you notes to those who gave assistance or those who were especially supportive. The process can be a heartwarming reminder of all the support and love you have received and the recipients will be touched by the gesture.

WHEN THE DEATH OCCURRED IN YOUR HOME

If your child's death occurred in your home, entering the space could potentially cause additional trauma, flashbacks or freezing. It is okay to take as much time as you need before returning to your home. If you feel anxious about going back, it is a good idea to bring someone with you for support.

If the death was caused by suspected or actual criminal activity, the coroner and police investigation may require that the space remain untouched; for a period of time you may not be allowed in your home. Medical responders and coroners who come to the scene will not clean the space or return it to how it was before your child died there.

In the case of violent death there will be reminders of that violence remaining after the body is removed from the area, which will also need to be cleaned up. Because it can be an extremely painful and difficult task, it is important that you do not try to do the cleanup yourself and that arrangements are made to have the task completed before your return.

Specialized companies are available to provide cleaning services in these cases. You can locate a bio-cleanup company by doing an Internet search using keywords such as *crime scene cleanup*. You can also consult with victim services, your phone directory or local police department for resources. In these situations, it is essential to have support and guidance from a qualified professional to address the trauma associated with the physical space.

POSSESSIONS

Parents address their children's possessions in countless ways. Some do it bit by bit, some do it all at once, some do it right away and some wait years. There is no prescribed protocol for when or how you choose to take on the task, but ultimately you will help yourself by taking care of this matter.

Choosing to avoid these reminders can, over time, contribute to stagnation in your healing process and limit your ability to look to the future and the possibilities it holds.

Peter related how he and his wife handled returning to their home after their baby died:

> *Before we even left the hospital we asked family to move the crib and baby things out of our apartment. Some people thought it was drastic, but we couldn't bear the thought of walking into a deserted nursery. It gave us some time and allowed us to go through the boxes when we were ready.*

Your child's possessions serve as a connection to a time when your child was alive and are reminders of his or her presence. At first your attachment to some objects may strengthen. Terri, one mother, told us:

> *I slept with my son's blanket for months after his death. Gradually it made it to the bedside table, then, when it felt right, I put it in his memory box.*

If your child had already left the family home, you may find yourself searching for items in boxes or approaching in-laws for a possession that has become important to have. This impulse comes from a desire for the physical presence of your son or daughter.

Your relationship with your child never really ends. Gradually, as time passes, it takes on a new form. As this occurs, you might begin to approach your child's belongings more pragmatically and start to think about parting with some of them or putting them away. It's important to note that this process often marks a transition to a new understanding of your relationship with your child, from a living, active relationship to a relationship of memory.

The act of going through possessions or even entering the child's bedroom can be daunting and terrifying. Some parents harbor the fear that they may find something they don't want to. When you are ready to start, there are a couple of things to consider.

First, some things that aren't important to one family member may be important to another. Before initiating the reorganization, ask family members what they would like to keep.

Second, no matter the timeline, the process of organizing your child's things will be emotionally challenging. Get help, take breaks, let yourself cry and laugh at the memories; do whatever you need to do to make the experience a healing one. The experience could bring an emotional release, perhaps even lifting some of the burden off your heart.

Consider finding meaningful uses for the things you are giving away. If you decide to hold a garage sale or sell items, use the funds for something special. Donate to organizations that helped your child or yourself. This can serve as a memorial for your child.

Here are some ideas for what to do with possessions such as clothes, toys, photos, furniture and recreational items:

- Make or commission a quilt made out of your favorite pieces of clothing
- Donate items to charity
- Give to younger siblings or cousins
- Distribute photographs among family and friends
- Have a garage sale
- Put items on consignment
- Donate to school programs, daycares or summer camps in which your child participated
- Choose photos and memorabilia you want to keep and add them to your collection
- Ask family members and friends if there is something of significance they want to keep

If your child was an adult without a live-in partner, you may be faced with organizing an entirely separate living space. In addition, you may be subject to time restraints regarding tenancy. This situation can add unanticipated financial and time pressures. If you are not ready to address what to do with your child's belongings but are pressed for time, consider hiring a moving company and renting a storage unit or asking family and friends to do the moving for you.

As part of the process of organizing your child's possessions, consider adding something in place of the things you take away. Choose a photo you love and put it in a prominent place in your home or in your child's former bedroom. Put together a memory chest of the things you choose to keep for yourself and for family members to revisit. Plant a tree or garden. Hang a piece of your child's artwork. These small gestures are a comforting reminder of the continued presence of your child in your life and family, albeit in a new form.

THE FAMILY HOME

Parents have very different experiences within their homes after the loss of a child. Some find it extremely difficult to be in the home because of pervasive memories or because the death occurred within it or close by. Others experience the home as a sanctuary where they can release emotions freely and reflect within spaces that contain happy memories.

In the aftermath of a child's death, it is important to give yourself some time before making any major decisions regarding your home. Someday the painful memories that trigger when you move about the space your child once lived in may become comforting reminders of happy times. Moving to a new home shortly after your loss can have the effect of a secondary loss, particularly if there are other children involved. It may mean losing friends, school and a sense of familiarity and belonging. For some, this second loss can compound and complicate the grieving process.

As time passes, your attachment to the home may transform, just as it might with your child's personal possessions. As life changes occur and you feel more able to look toward the future, you may decide to move out of the house. Some parents struggle with feelings of abandoning their child's memory in these situations. Moving to a new home is a natural life transition and your ability to do so, if well thought out, can be a positive change. Take heart: the walls surrounding you do not define or change the love you feel for your child.

Overall, trust your intuition when it comes to this decision. Carefully consider the impact on your long-term emotional health and on the health of your family.

FINANCIAL LOSSES

Costs associated with your child's death can exert a heavy burden and can come from lost wages, travel expenses, medical bills and funeral expenses. In some cases, circumstances can lead to secondary losses such as loss of a job, home or financial stability.

Michaela recalled what happened at her job when her daughter was dying:

> *I took a leave of absence to be with my daughter as she was fighting the cancer. Eventually I got a call from my boss letting me know that they had to find someone to replace me. I really loved my job. I was so wrapped up in taking care of her and then in the grief that it wasn't until months after my daughter died that I realized how upset I was that I had lost my dream job.*

The emotional impacts of these secondary losses sometimes go unrecognized initially, because they meld with your grief. Recognizing these secondary losses and addressing their impact is an additional piece of the healing process.

CHAPTER SEVEN

Dealing with the Criminal Justice System and the Media

I f a child's death attracts media attention or if it requires criminal investigation or legal proceedings, the layers of parents' emotional injury and
trauma can become more complex. Examples include death as a result of a
criminal act, from a motor vehicle accident or in combat.

Coming to terms with the reality that someone else caused the death
of your child is a deeply painful journey. As you struggle with the senseless and perhaps violent nature of the death, you may find your privacy
invaded by investigators and news media. Trauma is compounded if you
have been suddenly thrust into the foreign and seemingly unsympathetic
bureaucracy of police, courts and lawyers. Out of a need for justice and fair
treatment, parents are compelled to make every possible effort on behalf
of their child. The process can become a staggering series of re-exposures
to the details of the child's death, deepening the trauma and complicating
grieving. It is important that parents have guidance and support as they
navigate these unique challenges.

The focus of this chapter is to familiarize parents with the institutions, elements and risks specific to losing a child because of criminal,
questionable or unexplained causes. We include suggestions for accessing
support and resources as well as ideas that are helpful when the media become involved. Our intention is to provide guidance and to reduce any
stress you may encounter when navigating the criminal justice system and
media coverage.

CRIMINAL INVESTIGATIONS

Examples of sudden or unexpected deaths that require criminal investigations include:

- Death caused by the actions of another person(s) with or without intent or malice aforethought
- Suicide
- Overdose or suspected poisoning
- Suspected criminal involvement
- Act of terrorism
- Death without clear causal factors

Criminal investigations are carried out by the police force with jurisdiction over the crime. Jurisdictions may be municipal, county, civic, state, provincial, federal or military. The geographic location of the crime as well as laws and codes play a role in determining which investigative team is in charge. A criminal investigation might include a collaborative team of officers from different law enforcement agencies.

When a death is sudden and unexpected, the location where the death occurred becomes a crime scene and police restrict the area. The body remains in place and is considered "evidence" while a coroner completes a preliminary examination to determine if there is reason to suspect a crime has occurred. If authorities suspect a crime, they begin a criminal investigation and the body remains "in custody" until the forensic investigation is complete. The primary components of a criminal investigation include:

- Investigating the death scene
- Collecting physical evidence
- Interviewing persons related to the deceased and witnesses to gather evidence or information that may help solve and prosecute the crime
- Performing a forensic autopsy to determine cause of death and collect evidence that substantiates or disproves a criminal offense
- Identifying the perpetrator(s)
- Arresting and charging the perpetrator(s)

The full scope of the investigation could take several days, months or years. During the preliminary period, parents are not allowed access to their child's body. While the investigation is underway, parents need to be surrounded by loving support. Those who are with the parents need to maintain awareness of the parents' state of heightened sensitivity and vigilance. If you find yourself in or choose this role, try to provide a calm, quiet atmosphere, offer emotional and practical support and protect the parents from exposure to media intrusion or too many visitors.

CRIMINAL JUSTICE SYSTEM

The criminal justice system in North America and in some other countries consists of interrelated institutions which work toward the common objective of protecting individuals and society while enforcing the accused's right to just treatment. Responsibility for safeguarding laws and prosecuting violations is divided into jurisdictions. There are specific codes of law that determine what branch of the criminal justice system oversees investigation and prosecution of crimes. In most jurisdictions, components of the criminal justice system include police, courts, corrections and victim services.

Police

Police provide protection, enforce laws, maintain order, gather evidence necessary to obtain convictions in the courts and cooperate with prosecutors in criminal investigations and during trials.

Courts

Individuals who have primary roles in the courts are prosecutors (who represent the Crown or State), defense attorneys (who represent the accused), jurors and judges. The key responsibility of the court is to maintain the rule of law. The court is bound to discover truth and seek justice through the process of adjudication. When a criminal investigation has determined that a crime has been committed, the court will confirm charges against the accused and the case will then proceed to the trial process.

Here is a general overview of standard court proceedings for criminal cases. Court proceedings do not always follow a specific order.

- **Arraignment and pleading:** The accused is informed of the charges and her or his legal rights and asked to enter a plea of *guilty* or *not guilty*. A determination is made regarding whether incarceration or release prior to trial is appropriate. The prosecutor may request a family representative of the victim to provide facts relevant to the accused and the safety or danger of release. If the accused pleads *guilty*, the next court appearance will be at the sentencing.

- **Bail or Bond Hearing:** The bail or bond hearing sets parameters for release and takes place prior to trial. It may occur before, during or after the arraignment.
- **Jury Selection:** Jury selection is the process of interviewing prospective jurors who have been randomly selected from the community at large. The prosecutor and defense attorney conduct the interviews. The selection process may last anywhere from one day to a week or more.
- **Trial:** During the trial the prosecutor presents evidence that substantiates the charges, followed with counter-argument by the defense. Witnesses provide testimony during this phase. Trials have several stages that may include preliminary hearings, requests for continuances and plea bargaining or sentence bargaining between prosecutors and defense attorneys.
- **Finding of Fact:** This is the process of a jury or judge observing the trial, attending to evidence presented, hearing opposing arguments and considering the facts.
- **Deliberation:** Once both prosecution and defense have completed their presentations, the judge or jury goes into deliberation. This process includes reviewing all the evidence and testimony to determine whether the charges have been proven *beyond reasonable doubt.*
- **Verdict:** The formal determination by the jury or judge of guilt or innocence.
- **Sentencing:** If the accused is found guilty, a sentence is imposed. Sentencing may occur at the time of the verdict or a hearing may be scheduled for a later date. It is during the sentencing phase of a trial that the surviving victims are provided opportunity to submit victim impact statements before the court. The defense will also have opportunity to present testimony and witnesses to demonstrate why the accused should receive a certain sentence. The sentence parameters are set by codes of law and determined by the judge.

Corrections

Correctional agencies provide the services and facilities to house and supervise individuals found guilty of crimes. The primary components of corrections systems are jails, prisons and monitoring sanctions such as house arrest or electronic monitoring. Probation and parole agencies are also part of corrections.

Victim Services

Victim services' primary role is to provide victims with support and guidance through the criminal justice system. In North America, virtually all jurisdictions provide some level of victim support services. The agency that houses and oversees the victim services program varies. For example, one community may offer it through the local police, while another may offer it through the prosecutor's office. Ask your local police department how to access and register for this vital service. Services of the program include:

- **Emotional Support**
  - ▷ Assisting police with death notifications and providing support to the person(s) receiving the news
  - ▷ Supporting crime victims, witnesses and their family members in person and over the phone
  - ▷ Providing practical and emotional crisis support
  - ▷ Helping crime victims connect with personal support systems and community resources
  - ▷ Supplying referrals for counseling
- **Information and Court Support**
  - ▷ Providing advocacy and assistance in obtaining information regarding the status of the investigation
  - ▷ Informing crime victims of the justice system and court proceedings
  - ▷ Helping victims to prepare their victim impact statements
  - ▷ Furnishing information on the role of the various players in the justice system
  - ▷ Explaining the criminal justice system processes and proceedings
  - ▷ Offering guidance about the practicalities of testifying as a witness
  - ▷ Informing crime victims of updates on court appearances
  - ▷ Accompanying and supporting crime victims at hearings and trial
- **Financial Support**
  - ▷ Administering Crime Victims Compensation Programs, which provide compensation to victims for expenses such as medical bills, loss of earnings and funeral expenses
  - ▷ Assisting with filling out applications for services and reimbursements
- **Corrections Programs**
  - ▷ Providing resources for individuals to communicate their safety concerns about the release of a prisoner

     ▷ Assisting with safety planning regarding the offender's
       reentry into the community
     ▷ Facilitating a meeting at the request of the victim between the
       victim and offender while the offender is in confinement
     ▷ Notifying victims, witnesses and others enrolled for
       notification of the offender's movement within and through
       the prison system

To locate the nearest victim services organization, talk to your local police authorities.

WHAT TO EXPECT AT TRIAL

Every trial is unique to the circumstances of the criminal offense and jurisdiction. Parents often want to attend every stage of the trial, which may be difficult to accomplish, particularly if they have to travel far or miss work. The complexities and associated stress of trial proceedings complicate the emotional geography of parents' grief. Often grief is delayed as parents remain vigilant in pursuit of justice. Your love for your child and desire to see those responsible for her or his death held accountable is a powerful driving force.

At times it may seem as if the courts have no compassion or consideration for the plight of the victim's family. Expect to be challenged emotionally and physically. No sentence or restitution will ever match the value of your child's life or heal the wound of your loss; however, you may find some resolution through the legal process.

Next we detail some situations or emotional repercussions you may encounter as you go through the trial process.

Lack of Information

It is likely that you will not be informed of the details of the criminal investigation or evidence until the trial, when those details will be disclosed. This is a precautionary measure to ensure that the evidence is not compromised. You will be able to review all information once the trial has concluded.

Timeline Monopolized by the Process

The presentation of evidence and defense can be a confusing and drawn-out process rife with postponements and legal proceedings. Trials and hearings may be postponed or rescheduled on short notice. The prosecutor's office or victim services worker can explain the purpose of individual proceedings. Consider which proceedings are most important for you to attend; some may be less important than others. This way you can make informed choices when managing your schedule.

Facing the Accused

The accused will be present in the courtroom during trial and sentencing. This presence can be deeply unsettling and emotionally intense for parents. If possible, always have a support person with you. It is helpful to ask the prosecutor to show you photos of the accused prior to the trial, making your first experience of physical proximity less intense.

Unfair Balance of Rights

Courts must be unbiased, preserve the rule of law and ensure that the rights of both the accused and the accuser are respected. At times it may seem that the accused has more rights and protections than the victim. There has been a growing movement toward greater awareness of crime victims' rights. Parents need to be assertive about expressing their needs. Collaborating with victim services and appointing a representative to act on your behalf will help you to avoid overtaxing your internal resources.

Exclusion from the Courtroom

If you were a witness to the incident, you may be restricted from the courtroom until after you have testified. Speak with the prosecutor and ask if the restriction can be reconsidered. If you are not allowed in the courtroom, ask the prosecutor about your options: Can you be given a daily recap of the trial? Can you appoint a representative to observe the proceedings on your behalf?

Defense Tactics

The defense attorney may attempt to subpoena you as a potential witness in an effort to prevent you from being in the courtroom. If you did not witness the crime and will not be testifying until the sentencing, this can be overruled.

Rules of Order

Courtrooms have strict rules about behavior and protocol. Your victim services advocate can guide you on courtroom dos and don'ts.

Risk of Re-Traumatization

Evidence may include graphic descriptions of the crime scene and details of what happened to your child that may create painful imagery in your mind. To prevent secondary trauma, you may want to ask the prosecutor to inform you in advance if graphic or disturbing evidence is going to be presented. Then you can prepare emotionally or choose not to attend.

Hurtful Testimony

You may hear your child referred to as evidence; you may also hear hurtful words spoken about your child or his or her lifestyle. The defense may attempt to make it sound as if your child was responsible for his or her own death. Realize that it is the responsibility of the defense to represent the accused and ensure a fair trial. In your heart you know the truth about your child and no one can take that from you. Try to keep an emotional distance from any unkind statements.

Keeping Track of the Trial

Keep notes during the trial to help you remember what has occurred. Write down any questions or additional background you might be able to offer and discuss these with the prosecutor outside of the courtroom.

Behavior in Court: Control Your Emotions

It is important to remember that your behavior must not be perceived as an attempt to influence the judge or jury. You will be instructed to maintain a neutral appearance at all times. If you need to release your emotions, quietly leave the courtroom and find a private space.

This principle remains true outside of the courtroom as well. Do not talk about the case anywhere that you might be overheard and never speak to the judge or jury members. This safeguards the integrity of the trial and prevents any cause for mistrial.

Lack of Justice

The trial will not necessarily lead to a conviction. This is a tremendous disappointment for parents who have hoped for justice and it can be experienced as a secondary loss. A verdict of *not guilty* does not necessarily equal the innocence of the accused. It merely means the judge or jury determined that guilt was not proven beyond a reasonable doubt.

Sentencing According to Rule of Law

It may seem to you that the sentence imposed is out of proportion to the crime. Courts are mandated to uphold the rule of law and in some jurisdictions sentencing laws have yet to meet appropriate levels. Before imposing the sentence, the judge will consider sentencing guidelines, the criminal history of the convicted, victim impact statements and the requests of the prosecutor and defense attorneys. The sentence will not guarantee a sense of justice for parents, but it does bring an end to the trial phase of the criminal justice process. When the trial is over, the parents are released from the forced stamina of attending and can then turn their attention to mourning their loss.

WHAT ARE PARENTS' RIGHTS?

Parents have the right to be informed of:

- Legal rights within the jurisdiction
- The investigation case number
- Specific charges, potential penalties and court dates
- The rights of the accused

You also have the right to:

- Access victim services program resources and advocacy
- Be treated with respect
- Be informed of the layout of the courtroom and the flow of proceedings
- Ask questions, knowing that you will not always get answers immediately
- Express your concerns and needs to the prosecutor and victim services personnel
- Present a victim impact statement prior to sentencing
- Be informed of the prisoner's movements through the correctional system
- Retain a lawyer to advise you
- Refuse to talk to the media
- Appoint a spokesperson to handle all media interviews and communications
- Refuse to speak with the defense attorney

WHAT PARENTS MAY HAVE TO COPE WITH

Confusion

With minds and hearts already shocked and reeling from the pain and trauma of their child's death, parents suddenly find themselves thrust into the complex maze of the criminal justice system. Unfamiliar regulations, protocol and the seeming indifference of officials can be overwhelming and confusing.

Your logic and memory are compromised by the human stress response and grief emotions. Do not try to manage all the information at the trial; take notes rather than trying to remember details. Help yourself by having a friend, relative or advisor act as your advocate. Most of all, be gentle with yourself; as the shock subsides, your mental functioning will improve.

Secondary Victimization

Tragically, even when they are innocent in suspicious death or homicide investigations, family members are often the first people to be considered as suspects. This can deepen the emotional and psychological pain for parents, adding layers of anger, hurt and social stigma to their grief. Other forms of secondary victimization may occur with re-exposure to details of the incident through media or in court, exclusion from the court, facing the perpetrator and hearing his defense, failure of the criminal justice system to identify or prosecute the perpetrator and additional losses related to employment and finances.

Remain aware of your vulnerabilities; it is okay to take a protective stance and limit what you are exposed to. Avoid media reports and the comments of insensitive people. Discuss alternative work arrangements or additional time off with your employer. It will take time to process the layers of information, hurt and loss. Many people find journaling to be an effective method for contextualizing feelings and events.

Loss of Safety

The death may have been of a violent and brutal nature. Parents must struggle with the horror that somebody harmed their child, whether it was on purpose or by accident. Fearing retaliation from the perpetrator, parents may lose their sense of the world as a predictable and safe place. Reestablishing a feeling of safety after exposure to a violent or senseless act is a gradual process. Though you are forever changed by this experience, with time, you will begin to recapture your sense of choice, safety and control in the world. If you have reason to fear for your physical safety, let the police know and ask for their support and protection.

Traumatic Imagery

Parents may have witnessed the death or found their child's body. Even if they were not present when their child died, their minds may be awash in painful imagery as they attempt to imagine what their child's last moments were like. Reports and images of the tragedy in the courtroom or in print and electronic media catapult parents back to the first moments of emotional and psychological impact, deepening the traumatic nature of their experience.

Be aware that initially you are highly vulnerable and painful imagery will tend to replay in your mind. It is best to avoid re-exposure. Flashbacks are initially part of the human stress response and over time can be a signal of a more chronic nature. It is wise to have supportive treatment as soon as possible. (See chapter 1: *When Trauma and Grief Combine* for guidance on traumatic imagery and chapter 13: *Tools for Healing* for guidance on how to choose a therapist.)

Social Stigma

Society will seek a cause for sudden death and, simplistically, may blame the deceased or the parents for the child's death, which exacerbates parents' natural struggle with their own sense of failure or guilt.

Society's tendency to blame stems from a need to understand how a tragedy happened, with the intent of preventing a recurrence. Remind yourself that you did not choose for this to happen and would have prevented it if you could. Try to find out the true cause of death, meaning what exactly ended life in your child's body. Remember that, no matter what the circumstances were, they can never diminish your love for your child.

Frustration

Parents may become frustrated by the seemingly endless criminal investigation and court proceedings. Frustration also surfaces when the crime is unsolved or the death remains unexplained.

Frustration can build up in your body and disrupt your healing process. It is important to release frustration in healthy ways rather than let it fester and convert into anger, rage, anxiety or physical illness. Parents have limited control over the fluctuations or results of a criminal investigation or trial. Some ideas for what you *can* do are:

- Journal your frustrations
- Converse with the investigator or prosecutor to seek reassurance and information
- Involve yourself in pleasurable activities
- Meditate to release tension

- Seek counsel with clergy or a therapist
- Focus your attention on activities that provide you with a sense of completion or resolution

An Unwanted Relationship

Though uninvited and unwanted, the perpetrator becomes a person of interest in parents' lives, a shadow in their minds of which they are compelled to remain aware.

This is a relationship you did not choose with a person you do not want to know. Every parent must find her or his own way to cope with this relationship. Some parents find solace in compassion and forgiveness, sometimes promoted by involvement in restitution programs. Others are able to put the killer out of their minds completely, thinking of the perpetrator only when police, investigators or other authorities come forward with information about movement or parole hearings. Some must face and transform feelings of rage or desire for revenge. Whatever emotions you experience, it is important that you find a method to separate yourself from the unwanted relationship so you can find peace of mind. You have a choice regarding how the relationship will play out in your life.

Arrested Mourning Due to Protocols

As we've discussed, until the criminal investigation is completed, the authorities consider your child's body as evidence and will restrict access; this will delay your ability to see your child or begin planning for the final rites or funeral. Parents have described this time as agonizing; their heartbreak is frozen in disbelief, because they cannot see their child and have no "proof" that she or he is really dead. Parents may also have a strong impulse to be near their child and it is equally painful for them if that instinct is blocked by legal protocol.

When you long to be near your child, being told you must wait can be a painful, numbing experience. Though there is no simple comfort to lessen the suffering, the company of loving support can help. It is not a good time to attempt problem solving or to be exposed to public curiosity or media inquiries. Once the investigation is complete, you will have full access to your child to begin your mourning rituals. A victim services advocate can assist you with inquiries to the medical examiner and potentially arrange a viewing, depending on circumstances.

Grief Delayed by Vigilance

Parents are motivated by a desire to act on behalf of their child and attend to every stage of the investigation and trial. This often means that parents put their grief on hold in order to remain vigilant throughout a prolonged and complicated process.

You may choose to follow the criminal justice process every step of the way. Be aware that your grief will be deferred as you manage all the information and procedures that are involved. Doing so may be a source of comfort and purpose that helps you to cope with your loss. Once the trial is over, you may find yourself experiencing a renewed flood of emotion and grief. Take extra care to treat yourself kindly and engage all the support you can muster. In order to be able to look toward the future, we must travel through our grief. Grief will wait, no matter how long we postpone it.

Destabilization of the Family

With the family unit shaken and stunned by the death, stability is further eroded when parents must rearrange their lives around meetings, hearings and trials. Under the pressure of these added demands, parents risk emotional, psychological and physical exhaustion, which could negatively influence the family's recovery.

Helping your family to cope while facing the challenges related to the criminal process and your own grief is an onerous task. This is a time when families need to "circle the wagons" and draw strength from unity. It is also a time to utilize every offer of help from well-wishers, family and friends. The more you delegate routine tasks to others, the more time and energy you will have to give to your family emotionally and physically. Remain aware of your limits; it is okay to leave the dishes unwashed so that you can spend time with your partner or surviving children. Nurturing emotional relationships, giving and getting hugs, resting and letting go of peripheral worries will help you to manage the challenges ahead.

Surviving children experience their parent's preoccupation and may feel rejected and isolated. This may arouse feelings of resentment toward their brother or sister or they may experience guilt for having been the one to survive. See chapter 9: *Healing the Family System* for more information on the effect of loss on family members and ideas to encourage open communication.

Financial Burdens

The death, criminal investigation and trial process may cause financial strain from unanticipated expenses such as medical, funeral and travel costs or lost income from missed workdays.

Some of your expenses may be recoverable through victim services compensation, insurance plans or community agencies. Ask your victim services advocate for guidance; see the support groups, organizations and Web sites listed at the end of the book for contact information.

Disappointment or Outrage

A trial can result in unfavorable outcomes. It may conclude with a *not guilty* verdict or a mistrial. The defense may plea bargain for a lesser sentence. Sentencing laws may be unjustly lenient or the perpetrator may be released early due to overcrowded prison conditions.

Any of these outcomes could arouse a profound sense of disappointment or intense outrage toward the system you have depended upon to deliver appropriate legal justice. Keep in perspective that the justice system is society's most effective means of managing crimes, but it cannot always come to a satisfactory conclusion. You need to acknowledge your outrage and disappointment. Writing out your feelings will help to dispel some of the intensity and may provide some perspective. You cannot change the outcome of the trial and sentencing, but you can choose to live well in spite of it. Working through the outrage will allow your heart to soften, which will propel you further in your healing journey.

Ongoing Legal Process

A conviction does not necessarily mean that the process is over. The criminal defense may then launch an appeals process that could continue for years. Parents must also endure the parole process, which may mean reliving the tragedy each time a parole hearing occurs. Parents may also decide to pursue a civil suit against the person or institution believed responsible for the death. Civil suits require more direct involvement and personal costs and may take months or years to resolve. Be mindful of the impact of constant re-exposure to the trauma. It may be that over time you have to work to minimize your vigilance in order to allow yourself the time and space to grieve and properly acknowledge your loss.

Note: To remain apprised of any developments or changes, it is important that you keep your contact information up to date with the organizations that supervise and track prisoner activities, for example, victim services, the prosecutor's office and the parole board.

THE MEDIA

We live in a world of rapid communications, where information gathering and dissemination has become a way of life. As a culture, we look to the daily news as our source of information about the world we live in. Many journalists are ethically committed to reporting truth. However, over recent decades the role of media as an information source has shifted. Deadlines and competition for an audience can sometimes have a strong influence on journalistic style. There is often a rush to be the first to report sensational news, sometimes accomplished by using insensitive and intrusive strategies.

A high-profile tragedy such as a homicide, military death, motor vehicle accident or act of terrorism can provoke a frenzied media response. Parents' sense of privacy is intruded upon when reporters approach them, in public or at home, wanting interviews and asking questions that probe the most personal aspects of their lives. Reports with incorrect or presumed information arouse a sense of injustice and feelings of anger. Not only has their child been killed, but also the parents are confronted with a barrage of broadcast and print images about the incident. This constant exposure, in addition to intrusions into parents' private grief, heightens and sustains the parents' state of stress arousal, which potentially worsens the trauma injury.

There are ways to prevent or minimize the unnecessary emotional wounding caused by exposure to media. It is important that parents are aware of their rights and seek appropriate support when their tragedy becomes the object of media attention. Knowing your rights will help you make choices about how to interact with the media.

Parents' Personal Rights

- You have an absolute right to privacy regarding your personal experience as well as on your property.
- You have every right to decide what information you wish to disclose and in what manner.
- You have the right to refuse to communicate with the media.
- You have the right to request, in writing, corrections for incorrect, salacious or provocative reporting.
- You have the right to pursue legal action if slander or libel has occurred.
- You have the right to take care of yourself and your family first.
- You have no obligation to provide information to the public.

- If you are surprised by the media when you are in public, you do not have to respond and may state clearly that you want your privacy respected.

Here are some actions and precautions you can take to help you and your family deal with media attention:

- Choose a trusted person to be your spokesperson who can coordinate all information releases and interviews.
- Take time to meet with family and prepare a written statement.
- Check with the investigators to make sure that any information in your statement will not have an adverse effect on legal proceedings.
- Direct the time and place of an agreed-upon interview, limit the number of questions, ask to prescreen the questions, refuse any questions that you do not wish to discuss and end the interview at any time.
- Prepare a strategy for entering and departing the courtroom on trial days to prevent being mobbed by members of the media.
- Schedule a press conference to address media requests all at once rather than trying to address them individually.
- Avoid being alone in circumstances where you may be approached by the media.

REFLECTIONS ON MOURNING IN THE CRIMINAL JUSTICE SYSTEM

A parent's journey through the criminal justice system can be both stressful and challenging. Choosing whether or not to become involved with the process is a matter of deciding what is right for you. Some parents choose to follow every step and procedure, going public about their opinions, while others prefer to remain apart from it all. If you feel it essential to be actively involved with the criminal justice system, make sure you have an advocate who can support you and speak on your behalf. Knowing your rights and having guidance through the system will reduce stress. Keep in mind that whatever the outcome of legal proceedings, your grief will not necessarily be eased.

Participating in the legal process is much like an endurance race. In order to make it to the finish line you need to pace yourself, choose your battles wisely and keep balance in your life. Take time away from all the legal proceedings and spend these furloughs with family, relaxing or in healthy pursuits. Carol, one parent, reflected on the legal aspects of her child's death:

> *Sometimes I just had to pretend it wasn't happening so I could think about other things in my life.*

It is important to take good care of yourself, especially as you deal with painful realities as the criminal justice system seeks justice for your child who died a traumatic death.

CHAPTER EIGHT

Surviving with Your Partner

A spousal, civil union or long-lasting couple relationship is a distinctive and influential partnership in a person's life. The forces of love, attraction and choice bring a couple together. When something happens to one person, the other person is affected. Memories, goals, day-to-day routines and a unique intimacy are shared. Life transitions, such as entry into parenthood, are experienced together. Hardships are generally shared and endured together.

The death of a child is unknown territory for couples to navigate. It is often the first time a couple has experienced a shared loss of such intensity and it is profoundly challenging for a couple to endure. The force of the trauma, combined with the individual nature of grief, can cause unintentional rifts between partners such as:

- Difficulty supporting each other emotionally
- Changes in intimacy or sexual activity
- Feelings of distance, withdrawal or loss of connection
- Emergence of misunderstandings and miscommunications
- Changes in roles and responsibilities
- Feelings of blame, guilt or resentment

The ability for a couple to rebound from the death of a child varies. The resilience of the relationship is influenced by the existence of unresolved issues, the communication pattern of the couple, the degree of flexibility under stress and the amount of external stressors following the loss. After a loss, couples can regain a sense of common ground and connection through open communication, honesty and an ongoing commitment to nurture oneself and the relationship. Although sometimes it divides a couple, the death of a child often results in a deeper sense of intimacy and bonding through the sad shared experience.

In this chapter we discuss differences in grieving styles and how emotions, reactions and situations can change the relationship's dynamics. We share ideas for regaining connection and techniques for improved communication between spouses.

DIFFERENT GRIEVING STYLES

Grief is an individual journey that is influenced by a parent's personality, coping skills, loss history and relationship with the deceased child. This unique nature of grief becomes abundantly clear when partnerships experience a shared loss. Expecting your partner to grieve the same way as you can cause misunderstandings that deepen your hurt and create distance between you and your partner. Acknowledging that your partner's needs are different and that the two of you grieve differently encourages a more tolerant and healthy shared grief experience.

There will be circumstances when your grieving style conflicts with your partner's; for example:

- One of you may want to participate in social activities while the other wants seclusion and privacy.
- One of you may want to put together a photo album while the other cannot look at photos of your child without anguish.
- One of you may need to talk about the loss while the other chooses to grieve silently.
- One of you may isolate while the other craves intimacy and closeness.

It can be challenging to reconcile conflicting needs between partners. Discuss these differences openly and try to reach a compromise that respects and supports both your needs.

Imposing your own grief experience on that of your partner could cause incorrect interpretations of actions or words. For example, one partner may cope by returning to work right away, while the other feels unable and judges his or her partner as a result. Misunderstandings or arguments may indicate that you lack an understanding of your partner's coping style or that you are not communicating effectively. Take a moment to reflect and ask yourself: *Am I imposing my own needs or grief experience on my partner?*

In order to encourage a supportive and understanding environment within your relationship, recognize and acknowledge each other's unique needs. Consider making these promises privately or to each other:

- I acknowledge that we grieve differently.
- I recognize that we may need different kinds of support to cope with our grief.
- I avoid assumptions, judgments or expectations regarding my partner's ability to support my grieving process.
- I respect my partner's personal boundaries and needs.
- I do not take it personally if my partner needs some time alone.
- I seek support from friends, family, a counselor or clergy in addition to my spouse.
- I listen intently and provide support without trying to fix things.
- I let my partner know what I feel and need without expectation or criticism.
- I ask permission before offering suggestions.
- I recognize that my partner is suffering.
- I strive to be honest, respectful and patient.
- I do not impose timelines on my partner's grief process.
- I do not abuse drugs or alcohol.

Commitments such as these promote an open and accepting perspective regarding each other's grieving processes. Respecting your partner's way of healing and maintaining a neutral view of coping methods provides breathing space in your relationship.

Everyone has different timelines, grieving styles and forms of expression. It is impossible to know fully what your partner is going through, but you can connect by exploring each other's unique experience and identifying the emotional places where your grief is shared. In this chapter we discuss communication techniques for couples. These techniques provide strategies for creating a safe and respectful communication style that will allow you to listen to and feel heard by your partner.

Male and Female Grief

Gender is one of many factors influencing an individual's grieving style. Cultural understandings of gender roles and how men and women express themselves can play a role in how grieving individuals show their grief.

It is common for men and women to approach loss differently. According to Terry Martin and Kenneth Doka in *Men Don't Cry . . . Women Do: Transcending Gender Stereotypes of Grief,* there are two types of grievers: intuitive and instrumental. Both types have individual characteristics.

Intuitive Grievers

- Feelings are experienced intensely.
- Grief is experienced in waves.
- Grievers verbalize or talk about their grief.
- Ongoing supported emotional expression, such as counseling, aids in the resolution of the grief.
- Activities for emotional expression, such as journaling or making art, are effective coping mechanisms.

Instrumental Grievers

- Grief is experienced cognitively (through thought and problem solving) rather than emotionally.
- Grievers are generally reluctant to discuss their feelings.
- Emotional expression is rare or subdued.
- Grief is processed privately.
- Grievers work through pain by doing things, such as carving a memorial or building a garden.
- Social activities, such as shared projects or team sports, bring relief.

Most individuals are a blend of the two types of grievers, with a tendency toward one side of the spectrum. Women tend to demonstrate intuitive grieving while men tend to demonstrate instrumental grieving. There are times when men are more intuitive and women are more instrumental. Although gender may influence where an individual lands on the spectrum, it not an absolute determinant of grieving. One grieving style is not more effective or better than the other. They are simply different and require distinctive processes and coping mechanisms to incorporate the loss into the individual's history.

In the context of a spousal relationship, the information provided by Martin and Doka can help to shed light on the potential differences in emotional expression between you and your partner. Misunderstandings occur between partners when different coping methods are unrecognized or challenged. For example, a wife may believe her husband is not grieving enough because he does not cry or a husband may think his wife is struggling to move forward because she cries often. Consider whether you and your partner demonstrate intuitive or instrumental grieving. Some additional things to keep in mind:

- Appreciate the differences in your grieving styles.
- Avoid judging your partner's process or comparing it with your own.

- Allow your partner space and freedom to pursue healthy coping mechanisms.
- Maintain well-defined boundaries for your own process.

Different Grief Patterns

Grief has many ups and downs. In the midst of a long bout of sadness, a day of relief and relaxation may surface, but amidst that temporary lull you may find yourself unsettled when you face the grief and sadness of your partner. You may feel dragged down while your partner struggles to accept your good mood or vice versa. If this happens on a regular basis, it can negatively influence the relationship. Partners may begin to resent each other or avoid spending time together, because their grief patterns conflict.

The most effective way to address feelings of conflict with your partner's grieving pattern is to use open and respectful communication to discuss them. Let your partner know about your struggles and seek a compromise together that works for both of you.

STEPPARENT GRIEF

Stepparents have varying levels of emotional attachment to a stepchild that are influenced by the extent of co-parenting as well as the characteristics and duration of the relationship. The intensity of grief that stepparents feel is diverse. Some stepparents may feel and grieve as though they have lost their own child; others may feel it as a minor personal loss but are cognizant of the major loss for the biological parent.

A parent and stepparent potentially experience very different losses based on the relationship they each have with the deceased child. Some examples are:

- Stepparents may put aside their own grief out of concern for their partners' well-being.
- Stepparents may move through grief more quickly.
- Stepparents may hesitate to share the depths of their grief, because they do not believe that it is as legitimate as that of the biological parents.
- Stepparents may be more impacted by the loss of connection with their partners who are struggling with grief than by the death of the child.
- Stepparents can be valuable sources of support.
- Biological parents may feel that stepparents do not understand what they are going through.
- Biological parents may wonder why it seems that stepparents are healing faster.

The interplay between the degree of attachment and the intensity of grief explains why biological parents and stepparents may experience the loss of a child in different ways. Communicate openly and avoid assumptions or judgments regarding your partner's grief. If you find you are struggling to reconcile differences in your loss experiences, try some of the communication strategies detailed later in this chapter.

SHIFTS IN RELATIONSHIP DYNAMICS

Loss of Support

A couple's supportive dynamic often changes after a child dies; individuals who once functioned as a joint support unit are suddenly pulled apart as each parent struggles with his or her own grief. Some parents expect the same level of support from partners as they received previously, which may be difficult when partners' emotional reserves are strained. The push and pull between expectations and ability may wear on the relationship and in some cases partners may become angry or resentful toward each other.

Both you and your partner need to rebuild your own emotional, physical and mental reserves before being able to support each other again. To ease some of the pressure, seek sources of support outside of your spousal relationship, be alert to reverting to depending on your spouse for the accustomed support and, if appropriate, try to find alternatives. Spend time with close friends, talk with family members and participate in a local support group.

Heightened Sensitivities and Vulnerabilities

Often those closest to us bear the brunt of personal crisis. When there is a high-stress situation, for example a deadline at work, venting or decompressing is often expressed within the family or partner relationship before it manifests in external relationships. This phenomenon occurs because spousal and family relationships are considered safest and individuals can trust, for the most part, that they won't be abandoned as a result of their behavior.

When a child dies, emotional distress may influence interactions between spouses or partners. Wounded hearts are sensitive, vulnerable and overtaxed; grievers may find themselves with less patience and emotional balance and communication may be difficult. Unintended emotional injury can occur in conversation or disagreements. Here are some ideas for taking care of yourself when you're feeling vulnerable and recognizing if you are unintentionally hurting your partner:

- "Vent" your emotions with someone you trust.
- Engage in physical activity that gets your heart rate up.

- Remove yourself from the situation if you feel vulnerable. Ask, "Can we talk about this later?" and leave the room.
- Provide each other space and time to be alone and reflect.
- Do something nice for yourself and encourage your partner to do the same for him or herself.
- Take time to relax, restore, recharge.
- Pay attention to nonverbal communication of emotional vulnerability or hurt in conversation (for example, lack of eye contact).
- Be mindful of your language.
- If you tense up, take a break or a few deep breaths, count backwards from ten or meditate on a peaceful scene.

Changes in Intimacy and Sexual Activity

It is common for physical desires to change when a child dies; the degree of intimacy will vary from couple to couple. Over time, sexual patterns are usually reestablished as a couple regains physical comfort and an equal desire to be intimate. Here are some potential reactions to or impacts on intimacy and sexual relationships:

- You may experience diminished or absent libido.
- You may suffer guilt or discomfort over pleasurable activities or thinking about pleasurable activities.
- The desire for physical intimacy may increase in an effort to find comfort and express love.
- Trauma responses may shift both perceptual and physical responses to intimacy.
- Grief may leave you feeling physically, emotionally and psychologically exhausted, making sex a low priority.
- Sex may be associated with a fear of becoming pregnant and the risk of another child loss.
- You may feel guilty for wanting sex because it conflicts with your partner's desires.
- Sexual roles may change; for example, the accustomed initiator of sexual activity loses interest.
- There is a risk of partners engaging in extramarital relationships in order to find comfort or to avoid reminders during sex.

Here are some tips for working through changes or differences in libido and intimacy:

- Respect each other's sexual needs and vulnerabilities.
- Talk about your sexual needs and work to find compromises.

- Take small steps toward physical intimacy; kiss, touch or hug.
- Acknowledge that your heart's energy is focused on grieving rather than the relationship.
- Recognize any emotional associations you may experience with sexual activity and see if there are other ways you can address, change or communicate your feelings. For instance, if in the past you have felt that sex expresses love and you now feel unable or unwilling to participate, try to think of another way to show deep feelings to your partner that you both find satisfying.

Recovering from the effects of child loss on intimacy and sexuality takes time. Respect each other's comfort levels and allow time and patience as you gradually return to sexual intimacy. Sex and physical intimacy are an important source of shared enjoyment and connection for a couple. Working together toward a comfortable and enjoyable sex life is a significant step. It acknowledges a joint desire to connect with each other and to share the intimacy that makes your relationship unique.

Changed Roles in the Relationship

Child loss may affect partners' abilities to fulfill roles they previously held within the relationship and family circle. Roles within a relationship are practical, emotional and psychological. When grief is intense, role changes or adjustments often go unrecognized but have an impact on the couple's sense of stability. If you are feeling confused about the changes that are happening in your life, be assured that over time you and your spouse will gradually become comfortable with your roles again. For more information on role changes after loss, see chapter 9: *Healing the Family System.*

COMMON EMOTIONS COUPLES FACE IN CHILD LOSS

Blame and Guilt

As parents struggle to make meaning of their child's death, it is common to search for a cause—something or someone to blame. Two forms of blame may influence the health of a relationship: one parent blames her or himself or one parent blames the other for the death.

Often, parents blame themselves when they have guilt or feelings of failure associated with their child's death. Ongoing blame and guilt erodes an individual's sense of self-esteem and self-worth, transforming his or her interpersonal relationships and interactions with the world. Low self-esteem may cause parents to withdraw from relationships because they feel unworthy of love from a partner or anyone else.

When one parent consciously or unconsciously blames the other for the death, it is a painful and complicated situation. The "blaming" parent may find it hard to contextualize or understand her or his feelings and may feel unable or unwilling to discuss them. Despite this, the feelings will inevitably surface in interactions between the partners. If the laying of blame remains unresolved, the ability for the parents to trust each other will erode over time.

Self-blame, guilt and blame between partners needs to be brought into the open so it can be resolved. Some methods for unlocking these emotions include:

- Writing a letter to your partner or deceased child about your feelings
- Speaking to someone you trust about your feelings
- Seeking help from a couples' counselor to share and work toward resolution of your feelings
- Talking about your feelings of blame with your partner; she or he may be able to provide insight that helps dispel them

Loss of Connection

Grief can consume your energy and attention, which may leave you and your partner feeling disconnected from each other. Grief moves in waves and there will be periods when you feel remote from each other. The feeling of distance may surface quickly after the tragedy and could be in contrast to established patterns of closeness. Emotional withdrawal may originate from a desire to protect a partner from her or his own pain—or because a partner's pain is too much to bear. It may feel as though the relationship is uncertain or falling apart when, in a time of crisis, loneliness and distance occur rather than accustomed closeness and familiarity. Later in this chapter we provide suggestions for reconnection and communication that may help to address feelings of distance.

Resentment

Resentment between partners can stem from:

- Judgments about past decisions
- Unresolved conflicts
- A sense of abandonment, rejection or loss of intimacy
- Differences or misunderstandings over grieving styles
- Perceptions of being unsupported

- Feelings of having to unwillingly set your grief aside to "pick up the pieces"

Unresolved resentments can tarnish the relationship. Use the communication techniques found later in this chapter to initiate respectful and understanding conversations about the difficult feelings you both may have. Consider using a mediator or counselor to provide neutral observations or guide the conversation.

Anger

After a child's death, parents often feel a deep sense of injustice and anger. Generally, beneath the anger are deeper, more uncomfortable feelings of pain, fear or sadness. The anger may be toward yourself, your partner or the world.

Anger can block your ability to move through your natural grief responses, creating a buildup that spills over into your relationships. It affects communication and a partner's ability to see problems or issues rationally. Unaddressed anger can weaken the relationship, so it is important that you recognize the source of your anger. Try to sort out justifiable from reactive angers and avoid misdirecting your internal frustration toward your partner.

To address your anger, you may need to discuss specific issues or behaviors with your partner. Take time to focus your thoughts on paper; then set a time to speak privately with your partner. Anger is more easily resolved when considered as an issue separate from your relationship. Working to resolve angry feelings and find compromise as a team will strengthen your connection with each other and open your hearts to greater intimacy.

THE RELATIONSHIP AND CHALLENGING RESPONSES

Trauma Responses and Complicated Grief

Trauma symptoms can be low grade and ongoing or have a sudden onset. You or your partner may suddenly feel debilitated by trauma responses such as surges of anxiety, flashbacks or even memory loss; in the midst of grieving, you may find these additional symptoms to be overwhelming and frightening. (Use the list in chapter 1: *When Trauma and Grief Combine* to identify trauma responses you or your spouse may be experiencing and to help clarify what you are going through. For ideas on how to cope, see chapter 2: *A Dictionary of Emotions for the Grieving Parent* and chapter 13: *Tools for Healing.*)

Secondary losses—such as losing a home, a job, another family member or a close friend—complicate individual grieving experiences. The source of your emotions could be difficult to identify, overwhelming your ability to cope. Be mindful of additional losses or stressors that may be interacting with you or your partner's shared grieving processes.

Earlier we discussed the more debilitating responses to trauma and child death: post-traumatic stress disorder, complicated grief and depression. If you believe you or your partner may be suffering from one of these conditions, see chapter 1: *When Trauma and Grief Combine* for further information. PTSD, complicated grief and depression cause additional strain on relationships. All of these responses improve with appropriate treatment; seek assistance for yourself or help your partner to establish proper supports. (See chapter 13: *Tools for Healing* for additional guidance on how to find a counselor who meets your needs.)

Unhealthy Coping Mechanisms

Unhealthy coping reveals itself in activities or behaviors that are hurtful and harmful toward oneself or others. Manifestations of unhealthy coping include:

- Anger as an emotional outlet
- Physical or verbal abuse
- Self-medication, drug or alcohol abuse
- Workaholic behavior
- Persistent isolation
- Self-destructive behaviors (for example, binge eating, cutting, anorexia or bulimia)
- Suicide attempts
- Risky behavior (for example, gambling, compulsive spending or unsafe sexual activities)

Unhealthy coping complicates and prolongs the grieving process and is detrimental to the spousal relationship. The person employing these coping behaviors will need to take ownership of his or her actions before a change can occur. If you are attempting to find comfort or relief from your emotional pain in unhealthy ways, speak openly about it with your partner and seek support. If your partner is having trouble coping, you can show love, communicate and be supportive, but foremost, encourage her or him to engage in healthy coping. If necessary, seek the support of family and friends to secure healthy well-being for yourself and your partner.

Estrangement

It is a myth that the death of a child increases the risk of a divorce. Statistically, partners find greater strength and connection through their shared experience. Nevertheless, during the initial stages of grief, individuals may withdraw into themselves and partners may become estranged from each other. Estrangement between partners involves emotional seclusion, covering up feelings and generally ceasing to communicate. Without sharing experiences, feelings or thoughts, partners may start to question why they are together and the relationship may start to erode. While recognizing that each of you may need time to withdraw and process on your own, it is still important to commit to reconnecting with each other gradually and gently.

Questioning the Relationship

After a major loss, individuals usually question life, themselves and their choices. The death of a child often changes a person's sense of identity, including values, spiritual beliefs, interests and approach to the world. The death of a child puts strain on a relationship and may prompt a reassessment of the relationship itself. Partners may wonder: *Do I want to be with this person anymore? Is this the life I want to lead?*

If the couple was generally unhappy or dissatisfied before the death, these feelings of discontent may resurface and intensify. Persistent feelings of disconnect or a lack of healthy communication between partners could also be a reason for considering separation.

Making efforts to reconnect and communicate will either strengthen the relationship or help you reassess whether your partnership is well founded. Give this process time and make strong and ongoing efforts before deciding if you will remain in the relationship.

RESPONDING TO EXTERNAL STRESSORS

Stress from external sources may complicate the grieving process and influence the ability of parents to cope. The parents' relationship may suffer further damage if more stressors are present. Here is a list of potential stressors couples may encounter, along with ways to release some of the pressure that they may be causing:

- FINANCIAL STRESSORS: Seek help to manage your finances. Speak with a professional or family member who is skilled in money management. As a couple, form and agree on a financial plan. This process is empowering, gives a sense of control and reduces the stress money can cause.
- CO-PARENTING: Try to maintain a consistent parenting approach, discuss decisions for the family in advance and support each other when addressing concerns about the grief process of

any surviving children. (See chapter 9: *Healing the Family System* for more information about parenting grieving children.)

- HEALTH: If the health of either partner is compromised, speak about fears and the need for caretaking support. If you are unhealthy, make efforts to improve your health for the benefit of yourself and your relationship, if it is possible for you to do so. If your condition is terminal, support groups and resources for couples are available from doctors, through hospitals and in your community. To minimize the potential of complicated grief, seek help from a grief counselor to distinguish anticipated grief for your spouse from the grief for your child.

- DECISION MAKING: It is wise to avoid making any major decisions such as separation or divorce, the sale of a house or a change in jobs for at least one year after the tragedy. Coping with trauma and grief engulfs a person's vitality, unsettling one's perspective and sense of self. Big changes and additional losses in combination with the grief for your child can be extremely stressful and sources of later regret.

REGAINING CONNECTION

Much of this chapter discusses a couple's departure from a shared path as a result of the individual nature of grief. To help bring you back on a mutual course, this section provides ideas for reconnecting and sharing your grief experience.

Acknowledging the Parent Partnership and Your Child

Although we have highlighted the importance of recognizing and accepting your partner's unique grief, there is no one whose experience will be as closely linked to your own as your partner. Acknowledging your child in ways that recognize your shared roles as parents and the unique circumstances surrounding the death encourages appreciation for the depth and profound nature of what you have been through together. To acknowledge your shared grief and loss, you might try:

- Sharing stories or describing your loss experience to each other from your own perspectives;
- Planning and performing a joint ritual that honors and acknowledges your shared roles as parents to your child;
- Sharing memories of your child's life (for example, the birth story, toddler years, college, wedding);

- Donating to a mutually meaningful charity in your child's name;
- Choosing a project to work on together that symbolizes the love you have for your child;
- Participating in a grief support group or couple grief counseling together.

Relationship Nurturing

Your relationship needs healing and nurturing from the emotional distress, situations and changes that followed the death of your child. Listed here are some ideas for nurturing your relationship and reconnecting:

- Choose a day each week to spend time together.
- Take small steps toward intimacy—touch, hug and show affection.
- Go on a retreat.
- Go on a date.
- Choose an activity you have never done and experience it together.
- Reconnect with shared social relationships (for example, go to dinner with friends).
- Have a "do nothing" day.
- Revisit favorite activities.
- Celebrate your commitment to each other (for example, renew your vows, look at wedding photos or celebrate an anniversary).
- Go for a walk or hike together.
- Rent a comedy movie and laugh together.

Showing Appreciation

You may be so consumed by your own journey of grief that it is hard to recognize or appreciate all the ways in which your partner has supported you. As the haze of your grief lifts, consider the small and monumental things your partner did to help you. Showing appreciation for your partner fosters a sense of affection in the relationship. If it has been a hurtful journey for you and your spouse, showing appreciation conveys, "Despite it all, I still love you." This is a powerful message that can shift the communication dynamic in the relationship.

Here are some ways to show appreciation to your partner and communicate that the effort, love and support you received has not gone unnoticed:

- Say, "I love you, because . . ."
- Write a "Thank you for being you" letter.

- Express your love through words, gestures or touch.
- Make a special meal for your partner.
- Surprise your partner with a gift (for example, flowers, a massage or a weekend getaway).
- Tell your partner why you love him or her and why s/he is important in your life.
- Make a homemade gift such as a painting or carving.
- Deliver breakfast in bed.
- Say thank you often.
- Each day take turns completing the sentence, "One thing I appreciate about you is . . ."
- Do something significant with each other to acknowledge your shared appreciation and perseverance.

COMMUNICATION STRATEGIES

Effective and open communication between partners fosters respectful and appropriate support, despite emotional distress. After a traumatic loss, being able to share and voice your needs with each other contributes to a feeling of continuity and commitment within a relationship. Communicating about grief and the death of a child carries intense emotions and should be done with tenderness and respect to avoid hurt. This section outlines effective and healthy techniques for communicating that partners can use to discuss needs, grief experience, emotions and personal or relationship challenges.

Speaker and Listener Technique

This communication technique requires two willing participants and a few simple steps to get started. Partners should sit comfortably and face each other. There are two roles in this communication technique: the *speaker* and the *listener*.

The speaker is the person who has something to express to her or his partner. It is important that the speaker prepare for the dialogue in advance by focusing what needs to be expressed in clear and simple statements. Completing this sequence of phrases can be a helpful guide:

- When . . .
- I feel/felt . . .
- Therefore what I need is . . .

The role of the listener is to listen attentively to what the speaker has said without judgment or reinterpretation. Next, the listener repeats or paraphrases the speaker's words to make sure there is a common understanding between the two participants. The listener will then validate the speaker with a statement of understanding, followed with an expression of empathy.

If you want to discuss something with your partner, approach him or her to schedule a time that you both agree upon, preferably within a day. Make sure you have a quiet and safe space with no distractions. You must both honor the appointment you have made. If something comes up, it is essential that you ask your partner to reschedule with you. You can also plan a regular time when you meet to talk about how you are feeling or discuss any uneasy emotions. This chart outlines the steps of the speaker and listener technique.

SETTING ASIDE TIME TO COMMUNICATE

STEP	ACTION	EXAMPLE
Deliver the message to the listener	The speaker makes a statement.	"When I reach out for a hug and you pull away, I feel rejected and afraid and then I get angry. What I need is for you to let me know that you still love me."
Reflect the message back to the speaker	The listener reflects back what was heard.	"I heard you say that you feel rejected when I don't hug you back and then you get angry. Did I get that right?"
Confirm or clarify	The speaker affirms that the listener got the message correct or offers a clarifying statement.	"Yes, that is correct." OR "What I said is that I feel rejected and scared; *then* I get angry."
Continue the first three steps until there is agreement.		
Feedback and empathy	The listener then offers her or his understanding of the message. This is followed by an expression of empathy. It helps if the listener imagines how s/he would feel in the same position.	"It makes sense to me that you feel rejected when I don't connect with you. I can see why you would become scared and angry when you think I don't love you. It must hurt to feel cut off like that. When you talk about it I can see you feel really sad and lonely."

STEP	*ACTION*	*EXAMPLE*
Continue or close	The listener asks the speaker if there is more of the message that needs to come forward. If the speaker says yes, return to the first step. If the answer is no, the listener can ask if the speaker wants a response.	"Is there anything else about that you want to bring up?" OR "Would you like me to respond?"
Listener responds (optional)	The listener responds to the speaker. It is *very* important that the listener keeps the response clean and simple, avoids justifications and offers a resolution.	"I am sorry that I've seemed distant and it has hurt you. I will try to be more aware." "It would help if you just tap me on the shoulder and let me know you want a hug. Does that work for you?"
Change roles	When the speaker has stated that the communication is complete, partners can switch roles. Take a moment in between conversations to clear your thoughts and take on your new role in the dialogue.	

While performing this exercise, is it important for partners to remember some key points:

- If at any time during the dialogue you begin to feel defensive, your emotions become too intense or you feel overwhelmed, let your partner know you need a break. If you take a break, be sure you agree on a time to continue the discussion where it left off.
- Avoid using statements that begin with *you*. Accusative or presumptive language is certain to end the dialogue.
- Own your feelings and perspectives. Always work to speak from your own perspective and experience by using *I* statements.
- Treat each other with respect.

The first few times you try this communication technique it might seem a little forced or even silly. Practicing will help. Try doing a session using something neutral, such as what you are planning for dinner. (For example, "When I think about dinner I feel hungry. What I need is to figure out what to cook.") Addressing subject matter that is neutral allows you and your partner to become comfortable with the steps of communication in advance of more complex, emotionally-charged conversations.

Additional Suggestions for Healthy Communication

Here are some additional suggestions to help you and your partner achieve and maintain effective and open communication:

- Set ground rules or boundaries. For example, always ask first if it is a good time to talk. Respect when your partner does not want to talk and set up a time to talk with each other later.
- Consider working with a marriage counselor. Using a mediator who can provide neutral, reflective feedback often helps defuse misunderstandings or miscommunication.
- Always ask; never assume (for example, about feelings, needs, plans, etc.).
- Avoid feelings of exclusion or power struggles by sharing in decision-making and task assignment.
- Conduct check-ins; ask how your partner is doing. If your partner doesn't feel like sharing, it's okay. Asking shows you care. Even if your partner isn't expressing grief or seems to be okay, it's still a good idea to ask.
- If something is bothering you, ask for a dialogue. Unspoken hurts or thoughts can erode the relationship. Seek professional mediation if you think it is necessary.

Committing to open communication does not mean that partners need to share every detail of their grief experiences. In fact, it is common for individuals to go outside of the partnership for emotional support and companionship. Finding a balance between communicating with your partner and being self-sufficient in your healing is an effective way to ensure you and your relationship remain healthy.

MOVING FORWARD IN YOUR RELATIONSHIP

The death of a child is a shared experience like no other and the relationship you share with your partner will face previously unknown challenges. You have a shared loss that is life-changing and deeply painful. As your grief changes and evolves, you will find renewed strength and greater ability to comfort each other. Treating each other with tenderness, love and respect and communicating openly about your loss now and through the years will deepen your bonding and generate compassion and appreciation between you.

CHAPTER NINE

Healing the Family System

A family unit is a complex, interrelated group of unique individuals and relationships. Each family member is independent yet intrinsically connected to the greater whole. Imagine the family system as if it were a balanced mobile. When a mobile is disturbed, the entire structure reacts, shifting and moving as it seeks to rebalance itself. The same happens when a child dies: the family system is shaken and forever changed.

Every family has its own dynamic and unique communication style. Over time, roles and relationships adjust to meet new demands and include new members. Some families are scattered across continents; others are tight-knit groups with cross-generational support networks. This diversity, paired with the circumstances surrounding a child's death, makes the aftermath of a loss in each family unique.

In this chapter we explore and illuminate the grieving process of the family system and provide techniques to encourage communication and healing for the entire family. First, we focus on the nuclear family. We include sections on the family grieving process, parenting grieving children, sibling loss, blended families and communicating with children, adolescents and adult children. We also provide techniques for identifying support systems as well as ideas to encourage self-directed grief work by children. Second, we address the extended family with a section specific to grandparent grief.

THE NUCLEAR FAMILY

A nuclear family is defined as a family group consisting of a parent or parents and their children. When a child dies, that family system is thrown out of balance. Each individual within the system processes the death in a distinctive way and has unique mourning needs. Roles and routines that once seemed natural are disrupted and readjusted as the family deals with the emotional upheaval. Life may feel unpredictable or chaotic.

Parents describe varying effects on the family from the death of a child. Some parents feel the family and relationships are strengthened. Other parents feel relationships are severely fragmented as a result of the death. The ability of the family to cope is influenced by a number of factors including:

- Mental or emotional stability of the parents
- Family communication patterns
- Nature of the child's death
- Relationship between the parents and surviving children
- Degree of additional stress in the household from health, work or financial issues
- Spiritual or religious beliefs within the family
- Loss history of the family
- Presence of alcohol or drug abuse
- Existence of unresolved family issues

Facing a loss of this magnitude is challenging and requires communication, open and respectful emotional expression and shared mourning to restore balance in the family unit. The grieving process for you and your family is a lifelong journey and will unfold over time.

Grieving as a Family

Each individual—adult or child—experiences and expresses grief differently. Family members are emotionally wounded, which increases sensitivities and potential for misunderstandings. Acknowledging these facts and creating a supportive environment for emotional expression are powerful commitments that promote healthy grieving.

Some families have established emotional norms that may not be evident but may negatively affect the grieving process. For example, family members may believe that it's not okay to cry or express anger. They may also think they must "be strong" in the face of difficult emotions. Sometimes talking about the deceased is considered taboo. Gender roles may also influence what children think is acceptable. For example, a girl may hesitate to express anger or rage or a boy may hesitate to express sadness. If you feel comfortable and think it is age-appropriate, bring these concepts out into the open and discuss them.

Suppressing one's emotions potentially prolongs or complicates the grieving process. Families that promote open, respectful communication are more likely to progress through the grieving process and weather life's hardships with less difficulty. Some ideas for supporting healthy expression include:

- Share your own feelings.
- Create quiet spaces in the house.
- Make *Do Not Disturb* signs so individuals can claim personal time and space.
- Encourage self-care and creative activities.
- Spend quiet time together.
- Create grief guidelines for the family. Some suggestions are:
  ▷ We recognize that taking time alone is okay.
  ▷ We know it is okay to cry, feel angry and express grief.
  ▷ We love and support each other.
  ▷ We can always talk about our brother/sister/son/daughter.
  ▷ We can ask questions.
  ▷ We are patient and understanding with each other.
  ▷ We show respect for one another and one another's emotions.
  ▷ We look out for each other.
  ▷ We respect spiritual questions and needs.
  ▷ We know it is okay to seek help outside of the family.
  ▷ We listen without trying to fix things.
  ▷ We do not abuse drugs or alcohol.
  ▷ Hugs are always available.

Creating guidelines for the family engenders a supportive structure that encourages open communication and enhances family resilience in difficult times. Gather with the family to make a poster of the family's grief guidelines and hang it in a common space in your home to acknowledge the family's engagement in supporting one another. Commit to healing as a family and allow free, respectful expression to strengthen the support you bring one another in this shared experience.

Family systems struggle with different emotions and issues depending on how the child died. For example, if a child suffered from a terminal illness, how the family coped during the illness and onset of anticipated grief will affect the aftermath for the family as well as each individual. To encourage holistic healing, engage in conversation; acknowledge experiences associated with the nature of death as well as other emotions you feel outside your grief.

Self-medication, such as increased drug or alcohol use, often escalates after a painful loss, complicating the grieving process and creating issues in family relationships. Consult a counselor or healthcare professional if this is occurring in your family.

Mourning as a Family

Mourning needs to happen as a group for a family to heal after a child's death. Acknowledging the loss, sharing emotions and developing a new relationship with the memory of the deceased are important acts of family mourning.

Acknowledging the loss helps incorporate it into the family history and psyche. This is achievable, both formally and informally. Some ways to acknowledge the loss are:

- Perform rituals and ceremonies.
- Share memories.
- Create memory items (for example, photo albums, memory boxes or special paintings).
- Talk about the loved one openly.

Creating new connections with the deceased allows families to carry their love forward into the new reality of the relationship. This connection can be a cornerstone of comfort during the grieving process. Over time, forming and maintaining a connection contributes to the family's ability to look toward the future. Some ideas to encourage new connections for the family after the death include:

- Mark birthdays and anniversaries of the deceased.
- Plant a family memorial garden.
- Find a shared special place to sit and think about your son or daughter who has died.
- Become involved in an annual project in memory of your child, such as fundraising for cancer research or Mothers Against Drunk Driving (MADD).

Joining together as a family to exchange ideas about new traditions or projects allows each family member a sense of ownership and connection to the dead child. Acknowledging your loss and building a new relationship of memory recognizes the love you all share and helps to redefine the family.

SHIFTING FAMILY ROLES

Each individual has a distinct role within the family system. Roles are practical, psychological and emotional. Practical roles might include doing household chores, but psychological and emotional roles are often not as clear. For example, a child may be viewed as "the clown" or the "sensitive one." Parents are considered protectors, emotional supporters or caregivers. Over time, the roles in a family shift as adults' and children's needs evolve.

After a child's death, families go through a role adjustment period. Suddenly a gap exists in the family that is perceived on practical, emotional and psychological levels. Some aspects of the absent child's practical role may need to be filled. Surviving children may try to emulate characteristics of their deceased sibling to fill the void; others might be angry with parents for their inability to support the family as they used to. Some parents who had an easygoing parenting approach could begin to be overprotective; others might try to find someone to look after in order to maintain their accustomed caretaker roles.

Transitioning into new roles can be sudden or gradual. For example, a younger sibling may suddenly inherit the chores of the deceased, whereas with a longer transition, the family dynamic settles into a new set of un-spoken, subconscious roles. Family activities that are carried out in new roles further strengthen the newly formed family dynamic and identity. Furthermore, family activities can potentially create a sense of togeth-erness and form new, joyous memories. Some ideas for family activities are camping, going to the movies, planning a day trip to a new place or spending an afternoon playing board games.

SHIFTING FAMILY ROUTINES

The nuclear family becomes accustomed to routines that form around every-day activities and family needs. Routines create a sense of stability and pre-dictability for parents and children. When a child dies, those routines may change in both the short run and in the long term. Families are immediately expected to deal with the aftermath of the death, which may include making funeral arrangements or managing an influx of relatives. Concurrently and over the long term, the family feels the gap left by the deceased child; aspects of the family routine existed to meet that child's needs. To regain a sense of stability, new family routines need to be defined and established.

Families in which a child has died from a terminal illness experi-ence multiple shifts in daily routines. The parents' priorities were focused on caring for the seriously ill child, placing increased responsibilities on others, including extended family and siblings. Routines centered on the ill child were often structured around hospital visits, appointments and caretaking duties. When the child dies, parents feel the absence of those caretaking routines deeply; confusion may reign in the household as par-ents and siblings ask, "What do we do now?"

The routines of families with children with genetic disorders or spe-cial needs are often strongly influenced by the needs of the child. When such a child dies, it may seem as if a cornerstone has been pulled from the family's foundation. The family unit, particularly the parents, struggles to fill the emptiness and establish new routines.

Create new routines to help children feel safe and parents feel stable as they cope with their grief and trauma. Attempting to keep things as they were before can inhibit healing, because it fails to acknowledge the absence of the child. Establish new routines as soon as possible to help your family members ground themselves and find a sense of safety. Some ideas for reestablishing new routines are:

- Share at least one daily meal together as a family.
- Maintain previously-established behavioral standards to promote a feeling of continuity.
- Pick a day or evening of the week for a family-oriented activity.
- Encourage children to continue extracurricular activities, such as dance or sports.

CONSIDERING THE IMPACT OF TRAUMA WITHIN A FAMILY SYSTEM

Many factors determine whether a family member will be significantly harmed by the trauma of sudden loss. These factors include:

- Relationship to the deceased (age difference, dependency, in conflict or close)
- Level of involvement in or witness to the tragedy
- Developmental stage, emotional maturity and coping skills of the griever
- Degree of immediate support following the tragedy
- Griever's prior experiences with death and trauma
- Griever's mental health and resilience
- Griever's ability to access resources and support

Just as every person's grief is unique, so is each person's trauma. Some family members' trauma may resolve quickly, while for others it will take longer. Trauma could exacerbate preexisting negative patterns or inhibit an individual's ability to cope. In some cases, trauma has a debilitating effect on family members, making it difficult for them to fulfill their roles within the family system.

The more a family understands emotional, psychological and physical trauma symptoms, the more easily the members can communicate and support each other. (To better understand trauma responses or concerns about post-traumatic stress disorder, see chapter 1: *When Trauma and Grief Combine*. Familiarize yourself with the listed trauma responses to identify if any of your family members are suffering from trauma.)

Trauma is an injury that requires appropriate treatment for healing. If you find that one of your family members is suffering from prolonged trauma response, reach out to external supports such as a medical professional or counselor for help. (See chapter 13: *Tools for Healing* for information on choosing a counselor.)

Families with an Only Child

When an only child dies, parents who are now childless often struggle with a sense of purposelessness. Parents describe feeling empty; they have known fulfillment in their caretaking roles only to find themselves deprived of the source of their greatest joy and purpose. This sense of confusion, loss of identity and struggle to find meaning is a natural response when a child dies. The grief work required might leave little energy to attend to relationships with a spouse or extended family, which could deepen the sense of isolation. Relationships with extended family are discussed further in this chapter. (For information on grieving as a couple, see chapter 8: *Surviving with Your Partner*.)

It is important to be aware of your need for connection, support and reassurance as your search for meaning and purpose evolves. Avoid isolating yourself and be watchful for signs of depression, self-destructive behaviors and suicidal thinking. As you explore your life as a parent whose child has died, seek connections with others who have had similar experiences. Bereaved parents' insights and shared understandings can help in discovering who you now are. (For more information on the lost sense of meaning and identity that can accompany grief, see chapter 11: *Experiencing Identity Loss and a Shattered Worldview*.)

Blended Families

Due to divorces and remarriages, many nuclear families include a blend of stepparents and stepsiblings. In blended families, two dynamics play a role in family grieving: the relationship and communication level of the biological parents and the relationship of stepfamily members with the deceased child.

When a child dies, separated parents may find themselves challenged to make joint decisions. Their shared loss may heal or reopen old wounds, depending on the ability of the parents to communicate with each other. Separated parents could bond over the death or, alternately, direct blame at each other. The presence of the ex-partner and his or her extended family members has the potential to arouse discomfort at gatherings and funerals.

Though each parent has personal grieving needs, circumstances require that they communicate effectively with each other despite their history. If you are a part of a blended family dynamic, here are some helpful tips:

- Be mindful of how interactions with your ex-partner influence surviving children.
- If you are feeling blame toward the other biological parent, ask yourself if your relationship history is influencing your emotions.
- Recognize that your ex has distinct emotions and needs that may not mirror your own.
- Allow your ex some ownership over funeral arrangements.
- Be open to communication.
- Be aware of the potential for unintentional exclusion of ex-family members (for example, the nuclear or extended family of your ex).

In the wake of reinitiating contact with your ex, you may deal with old conflicts, emotions or vulnerabilities; if you struggle to resolve these issues, consider distancing yourself and resolving these feelings privately. Trying to resolve issues directly with your ex-partner may increase your vulnerability and create unwanted emotional injury.

All members of a stepfamily grieve differently for the deceased child, depending on the bonds formed over time. Respect the individuality of one another's grief. Make no assumptions—a stepparent or stepsibling can grieve with the same intensity as a biological sibling or parent, though it may appear as though stepfamily members are moving through their grief more graciously, quickly or intensely than you expected. (Use the communication techniques suggested in this chapter and in chapter 8: *Surviving with Your Partner* to promote open communication regarding differences in your grieving processes.)

Parenting a Grieving Child

A common assumption made by parents is that surviving children's grief is similar to their own. Although your surviving children may feel some of the same emotions, they are experiencing different grief. Children's grief depends on their developmental stages, the histories of the relationships they had with their brother or sister and their roles in the family system. Imagining yourself in your children's position is one way to understand how they might be experiencing the death. They have lost a playmate, a rival, a friend, a companion, an agitator and a shared love that is unique. Children may experience secondary losses within the family system; they witness their parents' sadness and stress as well as the reverberations of the trauma on the family; they feel this acutely. Children may become fearful about their own survival or that of their parents.

Applying compassion when talking with surviving children about their feelings may help put things in perspective and promote meaningful conversation. You might best assist your children by modeling openness, honesty and respect. This will help your children feel more comfortable speaking about their emotions and thoughts and teach them that open and honest communication is a desired family value.

The relationship with your surviving children will inevitably change. Each member of the family unit is profoundly affected by the death in spiritual, emotional and psychological facets. Over time, your connection will adapt and rebuild in this new context. Often, the strength of the relationship in advance of the death will affect how well it copes afterwards. If your bond was strained before the death, you may have to give the relationship extra attention in order for it to re-form. Here are some suggestions that may help:

- Make efforts to connect with your surviving children one-on-one.
- Do your best to make surviving children feel supported and loved.
- Acknowledge the joy you feel at having your children in your life.
- Express your appreciation for your children's unique qualities.
- Acknowledge your children's loss and how it is different from yours.
- Support your children's need to be heard and acknowledged.
- Encourage your children to talk about their brother or sister.
- Support new roles and dynamics.
- Share activities that are both related and unrelated to the loss.

Most importantly, committing to your own grief work will help support the family unit. Children are positively influenced when parents model healthy grieving and respectful emotional expression. Remember to balance your own needs with those of your surviving children. Some parents focus their full attention on the well-being of their surviving children; ultimately, these parents suffer in the end by delaying their own grief. If you feel overwhelmed, seek support; ask family, friends and neighbors for help. Spend time by yourself or with your partner; make time to release your emotions and heal.

DEVELOPMENTAL STAGES AND SIBLINGS' GRIEF

The developmental stages of your surviving children influence their understanding of the death of a sibling and the characteristics of their grief.

- EARLY CHILDHOOD: Young children ages two to five have a limited understanding of the permanence of death. They are conceptually literal and possess active imaginations. It may take many explanations and clarifications before they begin to understand that their brother or sister will not be returning.

- LATER CHILDHOOD: Children ages six to ten are able to understand the physical nature of the death as a body that ceases to function. Although able to grasp the permanence of death, they are not always able to understand or vocalize the emotions or spiritual experiences they are having.
- EARLY ADOLESCENCE: Young adolescents are aware of death and its place in human existence; they understand what death is. They begin to consider the spiritual and more abstract questions that accompany a major loss and are cognizant of the effect of the death on their relationships. They are more able to name and explain their emotions.
- ADOLESCENCE: Adolescence is a complex emotional, physical and psychological developmental stage. Teens are exploring their independence and developing a refined sense of self that is separate from the family identity. As a result, it is common for adolescents to turn to their peer groups instead of the family for support. Responses and needs of adolescents contain both child-like and adult qualities. For example, grieving adolescents may yearn for a comforting cuddle while privately struggling with their increased sense of mortality.
- ADULTHOOD: Adults fully grasp the cognitive, spiritual, physical and emotional aspects of grief. They are able to identify the meaning of the death in their lives and how it permanently changes relationships. In general, adults are independent and autonomous from the family unit. They possess maturity, experience and a personal loss history. They often have established support systems outside of the family. They are able to voice their needs, express themselves and access support independently.

COMMON EMOTIONS EXPERIENCED IN SIBLING LOSS

Siblings experience a range of emotions after losing a brother or sister. Some common emotions include guilt, self-blame, relief, resentment and fear of death or continued loss. Before they are comfortable with expressing their feelings, siblings often require encouragement, support and a feeling of safety. Children are sensitive to their vulnerabilities and those of their parents and may hesitate to share these very personal, sometimes "taboo" emotions. Parents can help by providing a space or medium that will encourage their children to express difficult thoughts and emotions. Some ideas include:

- Provide modeling clay or a pillow to pummel.
- Encourage physical activity.

- Enroll children in martial arts or sports.
- Participate in grief counseling.
- Encourage children to join support groups.
- Hold family meetings and pass around a "talking stick."
- Make music.
- Encourage letter or poetry writing.
- Provide supplies for painting, drawing.
- Explain and promote journaling.

The next section outlines and explores in detail the common emotions of sibling loss:

- GUILT/SELF-BLAME: Siblings often feel guilt or self-blame due to past actions or thoughts they held toward their sibling. Siblings may also feel survivor guilt. It is sometimes difficult for parents to identify feelings of self-blame or guilt. Your children may be afraid to share this history with you, because they feel ashamed or are afraid of upsetting you. Be aware of any self-destructive or self-demeaning language or behaviors. If moody, angry or confusing behaviors persist, try talking about it with your children. You may want to incorporate the support of a family counselor. Unaddressed feelings of guilt could affect your children's self-esteem and emotional health. Recognizing and addressing the source of guilt is crucial in establishing a healthier grieving pattern and preventing long-term emotional damage or self-destructive patterns.
- RELIEF: Siblings feel relief for various reasons. It may be because they no longer need to compete for attention or share toys. In cases of death due to terminal illness, they may feel relief that they have more time with their parents. Although relief is difficult to hear when expressed, take a deep breath and recognize the simplicity of the source of these emotions. Relief does not reflect a lack of love for the sibling and should not be interpreted in that way.
- RESENTMENT: Resentment may be felt toward the parents or the deceased sibling and can stem from a number of sources. The bereaved siblings may feel resentment toward the sibling for dying or for leaving them with unfinished business. If this is the case, writing a letter or having an internal conversation with the deceased helps to resolve these feelings. Surviving siblings may feel resentment toward parents for seeming to be more in love or more focused on the deceased child than on them. The resentment often passes as the family re-stabilizes and parents are

able to increase focus and energy on their surviving children. If resentment is not addressed, it leaves a potentially lasting imprint on the relationship between parents and surviving children.

Find ways to remind your children of your love for them. Words, small gestures or simply spending time together are ways to communicate your continued love for your children. These small moments of recognition and love are significant gestures to your children that help calm feelings of resentment.

- FEAR: After losing a brother or sister, siblings may express subsequent fears about losing parents or family members or dying themselves. Speak to your children about the child's death and the cause of death in simple and clear terms. Ask them to explain it back to you to confirm that they understand. If their anxiety is not dispelled, consider reassuring them by taking them to the doctor. Hearing information about death and health from an authority figure may ease your children's fears. Violent deaths highlight the uncertainty of safety in the world and fears could become more vivid. If your children are suffering from chronic fears or symptoms of anxiety, a registered counselor will be able to help your children work through their fears and rebuild their sense of safety in the world.

TALKING TO YOUNG CHILDREN ABOUT DEATH AND GRIEF

When you are expressing how you are feeling or talking about the death with your children, it is wise to remain mindful of your language. Young children may misinterpret information or generate images and fears that they may not know how to express. Use simple, clear language and explain death in physical terms.

Storytelling is an effective way to open discussions regarding emotions. Lead a story and ask your children to finish it or make up a story yourself to explain death or an emotion of grief. There are numerous children's books that explore death, illness, grief and associated emotions. Try searching online using keywords such as *children's books, grief* or talk to the staff at your local bookstore or library about effective books on the subject appropriate for your children's ages.

Although you may be eager to hear what your children are feeling, they will share when they feel ready. Be patient and receptive and encourage them to ask questions that will guide the conversation. Here is a list of ways to help your children express themselves in a non-forceful manner:

- Tell stories or read books.
- Provide memory boxes.

- Offer journals.
- Supply art materials and encourage painting and drawing.
- Sing and make music.
- Write and perform plays.
- Put together photo albums.
- Go for walks.
- Build a garden together.
- Share memories.
- Play make believe.
- Act and speak with honesty.

It is important that children express themselves freely. When your children do share their feelings, try your best to be present and attentive to what they are saying, although it may be hard to understand.

Children often express their feelings through play, art or actions rather than vocalizing how they feel. If your children are not sharing their emotions verbally, observe them during playtime for common themes or repetitive behaviors. Take note of body language or nonverbal communication and how they express themselves in creative activities. These signs may give you a sense of your children's emotional struggles. Respond with openness, encouragement and love and they will sense your support and readiness to help.

It is best to let kids be kids. You may find that they readily play, laugh and act goofy. This does not indicate that they are not affected by the death of their sibling. Children's emotions fluctuate more fluidly than adults'. They learn through play and interaction and will continue to do so even in the aftermath of losing a brother or sister.

<u>WARNING SIGNS</u>
If any of these emotions, reactions or behaviors occur persistently, your child may need additional support:

- Anxiety, panic
- Fear
- Chronic depression
- Denial of the death
- Self-harm
- Estrangement from parents, withdrawal
- Clinging, fear of separation
- Expressed desire to "join" sibling
- Suicidal thoughts

TALKING TO ADOLESCENTS ABOUT DEATH AND GRIEF

Adolescents who are facing grief are often treated as adults, but they require recognition of their child side as well. They yearn for support and love in the face of their emotions. At the same time they may not respond openly or share their feelings as they seek independence from the family unit.

One of the key desires of adolescents is to maintain normalcy. As a result, they often withdraw from the emotional chaos of the family and focus on relationships with peers or activities outside the family. In an attempt to maintain a sense of normalcy, they may act indifferent or unaffected by the death.

Adolescents may be unwilling to talk about their thoughts or emotions. Pose general questions without forcing the conversation and create opportunities for your teens to share feelings. Doing activities together often provides a sense of safety in which your teens may open a conversation about their grief. Here are some ideas for activities to do with your teenagers:

- Engage in physical activity (e.g., sports, walking, biking).
- Go to the beach, park or somewhere else in nature for the day.
- Join with or support your teens in an activity of their choice.
- Go for a drive.
- Cook a meal or a special dessert together.
- Listen to music together.
- Create something together (e.g., a poster, memory book or other creative project).
- Play a board, card or video game.
- Go out for dinner and a movie.
- Hang out together.

Spending one-on-one time in safe spaces encourages open conversation and storytelling, through which your teens may share their experiences and emotions. This time together also demonstrates your love and support, even if the topic of the death is never breached.

When outbursts or new behaviors emerge, it is often difficult to discern if they are a result of grief or just normal adolescent exploration and boundary testing. It may be challenging for parents to determine how to respond. Speak honestly and openly about your concerns, but withhold judgments or corrective action until you determine the root cause of the behavior. If your teens are unwilling to share with you and you are feeling concerned, consult with counselors at your teens' school or parents of your teens' close friends to get their impressions of the behavioral changes.

It is common for adolescent grief to unfold over a longer period of time. Special occasions or milestones may be a catalyst for an episode of grief or may raise feelings of loss. When painful emotions surface, remind yourself that teen grief might be delayed. This will help you address the situation more appropriately.

WARNING SIGNS

If any of these emotions, reactions or behaviors occur persistently, your adolescents may need additional support:

- Delinquent behavior
- Poor emotion regulation (for example, mood swings, excessive or inappropriate anger)
- Chronic depression
- Self-harm
- Suicidal thoughts or attempts
- Violent behavior
- Drug or alcohol abuse
- Remoteness from family and friends, withdrawal, isolation
- Noticeable drop in school attendance and grades

TALKING TO ADULT CHILDREN ABOUT DEATH AND GRIEF

Your adult children's willingness to communicate will depend on your relationship dynamic and history as well as their emotional health and maturity. As you would with any other adult, practice open communication; ask them how they are and share your experiences or emotions honestly. Recognize that your adult children have adult needs and acknowledge their independence. Approach conversations with equality and respect; minimize the parenting role. If you have advice to offer or helpful ideas for their healing process, ask permission to share them. Assuming you know what will make it better for them is unrealistic; it is always a good idea to ask first. Here are some additional ideas:

- Include adult children in the funeral planning.
- Mention the deceased child's name.
- Ask, "How are you doing with your grief?"
- Let adult children know that you are open to questions about your emotions or experience.
- Be willing to learn from adult children's ways of grieving and mourning.
- Ask if there is anything you can do to help.
- Commit to making regular contact in person, through phone or by e-mail.
- Invite adult children to spend one-on-one time with you (for example, attending a movie, going to dinner or taking a walk).

- "Just be" with adult children.
- Discuss and plan together a death anniversary, birthday or holiday memorial activity for the deceased.

The extent of sharing between you and your adult children will depend on the history of your relationship, the success of your children's entry into independence and the degree of unresolved issues between you. Talking about your grief can create or break down barriers, depending on how it is approached and the level of respect you show toward one another. Respecting your adult children's boundaries and limitations, asking permission before offering advice and listening intently will encourage healthy communication and connection.

Warning Signs

If any of these dysfunctional reactions or behaviors occur persistently, your adult children may need additional support:

- Excessive or inappropriate anger or rage
- Increased substance abuse
- Risk taking (for example, illegal activities, gambling, overspending, unsafe behaviors)
- Violent behavior
- Emotional lockdown, isolation
- Chronic depression
- Self-harm
- Suicidal thoughts or attempts

Building Support Systems

It is understandable if you feel drained and unable to help your children while facing your own grief. It is *okay* to reach out and ask for help from others. Contact mentors, friends or family members who have special relationships with your children. Ask them to check in with your children occasionally and do activities with them. Providing opportunities for your children to confide in supportive adults relieves some of the pressure you feel and frees time for you to recharge and restore your energy.

Many communities host grief support groups for children and adolescents. Your children may feel as though current peer groups don't understand what they are going through. Introducing your children to peers who are familiar with grief and loss will address their feelings of isolation. Hearing peers discuss similar feelings and experiences normalizes grief for the bereaved. Support groups also provide time away from the family and a safe place for personal expression.

In addition to face-to-face support groups, you may access online forums and information for children and adolescents who are grieving. Spend some time exploring online resources with your children to find information about what they are experiencing and discussion groups to join. Books designed for teens and children that explain grief and provide self-care and healing guidance are also available.

Talk to teachers and school counselors. Make them aware of the situation and see if they are able to reach out to your children at school and monitor progress or any concerning behaviors.

Children will also begin to build their own support systems. You may be surprised to learn that your children have been very open with someone outside of the family regarding their feelings. Your children have an impulse to protect you as much as you do them. In an effort to shield you from additional pain, they may go to others for support. Do not take this act personally and be grateful that your children have taken the initiative to find and talk with someone they trust.

Your love, nurturing and support are valuable sources of healing for your children. If it is all you are capable of, commit to one action a day, no matter how small, that demonstrates love to your children.

Having an Additional Child or Children

The death of a child affects the parental relationship with subsequent children along with surviving children. Parents describe a range of feelings, thoughts and reactions regarding children born after the deceased, including:

- Struggle to gain a sense of connection
- Sense that the new child brought healing
- Fear of the child dying and related difficulty bonding
- Resentment toward the child for being alive while the other child is not
- Greater ability to love
- Heightened sense of anxiety or overprotectiveness
- Feeling of relief and restoration
- Change in parenting approach

If you are struggling to connect with your subsequent children due to your feelings of anxiety, vulnerability or resentment, unresolved grief and trauma may be influencing your perceptions. In order to promote a healthy relationship between you and your children, it is necessary to separate your subsequent children from any negative associations regarding the death of your previous child. This process is vital in dispelling potentially lasting effects on your parent-child relationship. Use emotional release exercises and work with a professional counselor to address your mixed emotions. (For more information, see chapter 13: *Tools for Healing*.)

The Extended Family

The extended family includes aunts, uncles, cousins, in-laws and grand-parents. The dynamics between the nuclear and extended family vary. In some cases the nuclear family is isolated from the extended family due to distance or a family culture of independence. In others, the extended and nuclear families are closely integrated and members support one another in day-to-day activities as well as provide support during crises.

The death of your child has sent a shockwave through the family system, regardless of relationships or makeup. Initially, all focus is directed toward the immediate needs of the nuclear family. Extended family members may rally to the parents' aid, offering practical and emotional help immediately following the death. People's desire to connect, help and comfort can be reassuring as well as overwhelming. Remember that it is not your role to take care of others' needs. It is a tender and fragile time for the nuclear family and the help and support offered by friends and extended family is invaluable. Appoint a key person to be your representative, make phone calls, coordinate and delegate tasks and filter out emotional conflicts that may arise.

Family members are often unsure of what to do or say to support you. Here is a suggested list of tasks that will help family members understand your needs and ways they can help. Make your own list and keep it on hand to meet your needs and to convey to others.

Practical needs
- Prepare meals.
- Provide child care.
- Assist with financial management and banking (for example, make deposits, write checks, sort mail).
- Perform household chores.
- Care for pets.
- Shop for groceries.
- Transport children to and from school or activities.
- Mow the lawn.
- Help create a list of things that need to be done.

Emotional support
- Speak about my son/daughter at any time.

- Be patient with me.
- Remind me to take care of myself.
- Spend time with me; I'll let you know if I need to be alone.
- Remind me to take a nap.
- Recognize that tears are not personal; accept them and comfort me.
- Listen to me—you only need to listen, not fix.
- Say things that support me, not things that try to take the pain away.
- Reach out to me (for example, invite me for tea, a sports event or a walk).
- Show me you care.
- Give me a hug.

Incorporating extended family members into ceremonies, rituals and family remembering can be a source of support and comfort. Acknowledging the impact of the death across your larger family sheds new light on the influence your child had in the world and the degree of love felt for him or her and your family.

In some cases, the grief of extended family members will cause them to impose demands on your family, such as special requests for the funeral. Some family members may try to make decisions on your behalf without consulting you. Confronting family politics and asserting yourself against someone's demands or choices while worn with grief can be overwhelming; bring in a third person to mediate. This will help to prevent the situation from becoming hurtful and harming the relationship over the long term.

In the aftermath of the death, parents may feel emotionally conflicted about attending family events, because the absence of their child is felt more acutely among relatives and other families. Interactions with extended family may be particularly difficult for parents whose only child dies, as it reminds them not only of their grief, but also of their uncertainty regarding their role and relationships now that their child is gone. Be mindful of your emotions and allow yourself the choice to leave the event if you need to.

Estranged family members or extended relatives who are from previous marriages or relationships may feel disconnected from the family memorials or rituals and unsure of how to express condolences to you. If you feel comfortable and safe enough to do so, consider reaching out to them to acknowledge their roles in your child's life. Giving estranged family members an opportunity to share their sorrow with you will acknowledge the circle of love your child's life created. However, do not reach out to estranged members if you believe it will reduce your ability to cope.

Although it is not the role of the nuclear family to help or address the grief of the extended family, often these interactions or discussions leave the nuclear family feeling additionally loved and supported. Be aware of your vulnerabilities with extended family members who negatively influence your emotional well-being. Otherwise, be open to the support that is offered and know that your family doesn't need to do this alone.

Grandparent Grief

Grandparent grief is complex and often referred to as a "double-edged sword." Grandparents' grief for the lost grandchild interplays with an equally intense pain felt on behalf of their child. Grandparent grief is often under-acknowledged in families and by society. As a result, grandparents often carry unspoken feelings of exclusion. They may feel their emotions are not legitimate in comparison to that of their bereaved child and may hesitate to express what they are going through.

Involving grandparents in the family grieving process can ease their feelings of exclusion. Perhaps discuss support for grandparents with extended family. Once things feel settled and you feel able to talk, take time to acknowledge shared and differing loss experiences. You may also consider organizing a ritual with the family and asking grandparents to say a few words or contribute their own ideas if they haven't yet had the opportunity.

Here are some tips for grandparents on how to support themselves and their adult child. Consider giving this to them as a guide and to communicate that it is okay for them to show their grief in your presence.

SUGGESTIONS FOR GRIEVING GRANDPARENTS:

- Share your feelings with me.
- Express your needs to family members.
- Acknowledge the magnitude of your loss.
- Recognize the legitimacy of your grief.
- Consider the effect of your loss history on your grief.
- Offer concrete support such as practical help.
- Acknowledge that there is no way to make it better.
- Listen to me without trying to fix my pain.
- Respect my needs and I will respect yours.
- Share your memories with me and other family members.
- Be a source of support to yourself as well as me.
- Respect our differences in spiritual needs.
- Allow me distance if that is what I need.
- Take space if you need it but let me know why.

REFLECTIONS ON GRIEVING
IN THE FAMILY SYSTEM

The death of a child changes forever the individual and family dynamics and relationships within both nuclear and extended families. Recognizing the unique nature of each family member's grief and encouraging open communication will lead to a healthy, healing environment for your family. Continuing to acknowledge your son or daughter throughout your lifetime will bring a new relationship of memory founded in love into your family. Over time, continue to support one another in your grief and ensure that your child lives on in your memories and actions as a family.

CHAPTER TEN

Managing Social Relationships

Before the death of a child, parents have established social circles and relationships built on friendship and memories shared over time. After the death occurs, parents face social interactions in a state of heightened vulnerability and uncertainty. Navigating public outings and facing the reactions of close friends can be challenging and potentially hurtful. As a result of changed emotional circumstances, parents' social circles and friendships frequently shift after the death of a child. Over time, parents may notice an entirely new social landscape has come into being.

In this chapter, we highlight the challenges parents face in social relationships and offer guidance for addressing uncomfortable or stressful situations such as being in public, meeting new people and returning to work.

HOW SOCIAL SYSTEMS REACT TO THE DEATH

Often, friends and social circles are unfamiliar with a trauma and death so profound as that of a child. Parents have spoken to us of being aware of others' discomfort and nervousness. You may encounter people who feel unsure of what to say to you or of appropriate ways to support you.

Amarah discussed her reaction to others after her child's death:

I found it hard to talk about it, because I found people were uncomfortable. They don't know what to say, if they should talk about it or not talk about it. That's hard, because in a way you don't want to talk about it all the time, but you have to—you have to express.

Without taking on responsibility to support them, it can be helpful to offer suggestions to ease social discomfort and help you define your needs, such as:

- "It's okay to talk about my child and my child's death."
- "I appreciate it when you check in, call or write to me."
- "Why don't we make a date to have coffee or take a walk?"
- "I feel better when you say 'I love you'."
- "I value being sent flowers and cards."
- "Please don't make assumptions about what I need. It's okay to ask me."
- "It helps me when you share memories of my child with me."
- "When I seem far away or overwhelmed, please give me time; your presence alone is comforting."
- "When you approach me with compassion, patience, love and acceptance, I feel safer and remember that I am in a healing process."
- "Continue to invite me out for dinner or to social events, but respect if I don't feel able to go."
- "Your small, thoughtful gestures mean a great deal to me and comfort my aching heart."
- "Please feel free to offer help with household chores."
- "Sometimes what I need most is for you to listen quietly to me."
- "Times when we can just be together with no agenda are helpful."
- "Have no fear of continuing to acknowledge my child in the years to come; I want my child to be remembered."

Our society encourages people to address emotions privately. Although it is not the norm, being open and talking about what you are experiencing can generate healing in your grieving process and help others to understand. In regards to your social circles, your openness is an effective way to:

- Signal it is okay to talk about your child and your loss;
- Communicate your desire for support;
- Communicate what your needs are;
- Feel that your grief is acknowledged.

Harriet Sarnoff Schiff writes in *The Bereaved Parent* that "People are basically decent . . . But, as in many human endeavors, people need guidance . . . We are the ones who must set the tone and pace for social relationships. If we don't, we may find that no one will." Being open about what you are going through and what you need are ways to maintain communication with friends as you move forward in your grief.

Societal Understanding of Death

Grief is understood by many as a feeling to be overcome; it is something to withstand and which eventually ends. These perspectives are in conflict with the nature of child loss. The death of a child is life-changing for parents and does not fit into the accepted pattern of "normal" grief. Because the death of a child is outside the accepted norms of our society, there is not a common understanding of the complexities of parents' grief.

A reflection of the social perspective on grief surfaces in messages or statements from others that imply that there is a point when the parents should be over it, moving on or keeping their chins up. These kinds of sentiments can leave parents feeling misunderstood or pressured. Parents may wonder if something is wrong with them, because they struggle with intense grief and can't seem to "move on" as quickly as others expect.

You will move through your grief at your own pace and in your own way. There are no set timelines or predictable phases of grief. If interactions leave you feeling judged or questioning the validity of your emotions, acknowledge that societal or cultural understandings of grief are not necessarily reflective of how your grief truly unfolds.

Rapid Loss of Support

Right after their child's death, parents are surrounded with an abundance of support, but this support may wane quickly. Even within a few weeks, acquaintances may stop offering help, checking in or being cognizant of parents' needs and sensitivities. Society's understanding that grief is linear and should be "over" may lead friends and social circles to assume they shouldn't mention the child anymore or that parents no longer need support.

For everyone else, life returns to "normal," except that the grieving parents are still coming to terms with the permanence of their loss. This can leave parents who are grieving feeling abandoned and isolated. It is helpful for parents to understand possible reasons for their friends' behavior:

- Friends may be unsure whether they can continue to talk about the death, for fear of upsetting parents.
- They may be unaware that parents still need support or may be unsure of how to express it.
- They may feel the family needs privacy.
- They may never have experienced a major loss and do not understand the grief process.
- They may be struggling with their own fears of mortality.
- They may be caught up in their own busy lives.

A further difficulty for parents is that family, friends and community may avoid mentioning the child, thinking it may upset the parents. Feeling this discomfort in others can deepen parents' sense of isolation and estrangement from the world they live in. Marlee, a mother whose son died in infancy, commented:

I used to try to refrain from talking about Bobby. But now I think differently. He's my son; why shouldn't I acknowledge him? So I do things and yes, some people get uncomfortable sometimes, but, well, this is my life.

Though parents may hear the message, "Oh, you better not think about that; you'll feel bad," talking about a deceased child is not morbid. Rather, it is a validation of a very important part of parents' lives. It is the unspoken absence in the room and the denial of a child's existence that causes pain. Cheryl, one parent, shared a quote she heard at a Compassionate Friends meeting that speaks volumes on this subject:

If you bring up my daughter's name I might cry. If you don't bring up her name it will break my heart.

If you feel abandoned or unsupported, it's okay to tell your friends and family what you need. Let them know it is still okay to talk about your child and suggest a concrete task they can perform that will help you to feel more supported, such as going out for lunch once a week or calling regularly.

Fear of Death

A child's death may arouse fears in others as they face their own fragility and mortality. As individuals struggle with their own fears, they may be unable to reach out to parents, because they are afraid to show what they are feeling or do not want to face the reality that children do die and theirs might also. In an effort to maintain a sense of innocence and safety regarding their own mortality, people may avoid the subject of death and loss. This avoidance can leave bereaved parents feeling that they are being shunned—or that their loss is not acknowledged. Bereaved parents must live with the knowledge that they can no longer return to the innocent belief that bad things don't happen.

Connecting and talking with other bereaved parents can help with feelings of isolation and can provide a source of mutual understanding and shared support regarding the magnitude of your loss. See chapter 13: *Tools for Healing* and the support groups, organizations and Web sites listed at the end of the book for suggestions on how to connect with support groups.

Comfort Level with Difficult Emotions

Each person's ability to cope with difficult emotions impacts how she or he will respond to the death of a child and a parent's grief. It will influence how able or available they are to support parents. As Ralph, one parent, said:

*Some people are frightened by deep emotions, but they bring out
the best in others.*

Following a child's death, parents may find that their close friends have
not called or have been generally absent. This may be due to people's discomfort
with difficult emotions. In reaction to this situation, parents may understand
and forgive or they may find the absence inexcusable. Parents' perspectives and
flexibility regarding the situation and the friends' willingness to reconnect will
affect how this absence or lack of support will play out over the long term.

Cathy revealed one friend's discomfort:

*A man who was very close to my husband couldn't bear our
grief, saying our son Alex would have wanted us to be happy;
he was a constant visitor in our home before Alex died, a sort of
uncle to him, but abandoned us afterwards.*

Kristeen showed her own insight into others' issues with conveying
their feelings:

*When they have to, people show up where their strengths are.
They show up in the healing processes and celebrations of their
friends when they can. Some people are able to deal with it right
in the dirt and mud and pick up their friends and clean them
up and kiss them better and some people can't.*

Some time may pass before you realize that you still haven't heard
from a friend or coworker since your child's death. In that instant of realization, you may feel anger, hurt or curiosity. How you move forward from
there is up to you. Choose what feels will work best for your healing process
at this time. The important thing is that you do not want to harbor bitter-
ness in addition to the pain you already have in your wounded heart. Focus
on your needs and on healthy coping.

FRIENDSHIPS

Friends can be a crucial source of support for parents, particularly if family or spousal relationships are strained or not available. A friend who is
open and can offer honest, caring support often becomes an anchor in the
storm for parents. How friends choose to support bereaved parents varies
from person to person. The reverberation of a child's death can strengthen,
weaken or end friendships. Which friends play key support roles and which
ones shy away from the situation can be unexpected.

Maureen related the different reactions of several friends:

*I had three friends in my life whom I thought were friends for-
ever. I don't see any of them anymore, their choice. One said, "I
just want the old Maureen back." I could understand it to a point,
but it really, really hurt. I've come to the conclusion that when
you go through tragedies in life, the people who are the real woods
are still there. Whether their wood is a strong oak or bendable
willow, they are who they are; there is no veneer. The people who
are the veneers look really good in their packages, but everything
is for show. Be wary, because they haven't found who they are yet.*

Friendships can suffer because a friend withdraws from the situation.
The loss of close friends when they are really needed is hurtful and is felt as
an additional loss in the midst of an already painful experience. It also adds
a layer of uncertainty to parents' sense of self.

Parents may avoid contact with certain individuals out of fear of "in-
fecting" them with the pain, as if their grief and the nature of their loss
are toxic to others. As a result, friendships and social life can suffer. Being
overly concerned that your presence will hurt people may be detrimental
to your healing process and can make reentry into social situations more
difficult over time. If you find you are unable to reach out to your old social
networks, find communities and support groups of fellow bereaved parents
in which you can share without fear of surprising or hurting others.

Alex explained:

*Some friends just take too much out of you and you have
nothing left to give, so you just have to let go.*

As the death of a child creates a shift in parents' priorities, they may feel
disconnected from old social circles. They realize they no longer relate to the
values that once had meaning for them or take interest in the same topics of conversation. Friendships that revolved around families and children may be particularly difficult to maintain, because parents are reminded of what has been lost.

Friendships that withstand the hardships and transformations that
occur during grief and loss often evolve into deeply rooted, authentic bonds
between individuals. Friends who are able to support parents after a child's
death become sources of strength. Cultivate the friendships that have endured; express your gratitude for their support when you are able.

SOCIAL OUTINGS

The work of grieving a child is exhausting. As parents struggle with the
emotional weight of their loss, they may find that participating in social
events arouses their sense of vulnerability. Marlee told us:

I don't want to be in huge crowds and I don't want to run into
people I haven't seen in years. I've avoided people too.

Some parents avoid social events; other parents find that social events
are pleasant distractions. A few examples of challenges bereaved parents
may face in social settings are:

- The stimulation of social activities can be overwhelming, due to
  trauma symptoms.
- People may act uncomfortable or avoid conversation with the
  parents, because they are unsure of what to say or how to broach
  the subject of the child's death.
- Parents may feel unable to connect and wonder, *How can people*
  be so happy?
- Parents may experience feelings of discomfort or being out of place.

It may take a while before you feel the desire to be social again. Be
gentle with yourself. Over time, reentering social settings can be a positive
experience and offer a connection back to the world.

Here are some suggestions for engaging in social events in ways that protect your vulnerabilities and allow you to be true to yourself and your needs:

- You may find you have to be the one to bring up your child's
  death. Often, feelings of awkwardness dissipate once a person gets
  your message that it's okay to talk about it.
- If someone begins to ask questions that make you uncomfortable,
  reserve the right to say, "I'd rather not talk about it right now."
- If you feel overwhelmed, it's okay to take breaks. Go outside for a
  breath of fresh air and time alone.
- Ask someone to go to social events with you. S/he can be your life
  preserver if needed and his or her presence will help prevent any
  feelings of isolation.
- Avoid overconsumption of alcohol or drugs.
- If you are feeling uncomfortable, vulnerable or unable to enjoy
  yourself, it is okay to leave the event.
- Arrange your own transportation so you don't have to depend on
  someone else to leave.

WORK RELATIONSHIPS

For bereaved parents, returning to work involves reentering an accustomed
social environment as a changed person. Parents may feel nervous, awkward, resistant or eager to reenter the workplace. Parents may not have

an option and may be required to go back to work soon after their child's death; others may be able to take an extended leave before returning.

Annette described how difficult handling a job can be after experiencing the loss of a child:

> *I feel like I've been robbed of my grieving because all this other stuff is there. I have to put up a front every single day to go to work. I manage a retail department and I have to keep the sales up, because it's an important part of my job to do that. I want regular customers to be happy and come back and buy more stuff. I don't really know how to let all my emotions out and I can't do it at home, I can't do it at work, I can't let my grandkids see. I have to be strong.*

Some parents have stated that returning to their jobs helped them, because it provided a sense of routine and normalcy in their otherwise shattered lives. The workplace environment constitutes a fine balance between one's personal and professional lives and it can become doubly challenging to maintain that balance during a time of intense grieving. Parents may feel that:

- The workplace reminds them of what life was before or of the person they were before.
- They need to mask what they are going through in order to meet expectations and be productive.
- Relationships with coworkers are strained or awkward.
- They are distracted or unfocused and struggle to accomplish their goals.
- They no longer feel passionate about their work.
- Rumors are circulating regarding their situation.
- Coworkers are avoiding or tiptoeing around them.

Parents may compartmentalize their grief or suppress emotions in an effort to keep their grieving process separate from their work lives. They may ask assistance from their coworkers in this attempt; for example, a bereaved parent may ask coworkers not to mention the child.

In order to make the transition back into your work environment more manageable, consider these ideas:

- Have a conversation with your supervisor and coworkers and let them know about your needs and how they can help.
- Confide in one or more coworkers so you have support at work.
- Return to work gradually (start part-time) and slowly increase your comfort level.

- Host an information session during a lunch hour to answer questions, address rumors and express needs.
- Leave the workplace at lunch and go for a walk or meet a close friend.
- Choose inspiring or meaningful projects or start with the most enjoyable parts of the work.
- When possible, choose low-stress or easier projects to work on.
- If you find that work is too overwhelming, consider a leave of absence or finding alternative work.

It is most important that you communicate your needs clearly. Letting your coworkers know what is okay and not okay will guide them as well as define your boundaries. This will foster the process of integrating your working self with your new identity as a bereaved parent. Over time, your relationships at work will settle into a new pattern that leaves both you and your coworkers feeling more comfortable.

PUBLIC PERSONA

In order to deal with day-to-day life, parents often put on personas before entering social or public environments. To avoid judgment or attention in public environments, parents withhold emotions and cover up vulnerabilities. This emotional envelope is a protective measure that parents utilize to get through tough situations. It can be a struggle to cope with the dichotomy between your public and private personas, which can contribute to a sense of being split in two.

Benita exclaimed:

Grocery shopping is a challenge, because you have to go and you run into people.

Striking a balance between managing everyday life, protecting yourself from emotional injury in public and being true to yourself can be challenging. Being in a public space in the midst of emotional vulnerability is very stressful and can engender a sense of isolation or anxiety. Listed are tips for how to cope in public spaces:

- If you struggle going to public environments such as a grocery store, ask somebody to accompany you or to take care of your errands for you for a while.
- If you find yourself experiencing anxiousness, do not try to force yourself to keep going; find a quiet place to sit and take calming breaths.

- You may suddenly need to cry in odd circumstances; it's okay and much better to release the feelings. Remember to carry tissues with you at all times.
- If your emotions are triggered and you have an emotional reaction while out in public, be gentle with yourself and avoid judging yourself.
- Carry a touchstone in your pocket. Holding something can have a calming effect and provide a way to channel your energy.
- Keep in mind that you have choices. If it is becoming difficult to be in public, ask yourself, *What do I need right now?* and respond gently to your own needs.

PLATITUDES

In an attempt to comfort or support parents, people may say things that are intended to be helpful, but their words are actually hurtful. Platitudes can have the effect of causing parents to question themselves, their relationships or the ways of the world. As a result of things people have said, parents describe feeling:

- Judged, hurt, isolated, rejected, angry or shocked
- Reminded of the futility of the death
- Unsure of the level of support or understanding of the friend
- Inadequate as a griever due to their continued sorrow and grief
- Uncertain of their parenting or their child's quality of life
- That their child or their life with their child was unacknowledged
- That the depths of their grief was minimized or diminished

Kathy revealed:

I hate it when people say, "You're so strong." I'd like to respond with: "Should I have crawled into the cupboard? What choice did I have?"

Anne had a different reaction:

When the chaplain met me at the hospital he reached out to me and said, "I'm so sorry for what happened. Know that it was God's way of calling him to heaven." I felt a surge of anger and told him, "Don't tell me that. If that is true, then I will have to hate God. God would not have done this to my son." He was shocked by my words, but I knew that he needed to know how those words hurt me. I wished he had just stopped at the "I'm sorry" part.

When statements or well-wishes are meant to communicate deep feelings but have a trite or worn-out feel to them, they can sometimes cause more harm than good. Some examples of platitudes that can be hurtful to parents are:

- I understand how you feel.
- You'll see him or her again.
- He or she isn't suffering anymore.
- He or she is in a better place.
- God only gives us things that make us stronger.
- Give it time.
- Keep yourself busy.
- At least s/he didn't suffer.
- It is for the best.
- It was God's will.
- This is a blessing.
- It's time to move on.
- He or she would want you to be happy/wouldn't want you to be sad.
- Try not to think about it.
- At least you can have another baby.
- At least you still have your surviving children.

People who use these phrases to be supportive are speaking from learned practice or religious faith, but to parents, these phrases may seem like judgments about the validity of their grieving. It is likely that the intention of the person is to voice his or her support. If you are confronted with these sorts of comments and feel hurt or offended you can:

- Say thank you and move on.
- Use it as an opportunity to gently let the person know how the words affect you.
- End the conversation and leave to address your feelings privately.
- Let the person know that the words are not helpful, that you appreciate his or her caring but just need him or her to listen, hug, make tea.
- Know it is not your responsibility to help others cope and then choose the action needed to care for your own wounded heart.

MEETING NEW PEOPLE

Common questions that people ask in conversation when first meeting somebody can be painful reminders of what a parent has been through, particularly:

- How are you?
- Do you have children?

- Is this your first or only child?
- How many children do you have?
- How did your child die?

When faced with uncomfortable questions, bereaved parents may experience feelings of vulnerability, anxiety and uncertainty about how to respond. They may wonder if they should acknowledge the child and bring up the death. If parents decide not to disclose information, they may feel guilty, deceitful or disloyal for not acknowledging their deceased child. If they choose to share, parents may be confronted with people's reactions of shock, curiosity or sympathy. Parents sometimes find that when a newly introduced individual is not taken aback and is open to discussion, it can facilitate a very honest interaction between strangers.

Dania talked of why she now shies away from others:

I avoid a number of social relationships, because I don't want to have to explain or talk about her. [It's awful] in public when somebody asks a question. Someone I didn't know asked me, "Do you have any other kids?" I just burst into tears. Sometimes [when people ask] I can be really cool about it and say, "I have two" or "I have one." Sometimes I can say I lost a daughter, but a lot of the time I just kind of freeze.

Rachel brought out her feelings:

I try really hard not to hide what I've been through when I meet new people or make new friends. People ask questions sometimes. Because my surviving children are four and a half and seven months old, I often have people who don't know me ask why they were born so far apart. At first I didn't really know how to respond to that and I would not say anything. And then I realized I'm not really doing myself or anyone else any favors by not saying the reason that they are that far apart in age. I was at the gym one day and I dropped the kids off at the day care and a woman made a comment about them being far apart in age. I just said, "Well, I actually lost a baby in between." I said it in a matter of fact way and moved on . . . Rather than trying to figure out in my mind how to explain the gap without mentioning the death, I just said it and ever since then, whenever things come up where it would be appropriate to explain that I've lost a baby, I just do, because I think it's probably better for everybody.

Bereaved parents may find that the answers to questions regarding their children transform over time, depending on where they are in the grieving process. If you find yourself uneasy with questions regarding your child, it helps to plan ahead and formulate a few answers with which you are comfortable. You may find in more vulnerable moments or days that you choose not to bring up the death. On other days, when you feel more emotionally grounded, you may be comfortable discussing it openly with strangers. Experiment with different answers until you find ones that work best for you.

RECONCILIATION

Grief can be difficult for others to understand, confront or comfort. Painful and hurtful things can occur in relationships in the aftermath of such a profound loss. A relationship can be changed or damaged to the point that you no longer wish to continue connecting with the person. Sometimes a rift opens in relationships and you are uncertain of how to repair it. If you find yourself distant from a friend because of something said or done, it can be helpful to consider the motivations and circumstances related to the friend's actions and words. By doing so, it can help you to determine if you wish to reconcile with the person or not. Here are a few questions that may help with this process:

- What was the underlying intention of my friend's words or actions?
- Was s/he making an effort to help?
- Does the current conflict highlight an ongoing clash in values?
- Has it historically been a healthy or unhealthy relationship?
- Were my expectations of my friend's support reasonable? For example, did I expect him or her to make me feel better?
- Do I want to forgive what has happened?
- Would I like to reconcile?

If you determine that you want to attempt reconciliation, here are some ideas for resolution that can be done privately as well as with an esteemed friend:

- Write a letter. Write out your feelings freely as if the person will never read it, then wait a day or so and review it to choose the most important points you wish to make. Rewrite the letter and mail it.
- Have a conversation letting the person know that you want to reconcile but that you need to discuss difficult feelings. Plan out what you want to see happen, perhaps even making notes, and set a time to meet.
- Schedule a joint meeting with a mediator who can be a neutral support for the process.

Reconciling a difficult situation in a relationship can be challenging and unpredictable. Be sure to:

- Give yourself the time you need to work through your feelings and thoughts
- Let the person know you are taking a time out from the relationship if you think it's necessary
- Never force yourself to pretend that everything is okay when it really isn't
- Keep your expectations for reconciliation realistic

NEW RELATIONSHIPS

As a result of their child's death, bereaved parents often form new relationships. Relationships built on a foundation of mutual understanding and respect of how child loss is life changing provide a touchstone of normalcy in parents' lives; a place where they feel truly seen and accepted for all that they have become. Cathy shared with us:

> One of my best friends now is the mother of the boy who was with Alex when he died. I had only met her once before Alex died. She sat beside me crying for days after Alex's death. We find we are alike in many ways. I consider her friendship a gift Alex gave me.

These new relationships will stay with you and continue to be a source of support as your life progresses and you move forward in your grief.

LOOKING TOWARD THE FUTURE

The landscape of parents' social relationships will change after the death of a child. It is not always easy for friends and social circles to understand the experience, needs and grief of bereaved parents. Many bereaved parents have commented how the experience of their children's deaths and their grieving processes transformed their address book listings. Often, parents find that the friendships that remain are more authentic and trusting.

Though grieving your child is a personal journey, the support you draw from your relationships with others is crucial to your recovery. It is important to remember that you have choice in what manner of support you want, from whom and to what degree. Exploring and rediscovering who you are as a bereaved parent is an essential task of mourning. This may involve redefining your social and workplace relationships in ways that are healthy and aligned with your new sense of self.

CHAPTER ELEVEN

Experiencing Identity Loss and a Shattered Worldview

Most cultures accept that parents are not supposed to outlive their children. Parents trust that if they are caring and loving toward their children that they will grow to be adults, have their own children and mature toward old age. When a child is diagnosed with a terminal illness or fatal genetic disorder or when a child dies suddenly, this breaks all the rules and contradicts parents' established sense of right and wrong. Thrust into unknown territory without the guiding force of their accustomed worldview, parents are left searching for meaning and reason amidst the rubble of what they once believed their lives to be.

Anne related her shock at learning of her son's death:

> *I kept asking [my son's friend] to repeat himself, because I was sure I was hearing him wrong. When the words finally sunk in, it felt as if the world stopped turning on its axis and all of reality came crumbling down around me. Nothing made sense; everything was wrong. I felt as if I had been transported into a nightmare world where the most horrible things lived. In that moment, I knew my world had changed forever; nothing has been the same since.*

The tragedy of a child dying has an irreversible effect upon parents' worldviews. Parents must struggle to redefine themselves and their concepts of the world. Recovering a sense of self, purpose and meaning in life becomes the focus of your journey.

This chapter reflects upon how this transformative experience can be simultaneously confusing, tumultuous and empowering. We discuss the process of redefining one's identity and worldview by exploring the questions: *Who am I now without my child? Who am I becoming?* We also talk about how child death arouses feelings of powerlessness and suggest ways that parents can recover a sense of choice and control in their lives.

WHAT IS WORLDVIEW?

The term *worldview* means your conception and understanding of the world. It is the way you define yourself and the world you live in and is influenced by your basic assumptions, beliefs, principles, values and experiences. It is through the lens of your worldview that you interpret the past, determine choices in the present and plan for the future. Your worldview also informs how you see yourself in relation to the world around you.

As a person grows from childhood into adulthood, she or he develops a concept of the world that incorporates internal perceptions, family teachings, cultural influences, religious or faith-based ideologies and life experiences. From this, a person shapes ideals, social rules and personal beliefs that s/he applies to everyday life. One learns to trust that certain facts of life are predictable and that one will reap positive outcomes if cultural, religious or social rules are followed. It is through this assumption of predictability that people find a sense of continuity, control, safety, purpose and meaning in their lives. When an event occurs that contradicts one's worldview, such as the death of a child, it forces a confrontation with the unknown, challenging one's ability to make sense and meaning out of what has happened.

THE WORLD IS NO LONGER WHAT I THOUGHT IT WAS

The potential for children to suffer or for parents to outlive their children is not a part of our cultural understanding of the normal course of the lifecycle. You expect your child to live a full life and guide you through your final days. Consequently, there are few guidelines from which a parent can draw to make sense of the world after a child dies. In the instant when a terminal diagnosis is pronounced, when the heartbreaking words, "Your child is dead" are spoken, the world is irrevocably changed.

Maureen shared her feelings about parents' hopes of their children living after them being dashed:

> We seem to have this theme of entitlement about our children.
> We are entitled to have our children and they will outlive us and

look after us when we are old. They will bury us and that is how it is. Our children do not die at birth. We have a good medical system. Our children are not going to be killed before we are. And we have the false sense of entitlement. I'm not sure where it came from, because if you look back in history, women did not expect to give birth to a live child with every pregnancy. Seventy years ago WWII was happening; women knew their sons were going to be soldiers and not come home. But now we think, that's not right. We live in this false, antiseptic world [where] we think we are entitled to have our children beside us until we are old.

Grief is a place where we reassess our fundamental perspectives and assumptions. A world without your child in it is contrary to everything you have known to be right and true. As you try to make sense of your tragedy, it is a natural part of the grief response to ask and revisit questions such as: *Why? What does this mean? Why wasn't it me instead? What world/ higher power would allow a child to suffer?* This process of questioning can leave you feeling frustrated, confused and dispirited. It is part of the work of integrating the painful reality that you are now a bereaved parent into your worldview.

When the effect of a tragedy is a deconstruction of a person's worldview and the world no longer makes sense, many thoughts and feelings emerge. Some of the changes parents may grapple with include:

- No longer caring about things that once seemed important
- Feeling as if life is no longer purposeful
- Feeling rage at the betrayal of faith or belief in a fair and just world
- Questioning long-established spiritual beliefs
- Reevaluating values and ideals
- Awakening of new spiritual awareness
- A heightened sense of presence in the now
- A new appreciation for life and relationships
- Frustration with petty concerns or shallow conversation
- A sense of powerlessness or helplessness
- A sense of surrender to something greater than self
- An emergence of motivation to help others
- A major shift in priorities: work, principles, relationships
- Increased sensitivity and compassion for the pain of others
- A lifting of old burdens

The breaking apart of parents' worldviews and the onset of their quest to make sense of their child's death can be described as standing at a precipice, stunned with searing heartbreak and filled with a strange sense of grace and sacredness. Though not knowing where it leads, parents know they are stepping into a world in which they are forever changed and in which every footfall is on unfamiliar ground. How a person's worldview transforms after the death of a child is different and unique for everyone. Some variations include:

- The experience of an epiphany; a sudden and irrevocable shift in perspective that surges with new motivation and fills the parent with a newfound purpose
- The affirmation of long-established traditions and beliefs, which bring comfort and meaning to the tragedy
- The gradual development of a personal awakening that forms the basis of a new lifestyle and value system

Rebuilding a new way of knowing and seeing the world can seem like an onerous task. It is not without challenges, pitfalls and leaps forward and backward. What is important to remember is that when your worldview shatters, you are set free to recreate from scratch. You are the ultimate author of your worldview.

A major part of rebuilding your worldview is to re-envision your future while reconciling yourself with the painful reality that your child has died. Another part is to create new ways of being in the world that allow you to incorporate your loss with a new sense of purpose. What is most important to remember is that there are no simple answers that can make sense out of your tragedy or that define the meaning of your life. Your child's death has brought a change to your worldview that is irreversible and transformative. Take things piece-by-piece as you form a new perspective that shapes your present life.

FEELING POWERLESS IN THE WORLD

From unborn infant to mature adult, parents protect their children from a myriad of mishaps. Mothers and fathers are guided by an innate sense of responsibility toward their children as they make decisions and choices that steer the course of their children's lives. They watch over their children, teach them how to be safe, fix broken toys, soothe away bad dreams, bandage scraped knees, patch up broken hearts and help repair broken faucets. The death of a child imposes an irreversible barrier upon parents' most basic instinct: to nurture and protect their children. Parents often experience surges of anger and frustration when they realize that they are powerless to control or change what has happened. Feeling unable to soothe their own pain and grief deepens their helplessness. The crushing realization that even with the best of efforts bad things do happen provokes a sense that there is no real control in the world. Virtually all parents experience this overwhelming feeling.

Amarah conveyed the despair she felt:

> *We found out very shortly before she died. It was a crashing of hope . . . You have all this new hope, that beginning hope that hasn't really materialized. Then she materialized. It was just a pressure cooker from the moment my water broke. I was trying to hold on and give her a chance and my body was not . . . it was minute to minute. You're in this thing, your life is suddenly minute to minute, with the phone calls and the hospital and back and forth. Every moment was the hope that she would get better. They were talking with us about going home, what it would be like. I was pumping my milk and freezing it. Making plans . . . and then in less than a day she got an infection and died. It was a huge loss.*

Your child's death was not your choice, yet now you must learn to cope with the irreversibility of your loss. In the aftermath you may feel as if you have no control, that you are powerless. Through your tragedy you have come to know that there are no guarantees in life.

TAKING BACK YOUR POWER AND CHOICE

Your personal healing includes taking back your sense of power and choice. Regaining your sense of power in this world is not a direct path, but rather one that moves in small increments. Directing attention toward what you *can* choose and what you *do* have control over helps recapture your self-empowerment. Each little thing that you discover is a building block. For example, you might tell yourself that you had no choice about your child dying, but you *do* have a choice to brush your teeth or take a walk or sit down for a while. It sounds silly, but this patient and minimalist approach will help. It is a matter of finding balance between the painful, helpless feelings and the fact that you still have choices. Next we offer an exercise to help with this process.

REDISCOVERING CHOICE

Initially, this is a free association exercise, which means you write out your thoughts as they come to your mind without planning or editing.

1. Find a quiet place to sit without interruption.
2. Open your journal or notepad to a fresh sheet and draw a line down the middle.

3. On the left side of the sheet write down all the thoughts you have been having about what you cannot control or that you have no choice about.
4. Take a pause and allow yourself to think about what you do have choice about. Search for the smallest things that demonstrate that you can or have made a choice. Examples are: what shirt to wear today, how to quench your thirst, whether to speak or listen. Write these in the right column on your sheet.
5. If you fill a page and have more to write, continue on a new sheet of paper.

You are now ready to apply this technique during your normal activities. As you go about your day, notice when you are using powerless or helpless self-talk in your mind and in your speech (sentences that contain *can't, won't, don't, never, always, shouldn't* and *couldn't*). Immediately upon noticing your negative self-talk, complete the phrase, "Yeah, but I can . . ." For example, if the thought is *This heartache is going on forever; it will never get better,* follow it with, *Yeah, but I can get a refreshing drink of water right now.* Through this process you slowly begin to affirm that you *do* have choices and you *do* have some power over your own life.

In the book *Man's Search For Meaning,* Viktor Frankl explores how a person copes with and recovers from tragedy. He states, "everything can be taken from a man but one thing: the last of the human freedoms—to choose one's attitude in any given set of circumstances, to choose one's own way." Shifting your perspective in small pieces allows you to gain ground in your life. Remember, though the worst has happened, you do have choice about how you are going to cope with it.

WHO AM I NOW WITHOUT YOU?

Mothers and fathers experience a feeling of bereft emptiness where the relationship with their living child once was. Parents define themselves through their roles as caregivers, providers, mentors and protectors of their children. Everyday activities, relationships and household patterns are the threads from which one weaves the fabric of life. Parents come to know themselves as they are seen through their children's eyes as well as their own sense of purpose in their roles and expressions of parenting. When that relationship is tragically severed, fathers and mothers face the conundrum of what to do with the reality that they are the parent of a child who is no longer living. Lynn, who lost her only daughter, echoed the feelings of many parents when they face the death of a child:

Catherine and I have been pretty much on our own since she was a little girl. She was my greatest joy in life and everything I ever

did since she was born was because of my love for her and my
fulfillment in seeing her grow into such a fine young woman. Since
she died in a car crash I have felt so lost. What is the point of it
all anymore? I did the very best I could as a mother, but I couldn't
keep her from dying. I don't know who I am or what to do with
myself anymore. I still feel like her mother, but she isn't here.

Bereaved parents express that it is difficult for them to figure out what their purpose in life is after a child has died. Gerard, one father, stated:

I still have all the feelings and all the parts of me that are a
father. I don't want to lose that. It would be like erasing that he
ever existed. What I need to do now is find ways to show what
being his father means to me.

The part of you that has been mother or father to your child does not die with the child but lives on in your heart. It is essential to remember that even though your child has died, you will always be her or his parent. It is a role that has been forever changed by a tragic turn of events but nevertheless a role that is part of who you are.

Every parent struggles with how to make meaning and value out of the child's life and how to validate the part of him or herself that will always be the child's parent. The ways you choose to express your parenthood will be influenced by how you wish to remember and represent your experience with your child in your life. It is helpful to connect with other bereaved parents for support and to explore and exchange perspectives and ideas with them. (See the support groups, organizations and Web sites listed at the end of the book for suggestions of supports that are available.)

WHO AM I BECOMING?

The question that often resurfaces for parents is: how do I go on with my life still feeling like I'm a parent to a child who is no longer living? Grief and mourning is a process of building a new kind of relationship with your child over the years. Emotions and thoughts evolve across a spectrum. Each parent develops his or her own unique relationship with the deceased child that endures through memory and love. As time passes and the acuteness of your grief lessens, you will begin to explore and discover new ways that your role as a parent to your child can be expressed.

Brea talked of the differences in her life since she has lost her son:

My life has changed irrevocably and I have had to learn how
to accommodate the death into my life so that although it's not

*normal to me that my son isn't here, it is what it is. The relation-
ship that I have with him now is one of memory. It's ongoing,
it's different. When he first died, just the thought of him felt like
somebody was ripping my heart out of my chest. But now it's
okay for him to be with me and I don't feel like I'm going to die.
I feel like, he's here! And I fill with gratitude for all that he has
brought to my life and for his presence in my life today.*

One of the more public examples of how a bereaved parent found
purpose in her grief is Betty Fox, the mother of Canadian hero Terry Fox.
Twenty-two-year-old Terry set out to run across Canada to raise awareness
about cancer after losing a leg to the disease. After Terry died, Betty Fox
devoted her life's work to upholding her son's legacy by raising funds for
cancer research. Parents have found many ways to express their love for
and continuing relationship with their deceased children. Many parents
express the desire to "live on" for their children, to face life with passion
and to carry on the good qualities or lessons from their children. This desire and new sense of purpose manifests in the many amazing and subtle
acts that bereaved parents perform on behalf of their deceased children and
themselves, such as:

- Helping newly bereaved parents
- Joining projects that represent the spirit and character of the child
- Creating a special place outdoors to visit, remember, reflect
- Talking openly about grief and the child with others
- Becoming a grief counselor
- Volunteering at a children's hospital
- Donating a bench in a park that provides a resting place for the
  weary
- Donating an adult child's household belongings to a needy family
- Writing and publishing a book of poetry for the child
- Starting a fund or not-for-profit to continue the work of the child
- Creating a scholarship fund in the child's name
- Planting flowers along the stretch of road where the child died
- Working with troubled teens
- Lobbying for stiffer laws against drunk driving
- Becoming a "second parent" to homeless teens

Though you may wonder who you are now that your child has died,
remain open to what unfolds and what resonates with your true self. Your
journey to redefine is uniquely your own. Search inside yourself for ways
that express the love you feel and the meaning your child's life brought to
your world. Remember that the part of you that was a parent to your living

child remains a parent always. Giving voice to *what was* in the context of *what now is* can help to heal the empty place you feel in your heart.

CHANGED PERSPECTIVE

Bereaved parents experience their grief as an ongoing, living organism. The death has changed their lives and is a fundamental part of the life they now live. It will flow and change and evolve with each passing day. When a child dies it changes the fabric of parents' way of knowing. There is no set timeline for the process. Parents move forward one step, one experience, one conversation and one sunrise at a time. Each moment becomes integral to the fabric of a new life.

As a parent is able to reflect on his or her experience and the person s/he has become, s/he may find an entirely new person wearing his or her clothes. The death of a child brings new perspectives and life lessons that define the future of a parent in unexpected ways. There is a strength and empowerment that comes with surviving the worst. The experience defines what is important, what is not, what is worth spending time on and, most importantly, what is true to oneself. Have faith that your power will return to you and you can do amazing things with the lessons you have and will learn about yourself and the world around you.

RECREATING A WORLDVIEW

The unspeakable has happened. Your child has died. In that moment when the devastating news pierced your heart and mind, the world that you knew and the rules that you lived by were shattered. You were thrust on a difficult and painful journey without a roadmap and the world did not make sense anymore. Now, with each passing day, you face the questions that begin with *why* and struggle with the questions that begin with *how*. Alex expressed her understanding:

> *There is an insight gained to what we have. Every little thing, even the small things, can be so precious, so much more notable. These moments that we have or that relationship or our aware- ness of another person's pain is more vital, more alive.*

Your search for meaning is a natural part of your grief. Rebuilding your life and weaving in the threads of your new experience and perspec- tive is how you will redefine yourself as a bereaved parent. It will take time as you explore and experiment with new ways of seeing yourself in the world. Bit by bit, you can recapture a sense of self-empowerment that balances with knowing true powerlessness.

Taking small steps, taking time to notice the little things that count and caring for your wounded heart are paramount to your progress. You will always be a parent to your deceased child; what you are now exploring is how that relationship will manifest in the present. It can become an opportunity to make good from bad as you find ways to ensure that your child's life was not in vain. Only you will know what is right for you, but it will not help to isolate yourself in your struggle. Seek the company of those who have walked this path before you. It is from the wisdom and experience of parents who have lost children that you can find support, changed perceptions and new strength.

CHAPTER TWELVE

Facing Spiritual Emergencies

There are spiritual components to parents' bereavement experiences and the degree to which the death impacts spirituality is diverse. The personal nature of spirituality and spiritual understanding of the world is rooted in an individual's cultural and social background, history and beliefs.

After a child's death, some parents maintain the same spiritual view of the world with new understandings that deepen and strengthen their faith. Others enter an entirely new spiritual territory as a result of awakenings or discoveries after the death. Parents have described a period of uncertainty and doubt about previously sound spiritual beliefs. Questions about life and death drive the quest for a deeper understanding of what has become of the child. Does God exist? What happens after we die? Is there an afterlife? What gives life purpose and meaning?

The term *spiritual* refers to the spirit as human experience and the sense that there is something beyond physical reality or that there are things that we don't fully understand. It is the mystery of the world and the universe that causes us to explore and define our spiritual beliefs. In this chapter we do not focus on a particular religious belief, though we do touch on places of loss or peace within personal faith that mark the journeys of some parents. We outline the spiritual aspects of the parent-child bond, the spiritual opening or break that often occurs as a result of the death, the types of mystical experiences that mothers and fathers encounter and the process of redefining one's spirituality in the world.

THE SPIRITUAL BOND WITH YOUR CHILD

The bond between a parent and child is unique from all other relationships. The entry of a child into parents' lives has a quality of miracle and wonder.

New parents gaze in amazement at this sacred, vulnerable being that has entered their lives, that they are responsible for, that they must love, protect and embody values for. Parenting is fundamentally selfless and is done, as Dennis Klass writes in *The Spiritual Lives of Bereaved Parents*, "with the best part of ourselves." Entry into parenthood forces a redefinition and re-aligning of oneself that is inspired by the sacred nature and responsibility embodied in the spiritual bond between parent and child.

Beyond the parent, this bond goes back through the generations. Children represent continued life and ancestry. As a parent, you give a self-less investment of unconditional love to this being who carries on your heritage. To be a parent is to be gifted with this life to nurture, protect and prepare for the future ahead.

When a child dies, parents may at first feel as though the bond is sev-ered, because the child is no longer physically present in the world. The in-congruity between physical reality and the bond one feels with one's child is where there is a noticeable emptiness. The thread that ties parents and child together through heart, love and experience needs to be redefined. Manifestation of the bond changes and it is reintegrated in parents' lives in new ways: through memories, rituals and a new spiritual understanding of the world. For example, some parents redefine their child as a constantly present guide, angel, consultant, inspiration or advocate on the other side.

SPIRITUAL BREAK

The death of a child shifts parents' internal and external life experiences. The moment of realization that their child will die or has died is unlike any other in human experience. Some feel a breaking open sensation or a sense of being transported out of body, no longer rooted in their known world. In that moment, time seems to stop and senses became so acute that in the awe of that peak experience, they are stunned with a sense of wonder at the depth of love within themselves. The surge of raw emotions forces an instantaneous return to the core fundamentals of what it is to be human and what it is to be oneself. Anne expressed her experience:

> When the words "he's dead" came through the receiver, I recall
> seeing the world before my eyes fade to a dark sepia brown and
> feeling as if the movement of the universe had suddenly frozen . . .
> all that I had known to be my world shattered before me. I could
> feel the life force draining out of me. My perceptions were com-
> pletely distorted. Suddenly I was standing before a long tunnel.
> At the far end of it I could see a light. I intrinsically knew that I
> could walk toward that light and find my son . . . I was standing
> at the gateway between life and death and I knew with every

fiber of my being that I needed only to decide to step toward the light. In that instant of profound consideration, I knew that I had a choice: join my son, reach out to heal his pain or embrace living and step into a strange world that included the reality of having a murdered son. In that terrifying moment it became so real to me that there is a place outside of the known world where love is an infinite source. Somehow, to the core of me, I knew he was safe.

Amarah told us how she felt when she learned of her child's death:

[When Marie died] it was so intense . . . I think of it [as] this incredible experience. I don't want to say it was a healing, because that came after, in a sense. But it was a spiritual moment. I was holding her and I knew she was dying . . . It was just as if the whole room exploded in light. And it's still the most powerful experience in my life. It just exploded and there was this bright light and there was this overwhelming feeling of love in the room. I was just sitting there with her body. I couldn't say anything to anybody, I didn't know if that's what they felt, but for me that was exactly what happened. I felt this incredible love. I was very close to my grand-mother when I was growing up and I just saw her standing there in the room. And in that instant . . . in that moment, for me, all those questions were answered and I have never had a bit of spiri-tual fear since . . . All of those seeking questions that I had when I was younger, I just don't have them anymore. It was experiential and it's my truth. It has guided me ever since then.

Parents have described undergoing an abrupt awakening to an aware-ness of their own mortality, an ending of innocence and an unbidden mo-ment when the line between reality and the sacred blurs. In moments of such intensity there is an *undoing* that gives view to the unexplainable or the unknown. This flooding and opening can rarely be described in terms other than metaphor, because it defies language. No two parents give the same description, but there is a theme that is consistent. It is unlike any other experience. It is accompanied by an awareness of profound signifi-cance and is often mixed with a sense of a presence beyond the physical, heightened sensitivity, unreality and timelessness. It is in this place, where the sacred and profane collide, that questions of a spiritual nature arise.

SPIRITUAL CRISIS/CRISIS OF FAITH

The contradiction that this wondrous gift, a treasured child, was taken from the world can bring dogmatic aspects of a religion crashing down. In that moment of crisis, prior understandings of the universe and creation are no longer able to sustain the reality of the child's death. The dissolution or absence of faith is felt as another profound loss. Parents' belief systems are confronted with painful and immutable truths when their child dies. Bad things happen, no matter how good or faithful or deserving a person is; the innocent are not any less vulnerable than the wicked. It is a moment of spiritual crisis framed in questions not previously considered: Why? Why my child? Why would God/the universe do this? How could God/the universe hurt a child? Why did God/the universe abandon me? The questions frame an unfolding story of personal inquiry and discovery.

Joyce revealed the change in her that her child's death brought:

It was a huge mid-course correction for me . . . I was going along with my life all in order and the bottom dropped out. Then I had to rework my point of view about God and spirit. [My son's] death had to have some meaning, but all the ways I would have intellectually described it before no longer fit.

Some of the crisis is a reworking of one's own faith. The death of a child brings parents to *unknowing* themselves as much as they thought they knew themselves. The experience of the child's life ending, of hope collapsing, often provokes a tear in the fabric of their fundamental spirituality. The fearful part of this is the sense of losing one's identity and belief structure. Bereaved parents are challenged to become comfortable with the unknown and to allow the answers to unfold. The quest for finding a definition or purpose for the child's death becomes a profound journey of the soul as they seek new meaning to redefine their spiritual understanding of the world.

Parents describe a broad spectrum of responses to this spiritual crisis. Some examples are:

- Questioning the existence of God
- Feeling disconnected from God
- Feeling abandoned or betrayed by God
- Finding comfort in spiritual beliefs
- Feeling disappointment with clergy/religious community
- Finding support and comfort from a religious community previously not known to them
- Being angry at and blaming God
- Experiencing a loss of faith
- Having no sense of a world beyond the physical
- Experiencing a new sense of connection with spirit, soul
- Sharing an ongoing connection with the presence of the child
- Interpreting symbols and myths within their worldview in new and more profound ways

- Finding new and compelling worldviews and belief systems
- Feeling deeper compassion toward the suffering of others
- Rejecting a belief system or religion
- Awakening to a new faith and embracing a formal religion
- Returning to church after a long absence
- Discovering a newfound peace in knowing there is life after death
- Experiencing a complete and absolute shift in spiritual perspective

When a child dies, sometimes violently, sometimes after a prolonged battle with illness, parents are faced with the inevitability and unpredictability of life. They may have prayed to God/a higher power in search of comfort and answers that could ease their pain. Left to deal with their anguish and sorrow, bereaved parents may feel abandoned by God, alone in their grief and longing for their child.

Bereaved parents question if they will ever be able to feel emotionally engaged in life again. The idea of being with the child can seem far more palatable. A deeply spiritual dynamic is at hand in choosing life when this kind of challenge is before parents. They have lost a child, faith, purpose and identity. The effort of grappling with the deep questions of meaning and faith is an interior journey of searching and choosing. When this choice is made, bereaved parents embark upon a path toward exploring new understandings and new ways of being.

Marlee described her crisis with spiritual beliefs:

A lot of my questions are about why. I want to know about the God I love and know: Was He responsible for this or was it just a catastrophic accident? When we are born does God know when we're going to die? I know those are unanswerable questions, but those are what I ask. I understand [my son] is gone. I'll never accept it, but as my friend said, we learn to live with it.

It is a natural part of parents' grief to want answers that will ease the pain and offer meaning for their child's death. For some, answers are found in their religious beliefs. For others, the search may be philosophical or based upon the practical. What matters is that your search will require you to pursue answers to questions that may not be answerable.

A crisis of belief and faith arouses profoundly important questions. Exploring grief's questions moves parents deeper into the spiritual dimensions of their existence. Finding resolution may occur in a moment of epiphany or it may be an ongoing, life-long journey. There are no absolutely right or wrong answers that will suit the needs of every person. What is important is that you allow space and time in your life to grapple with your questions and cultivate the patience to let the answers unfold.

FINDING SOLACE AND PEACE
IN SPIRITUALITY AND FAITH

There are many ways that bereaved parents have found peace amidst the turmoil of loss. Parents may find comfort in their existing belief systems or in knowing that the child is now under the protection of God or the universe. It is faith that carries them through the dark passage.

Maureen shared:

For me, I knew that Andrew heard, I just knew that he heard, "Well done, my good and faithful son" before [he died]. That was cemented into me. I also knew . . . that every time I yelled out [or questioned God], a calm reassurance came over me . . . When the rubber hit the road, the only person I could truly count on was Christ and He was always there, even when I tried to chase Him away.

Mink told us:

My spiritual community is my strongest touchpoint. The people in the community are always behind me. Without their help when Joshua died, I don't think I would have come out on the other side as well as I did.

Spiritual beliefs can provide a solidifying structure in a world that has come unglued. The way in which bereaved parents define the world of the living and the reality of death is often through religion or an interpretation of spirit or soul. Examples of how parents have described what their beliefs, spirituality and faith gave them in their times of profound need are:

- Moments of solace and reflection in prayer and/or meditation
- A sense of stability and peace in faith
- A sense of being connected to a reality that transcends the self
- An association with something bigger than oneself that the child is now a part of
- The felt spirit of the child creating a bridge between the worlds of the living and the dead, of heaven and earth
- The comfort found in knowing there is an afterlife where they will reunite with the child
- The support of a community of people who share the same values and beliefs
- A sense of shelter and protection from the immeasurable pain of grief
- A source of answers to the bigger questions about life and existence

- A sense of comfort that there is a higher power with a divine plan
- Peace in knowing the child is part of a greater whole
- Belief that the child still exists in a different form, dimension or realm
- Emotional comfort in the embrace of grace and spirit
- A way to forgive oneself through compassion and love

MYSTICAL EXPERIENCES

Many parents have mystical experiences following the death of a child. These moments of connection that transcend the physical world can be strangely unnerving as well as deeply comforting. They highlight that there are things beyond the realm of what can be seen, touched or fully understood. Experiencing a communication with or presence of a deceased child also brings a sense of connection with something bigger than oneself that is beyond death, making the invisible visible. The boundary between life and the afterlife dissolves in these moments. Mystical experiences open one's mind to the mystery of life and often influence or form the basis for a new understanding of the world.

Sensing Your Child

Receiving visitations or sensing the presence of a child after s/he has died is a common and comforting experience. Parents have experienced their child's presence through all of the senses: they hear, smell, see or feel the touch of their child. Kathy shared her connection with her daughter's spirit:

> *Rather soon after Tammy's death I was looking in her closet and crying, knowing I would never see her in these clothes again. For some reason I pulled out her old red sweatjacket and started to put it on. As I did, a warmth spread from my arm around my shoulder and down my other arm. It was not a normal warmth, but a spiritual understanding that she was with me and hugging me, maybe for the last time. The euphoria I felt that day stayed with me and I wrote a poem about the experience. I know that there is another world that we pass into and now I don't fear death.*

Mystical connections with a deceased child demonstrate the sacredness of a shared love and how that love can endure across the boundary of the physical world. We are not attempting to verify or disprove the phenomenon; we only wish to share parents' stories and demonstrate how connections with a child beyond death bring deep and meaningful comfort to a parent's broken heart.

Mink described her vision of her son:

About three years after Joshua passed, [I saw him] sitting on the couch downstairs in almost a blue shadow. His face was like a picture, but the body was in a blue color. His teeth were white, his smile was there. It was like he was just here to tell me that things were okay. That he's in a different form, that he is here, that I just can't see him all the time, but when I slow down enough, I can. I can be with him in the cemetery or whenever I take time out to just sit and enjoy nature.

If you sense or experience the presence of your child, trust your intuition. Have confidence that there are things that we can't understand and that these moments are gifts. If you feel the impulse, strike up a conversation, let your child know how you are and how you miss and love him or her.

Spiritual Guides and Angels

Parents also experience connection with or messages from spirits and beings other than the deceased child. Family members and friends may also convey similar experiences to bereaved parents. Brea told us:

I heard a voice that said, "He is happy, he is loved, he is well taken care of." I know I would never have used those words and I would never have said he. I would have said Sean.

Similar to sensing the presence of your child, receiving messages in the midst of grief from spiritual guides, angels, God, the universe or elements of nature is often a source of comfort and reassurance.

Dreams

The dream state is an ethereal and mysterious realm. After a child dies, dreams can be a source of discomfort and fear or of connection and healing. Alex spoke of dreams of her daughter:

For several days after Shaughnessy's death, a great many people— students, friends, family and people I didn't know—had dreams about Shaughnessy. They all described her looking the same, with the same hair, same expression and wearing the same outfit. I had numerous dreams where she came to me—"spoke" to me [without] words [and] danced with me. I still keep a journal of all of my dreams as well as dreams others have shared with me.

Nightmares that follow a traumatic loss are an aspect of the trauma itself and of the cognitive process of trying to understand and integrate the event. Replaying the scenario or circumstances surrounding the death can occur in both waking and dream states of consciousness. In the dream state, the unpredictable and symbolic nature of the subconscious can intensify the fear and discomfort felt. If you are experiencing ongoing nightmares, consider it a signal that you have additional work to do to resolve your trauma. (For more information, see chapter 1: *When Trauma and Grief Combine* and chapter 13: *Tools for Healing*.)

In some dreams you may have a conversation or embrace your child. You may see your child in a new place or with other deceased family and friends. Waking from these dreams can arouse a mixed reaction: they can bring feelings of connection or be a reminder of what is missing in your waking life.

Dreams are also a mechanism for expression of emotions as well as a subconscious workshop where the mind works on problems, fears and unresolved issues. The dream state is a place that is free from the inhibitions that control our behaviors and thoughts. Fred, one parent, did not cry often when awake but spoke of crying regularly in his dreams.

Symbols and Messages

Parents often notice signs, symbols or messages in nature or in everyday life that act as a link between themselves and their child. These symbols come to represent the presence or continued existence of the child within their lives. Serendipitously, symbols or messages commonly present themselves at times when parents most need it. These symbols or messages often bring comfort and a sense of solace when encountered. Symbols are frequently found in numbers or nature totems: animals, flowers or plants. Judith relayed her son's last communication:

> *The last thing Kevin said before he went out was, "I'll come and visit you guys sometime." We didn't understand what he was saying at the time, but we remember him saying that when he was painting in a field and a little bird came and sat on the wire. Kevin was rubbing his eyes, because he was crying, but he knew that little bird was a message from [his deceased wife] and that she was visiting him through the little bird. I think what he was saying is that later we would know that when we saw a little bird he was coming to visit us. Now when I see a robin I say to [my husband], "There's Kevin," because I know that's what Kevin meant.*

Anne shared the messages she receives from her son:

Jake had an impish sense of humor and a way of really seeing through the bull. I've come to accept that when something really quirky happens that stops me from doing something stupid, it is Jake giving me a little reminder and I smile and thank him for watching over me.

Synchronicity often causes the transformation of something common into something with meaning. For example, a butterfly lands on a parent's hand in the midst of thinking of the child or a number constantly reappears following the death of the child. From that moment forward, when a butterfly or the number reappears, the parent thinks of the child. These symbols or messages are mysterious and powerful and provide a way for parents to sustain a sense of connection with the deceased child. If you can, smile, contemplate and accept them.

When Mystical Experiences Don't Happen

If a parent expects to have mystical experiences but they do not happen, it can be deeply distressing and upsetting. It can inspire further questioning or uncertainty regarding the workings of the world and personal faith.

There is no real answer to why some parents experience or feel the presence or ongoing sensory connection to a child and others do not. Some parents have described success at fostering this connection through meditation or spending time in nature, but there are no guarantees.

Even if you have not sensed your child's presence, it does not mean that your bond or connection no longer exists. The connection is in your heart and this can be cultivated through speaking to your child, doing personal rituals and remembering. It is healthy to continue nurturing your relationship and expressing love for your child. (See chapter 14: *Creating Personal Rituals and Memorials* for ideas.)

REDEFINING AND REINTERPRETING

Experiencing a spiritual break, reevaluating faith and having mystical experiences act as clues to spiritual answers. As parents move forward in their quest toward redefining their spiritual understanding of the world, they continue to seek answers and reinterpret values, traditions or religious beliefs. Over time, parents begin to make meaning of the death and apply or integrate their experiences in the context of the bigger picture. Maureen shared her view:

I'm starting to come to the realization that I don't need the answers; they don't matter.

Seeking Answers

Parents may seek sources of connection or guidance in an effort to have spiritual or personal questions answered. Kathy described her journey:

> *Through a spiritualist I experienced an incredible conversation with my daughter. We talked about her death and other personal things that just could not be duplicated by someone else.*

Ways of actively looking for answers may include:

- Consulting with clergy or spiritual leaders
- Reading books on spiritual transformation, life and death
- Visiting with mystics such as psychics, shamans or mediums
- Studying religious texts
- Thorough, directed or systematic questioning of a past belief system
- Seeking and returning to places that hold a mystical quality or sense of connection to the deceased child
- Going on pilgrimages
- Attending conferences that promote spiritual connection or development
- Reading poetry or literature that explores themes of death, life, grief and spirit

This more formal act of seeking answers is another step in how you interpret the meaning of your child's death and redefine your world. (For a listing of books related to spirituality and mortality, refer to the resources at the end of the book.)

Anyone Can Be a Spiritual Guide

Often, people enter into the lives of bereaved parents and serve as guides. These individuals can act as mentors as parents work to remold their lives. Brea shared:

> *My friend and I went to a bookstore I hadn't been to before. When I inquired about books dealing with grief, I met a lovely young lady. As we talked it became apparent that we had similar beliefs . . . Was it a coincidence we met?*

If you find that new people are entering your life unexpectedly and at the perfect time, pay attention. Cultivate these relationships if you can. These connections can provide guidance and inspiration as parents reshape their spiritual lives.

Finding Meaning

Over time, the emphasis of the search transforms from "Why did this happen?" to "How am I going to make value or meaning out of this experience in my life and what am I going to do with it?" With persistence, parents often form a sense of spiritual purpose to the loss. *Kairos* is a Greek word that means "a passing instant when an opening appears which must be driven through with force if success is to be achieved," according to the *Encyclopædia Britannica*. The death of a child often forces these moments of *kairos* when everything melds into one and the human spirit comes to the surface. The spiritual quest to redefine the world after the death of a child is challenging and takes time and dedication to pursue.

Ultimately, parents come to realize and become comfortable with the fact that the bigger questions may not be answered in their lifetimes. It is what they do with the journey that counts.

SPIRITUAL TIPS AND PRACTICES

There are many spiritual practices that take a variety of forms, some more formal than others. The purpose of these practices is to bring oneself to a place of solitude, introspection and interconnection with the non-physical aspects of one's life experience. Spiritual practices also provide a structure from which a sense of meaning and purpose can be derived. When performed in a routine manner, they can provide respite from the pressures of the outer world as well as grounding and containment for matters of the heart and soul. In no way are we attempting to endorse a particular practice. Find what is right for you. What matters is that the practice helps to bring you to a place where you experience a grounding connection with the inner dimension of soul or spirit. Some of these practices are:

- Praying
- Chanting
- Meditating
- Spending time in nature
- Practicing yoga
- Performing mindfulness practices (e.g., Tai Chi, walking meditation, breath meditation)
- Running, swimming or biking
- Connecting with things or places that fill you with wonder
- Visiting a place of worship

It is important for bereaved parents to have a source of connection and comfort as they carry their burden of grief and grapple with life's deeper questions. If you have not already done so, seek groups with similar spiritual beliefs or practices.

Speaking with spiritual guides, counselors, mentors, clergy or other bereaved parents can help parents as they wrestle with questions of soul and spirit. Exchanging thoughts, feelings and uncertainties with a trusted "sounding board" helps parents as they reflect upon old and new interpretations of their spirituality. It can be quite helpful to talk with someone who has training in grief and spiritual crisis.

SPIRITUALITY AS A GUIDE

There is no single path that will lead bereaved parents to the answers to their questions regarding spiritual matters. What is most important is that parents set out upon a path that helps them to find direction in their grief. It can be your own private path or one of the great traditions; whatever will support and guide you on your journey.

The movement toward a deeper relationship with spirituality that helps to heal your wounded soul need not be grand or complex. There may be times when it feels as if everything is overwhelming and nothing will ever make sense again. Often, inner quiet is found in the simple things. If you are having a bad day, attend to simple acts if that's all you can manage. Sip tea, gaze at the sky or feel the wind moving through the trees. It is often in the most simple that the wonder of spirit is found—that place where the profound presence of love for your child can transcend the ordinary and closeness with the greater whole is felt.

Connecting with the source of life conforms to your natural ability to heal and allows transformation to occur. It is important that you follow your heart and your spirit on your quest to resolve your deepest questions.

CHAPTER THIRTEEN

Tools for Healing

A t the moment of your child's death, all facets of your mental, physical, emotional, spiritual and psychological being were strained. You need to practice extreme self-care. This chapter is for the good and bad days. We provide ideas, exercises and reflections to guide you through your grieving process and your journey of self-discovery. Taking care of yourself and processing your grief includes small comforts as well as goals for long-term personal growth. Practicing reflection and seeking support in your process are healthy coping mechanisms. Grief for a child is a layered and complex experience that plays out over a lifetime. Revisit the techniques and suggestions in this chapter as you progress in your grief.

PERSONAL AFFIRMATIONS AND VOWS

Affirmations are personal promises and a powerful tool of commitment to oneself. Personal affirmations written in active language and in the first person are more effective in forming personal associations with the promises. Here is a list of affirmations you can use to guide your approach to your grief and to remind yourself to practice regular self-care. Add to this list with your own affirmations.

- I commit to healing.
- I express my emotions.
- I take ownership of my grief.
- I commit to movement within my grief process.
- I make changes when it feels like I am stagnating.
- I do not judge or critique my process negatively.
- I know what is best for me.

- I allow myself time for reflection, rest and restoration.
- I maintain a support system that works for me.
- I accept my vulnerabilities.
- I acknowledge my pain.
- I recognize there are good days and bad days.
- I move through my grief, not around it.
- I honor my experiences.
- I make self-care my first priority.
- I am gentle with myself and act within my emotional limits.
- I love and value myself.
- I accept myself and my emotions.
- I am honest with myself.
- I am patient and tolerant with myself.
- I have the power of choice.

Personal affirmations can be incorporated into your life in many ways. You can:

- Read them daily
- Choose one affirmation to focus on for yourself and write it out or speak it aloud a few times every day
- Post them in a place of prominence in your house (e.g., on your bathroom mirror)
- List them in a journal to revisit
- Use them as inspiration for an art piece or a song

Working with personal affirmations allows you to assert control over your healing process. They declare your intentions for moving forward and are a consistent reminder of your commitment to healing and being gentle with yourself.

PRACTICE REGULAR CHECK-INS

You are the best person to determine what you need to help you grieve and heal. Performing regular check-ins is an effective way to determine if you need to make any changes to your situation in the immediate moment as well as the long-term. The simplest personal check-in is the question, "What do I need?" This question can be used in diverse situations and is a great tool for determining your next steps or changes you need to make. It can be used when you feel your anxiety mounting or when you are pondering your direction for the future. Now is a crucial time to listen to your intuition and practice self-care. Other questions that can be used to check in on more specific aspects of your life include:

- Do I associate with people who help my progress?
- Do I make time to relax or spend time alone?
- Am I taking care of my body?
- Am I asking for help when I need it?
- Am I being honest with myself?
- Am I giving myself permission to love and grieve freely?
- Am I self-medicating?

GUIDELINES FOR HEALTHY COPING

Everyone's Grief is Unique

There are many incorrect assumptions about the characteristics of grief, such as the notion that it is a finite experience or that everyone grieves in similar ways. If you are confronted with these assumptions or myths about the workings of grief, it can be unsettling and cause you to question your process. By recognizing that grief is a diverse and individually unique experience, the pressure or judgment you feel dissolves. Grief is an ongoing personal journey with many layers. Over time the grief transforms, but it will always be there and will reemerge throughout your lifetime. Accepting this as reality allows your emotions to come forward for expression.

Keep it Simple

The less complicated your life the better. It is an intensive process to mourn your child and to reshape what remains of your life. As much as you can, keep your life simple. Make small goals for yourself; allow yourself the space and the time you need. When faced with decisions, ask yourself: does this improve the way I feel or make things more difficult? For the first while, don't get heavily involved in things and try to minimize stress in your life. Plan ahead if you can and break tasks into small, manageable steps. Call on supports and delegate to get things done if you have to.

Seek Information

While you are reforming your world, gaining a further understanding about the cause of your child's death or the grieving process can be comforting. If you have more questions, medical professionals and counselors can be valuable sources of information. There are also books and Web sites regarding grief and specific types of loss. (See the resources at the end of this book for suggestions.)

Give Yourself Permission to Grieve

You have just been through one of the most difficult and powerful experiences of human existence. Give yourself permission to do, say or feel whatever you think will help. It is okay to admit the pain of your loss. Avoid judging your process and keep your best interests at heart.

If you are having trouble releasing your emotions or are compartmentalizing your grief, doing activities that break down your boundaries or quiet your rational mind can help. Some examples are renting a tearjerker movie, listening to a special piece of music, going for a run or building a memory box.

Remember Honestly

Every relationship and individual is unique. People have faults and relationships have challenges. Idealizing your child or the relationship you had with your child can be a detriment. It can skew your relationship with others, such as your surviving children. Choosing to remember your child honestly opens yourself to the possibility of reconciling difficulties or accepting your child's faults as part of your process. Being truthful in your recollection encourages holistic healing.

In cases of perinatal loss, remembering honestly is about letting go of your imagined child and mourning the child as s/he was in his or her short lifespan.

Take Care of Your Body

The capacity to cope is directly influenced by your physical state. Grief and distress take a toll on your body. Rest, adequate sleep, proper nutrition and exercise are extremely beneficial in times of duress.

Inadequate rest or sleep increases disorientation and your ability to process information. If you have a chance, take small rests on the couch or bed throughout the day. Falling asleep and maintaining regular sleep patterns can be difficult in the early stages of grief and trauma. If you are having trouble falling asleep, try doing something to relax before bed. Take a bath or have a cup of tea or warm milk. The focused breathing exercise later in this chapter can also be used to relax as you are trying to fall asleep.

Eating healthy and nutritious foods is important for maintaining your stamina and health. Ask others for help in preparing meals to ensure you are eating healthy meals regularly. If you have lost your appetite and it is not returning, it may be worthwhile to speak with a doctor or nutritionist.

Exercise relieves stress and muscle tension, provides an avenue for emotional release and helps regulate sleep patterns. Physical activity is also a way to process thoughts and have some time alone. You may feel uninspired to do the types of exercise you used to. If this is the case, try something new or do something simple, like going for a short walk. Some other ideas are: swimming, running, hiking, doing yoga, playing a sport (e.g., basketball, football, soccer, volleyball, hockey), practicing martial arts or kickboxing.

There is an intrinsic connection between the body, soul and emotions. Alternative therapies such as aromatherapy, reflexology, massage, Reiki, energy treatments and acupuncture work to release physical and emotional tensions in the body. They are also very relaxing and a nice way to treat yourself. Many bereaved parents find alternative therapies to be beneficial and effective methods for emotional release and relaxation.

Tend to Your Spirit

Tending to your spirit means doing things that reconnect you to your core and calm your soul. Some ideas include spending time in nature, reaching out to your spiritual community or meditating. Refer to chapter 12: *Facing Spiritual Emergencie*s, where we discuss the profound impact child loss has on your spiritual understanding of the world.

Create Sanctuary for Yourself

Find places in nature or create calm spaces within your home or property where you can reflect, spend time alone and experience calm in the storm. Plan a vacation by the sea or go on a retreat. Sanctuaries are private spaces where you can feel safe and protected and can break away from the busyness of life. Places of remembrance and healing allow you to contemplate, feel emotional pain and mend in peaceful surroundings.

Grief Is Individual and Shared

In the midst and intensity of your grief it can be difficult to recognize the pain of those around you. If you find people's actions hard to understand, before reacting, gently remind yourself that this is a difficult time for everyone. Be aware that others will need space to grieve as well.

Take Breaks from Your Grief

Grief is exhausting and feels inescapable at times. Be careful not to associate your suffering with the love you feel for your child. Pleasurable activities are not an affront to your deceased child. The raw dichotomy of life is tears and joy. Create opportunities to set your grief aside for a moment. Give yourself permission *not* to think about it. Bring some laughter into your life. Rent a comedy, download amusing videos or go to a comedy club. Tell a funny story about your child and allow yourself to laugh. Laughter, like tears, is an excellent release and reconnects you to the joy in life.

Pay Attention to Your Reactions and Feelings

It's important to take time to reflect on your emotions and reactions. They can signal where you need to focus your energy or the changes you might need to make to facilitate movement in your grief process. For example, if you are highly irritable or acting out, you may have unresolved anger that needs to be addressed. Recognizing that something needs to be further explored in your emotional self is the first step to resolution.

Enjoy Small Pleasures

Taking part in small, simple pleasures is a great form of self-care. Here are some suggestions that you can use and add to. In adding to the list, ask yourself, *What activities or behaviors have comforted me in the past and which of them still work?* These small steps to wholeness are simple ways to regain connection with the joy in life.

- Eat an apple.
- Sip tea.
- Sleep late.
- Chop firewood.
- Look out the window.
- Organize your desk.
- Pick flowers.
- Watch the clouds.
- Go to a ball game.
- Finish a project.
- Go fishing.
- Watch the sunrise or sunset.
- Rearrange a room in the house.
- Go to a museum.
- Bake cookies.
- Visit the library.
- Feed birds.
- Go to a concert.
- Do nothing.
- Bask in the sun.
- Spend an afternoon lounging.
- Read a novel.

- Gather shells and stones on the beach.
- Learn something new.

Help Others

Helping others in simple or more committed ways is an enjoyable and effective way to reconnect with people and funnel your grief into something meaningful. Transferring your experience and lessons to something with personal significance can comfort you and make meaning from your loss.

Find Community

There is a direct correlation between the level of support a parent has and the parent's ability to cope. Commit to building a community for yourself through family, friends and support groups. The next section discusses building your support systems in more detail.

CREATING SUPPORT SYSTEMS FOR YOURSELF

It is important that you surround yourself with as many supportive resources as possible to help you on your healing path. Your well-being includes a balance of supports that address the needs of your body, mind and spirit. Here are some ideas and suggestions for building a team that is focused on helping you cope with and grieve your child's death in healthy and supported ways:

Social Supports

You are in a vulnerable emotional state. It is a good idea to be selective about with whom you spend your time. Surround yourself with people who are beneficial, who support your process, with whom you are comfortable and with whom you have mutual respect and love. Here are some questions to help guide you to the individuals in your life to whom you can reach out:

- Who understands me?
- Who is able just to be with me?
- With whom do I feel comfortable sharing my emotions and being open?
- Who is a good listener?
- Do I know anyone who has been through something similar?
- Who has emotional/spiritual strength or grounds me?
- Who does not leave me feeling judged?

Health Support

If you do not already have an existing relationship with a medical practitioner, this is a good time to establish that connection. Trauma and grief can have prolonged effects on physical health. You may have been so overwhelmed with the aftermath of your child's death that you have not been able to keep up with your health, diet or sleep. Your health practitioner can be one of your closest allies in your healing. Start with a basic checkup and let the practitioner know what you are dealing with. You and your health practitioner can then track your health status and address any issues you may be having (such as high blood pressure, symptoms of PTSD, anxiety, depression, sleep problems or digestive problems). It is important that you feel comfortable and connected with your health practitioner and never feel obligated to continue seeing her or him if you are uncomfortable. When you are looking for a new practitioner, it is always a good idea to ask people you know for recommendations.

There are a variety of health practitioners who can help you to address ongoing physical and mental health issues, including medical doctors, naturopaths, psychiatrists, homeopaths, acupuncturists, massage therapists and physical therapists. All of these practitioners can offer treatment approaches and guidance for your health and self-care.

Support Groups

Grieving parents are experiencing emotions and reactions, challenges and struggles unlike any other. This experience can be isolating and debilitating. Your grief can feel very lonely, even in the company of loved ones. Finding others who share the unspoken "knowing" of child loss can be an important and helpful step for you. It is without hesitation that we recommend that you connect with other bereaved parents.

There are several kinds of support groups:

- Groups facilitated by grief/trauma specialists with a structured meeting plan and predetermined time frame
- Peer support groups such as the Compassionate Friends and Parents of Murdered Children
- Informal gatherings of bereaved parents who have met one another through bereavement groups or other connections
- Support groups that are specific to types of loss (homicide, SIDS, AIDS, cancer, miscarriage, etc.)

Connecting with a support group that focuses on child loss can change the course of your grief and help you to find your way on this unmapped journey. Support groups in your area can often be located through local hospitals, hospices and victim services. (We also provide a list of support groups in the appendix.)

If you go to a formal support group and find the format does not work for you or you are uncomfortable, it's okay to stop going. Make an effort to find another bereaved parent with whom to speak. Talking to someone with a shared experience is extremely valuable and can help dispel feelings of confusion or isolation.

Psychological and Emotional Support

An integral task of your grieving process is to regain a sense of emotional resiliency and psychological wellness. The emotions and reactions that were aroused when your child died can be confusing and overwhelming. Left untreated, grief reactions can worsen and become chronic, debilitating issues that stall grieving and interfere with your life. It can be very difficult to sort through the maelstrom of feelings, thoughts and reactions alone. Your loss is profound and may be complicated by many different factors including trauma response, guilt, shame, anxiety and depression. Engaging in a relationship with a therapist or counselor who has training and experience with issues related to grief and trauma can facilitate a more productive, healthy bereavement.

A major part of taking care of yourself is becoming aware of what you are experiencing physically, psychologically and emotionally. Working with a counselor or therapist can help you understand, manage and treat any ongoing troublesome effects that the trauma of your child's death has caused. Counseling is a therapeutic and beneficial process. It provides an opportunity to speak openly in a safe, confidential space with someone who has no agenda but to listen and help you.

The next sections offer tips on self-assessment, what to expect from a counseling or therapy relationship and how to choose a therapist or counselor.

Self-assessment

The four most common responses that can prolong your grief and affect your ability to cope are complicated grief, depression, anxiety and PTSD. There are many treatments and approaches that can help you to recover from these "tricky responses." Each has specific signs and symptoms. The first step is to assess your experiences and identify if these complications are indeed what you are dealing with. There are a number of self-assessment tests available through reputable sources on the Internet. (See the appendix for links. For more detailed information about the signs and symptoms of complicated grief, PTSD and depression, see chapter 1: *When Trauma and Grief Combine*.)

Once you have done a self-assessment, you can then discuss your concerns with your healthcare practitioner or a therapist. She or he can

provide you with further assessment and support as well as help you to
pursue appropriate treatment. Appropriate assessment is critical for deciding the most effective course of treatment.

WHAT SHOULD I KNOW ABOUT THE COUNSELING/THERAPY PROCESS?

Having a realistic idea of the goals and processes of therapy before you
begin will help in managing your expectations. Here is some information
about participating in counseling:

- Counseling is a learning process. The goal is to help you to deal
  more effectively with problems and issues.
- Do not expect a "quick fix"; it will add undue pressure to your
  process. Keep your goals for improvement reasonable.
- Progress in counseling/therapy does not occur right away, nor is it
  always steady.
- Dealing with difficult emotional issues can be an uncomfortable
  process. You may experience periods when you feel tempted
  to skip appointments. Continuing to attend even when things
  are difficult will help you work through the issues that hold
  you back.
- To improve, you should be prepared to discuss topics that may be
  uncomfortable for you to talk about.
- It may take some time to get used to being in counseling. If you
  have doubts about whether to stay in counseling, it is often helpful
  to attend at least a few appointments and to discuss any concerns
  with the therapist before making a decision.
- The relationship between you and your counselor or therapist
  differs from that with your doctor. A medical doctor provides a
  patient with specific advice. A therapist is a skilled listener who
  focuses on helping you discover and identify your strengths as
  well as roadblocks that inhibit your ability to achieve your goals.

The majority of individuals who are willing to participate actively in
therapy find that counseling can help them to feel less troubled by grief,
anxiety and depression. They feel more able to cope and to resolve emotional and psychological issues.

TIPS FOR CHOOSING A THERAPIST

The best ways to get referrals for a therapist are to:

- Speak to people you know (e.g., friends, clergy, doctors).
- Ask staff at resource centers or programs that are familiar with
  grief (e.g., hospital/hospice grief and bereavement programs,

funeral directors, victim services staff, community mental health centers, bereavement support groups).
- Check online for referral resources provided by licensing or certifying boards.

Remember:

- You are selecting a professional who provides a service.
- You are looking for an individual who specializes in grief and trauma.
- It is appropriate for you to ask the therapist for references and to check credentials.

When you are looking for a counselor or therapist, the first step is to request a meeting for an initial, brief interview. This will help you to determine if she or he is the right person for you to work with. There should be no charge for this meeting. Key questions to ask are:

- What are your credentials and where were you trained?
- What is your training and experience working with grief and loss?
- What is your training and experience working with trauma?
- What is your theoretical perspective and approach?
- Will you help me to set goals for this process?
- How long are the sessions?
- What are your fees?
- What is your cancellation policy?

Maintain Support Systems

You may have already made forward strides in coping with your grief through the help of counseling, a support group or other sources of support. Expect your grief to go through cycles. There will be periods of time when you feel much better than other periods. Over time, the intensity of your grief will soften; your experience will evolve. The grief of child loss is a lifelong journey; trust the process and expect ups and downs. It is important that you attend to your emotional, mental and physical health on an ongoing basis. You will learn new and healthy ways to strengthen your coping skills. Recognize that maintaining supports in many forms will help you in your grief as it transforms with time. Here are some additional thoughts:

- Remain open to new support systems as your lifestyle evolves and your grief progresses.

- Relationships that have grown from your experience may deepen and become lifelong bonds.
- Activities that are integral to your healing process can be sources of new support.
- As you change and adapt you will build new relationships along the way.
- Your old support systems may fall by the wayside as you develop new ones.
- Always keep sight of your needs for support and be generous and compassionate in responding to them.

CREATIVE EXPRESSION

As you are grieving, you can use creative activities in a number of ways. Creative media can be used for a distinct purpose or be more free-flowing. When using these tools for emotional release and expression of your grief, it is important not to place expectations that you are creating finished art. Use any of the media listed to create a memorial for your child, to focus on one specific emotion in order to experience and release it or to free flow your state of heart in the current moment.

- Dancing and movement
- Painting
- Drawing and sketching
- Writing
- Sculpting
- Collage making
- Carving
- Woodworking
- Building models
- Scrapbooking
- Playing music
- Drumming
- Singing

It is common for parents to feel unable to return to old forms of creative expression after the death of a child. For example, an avid painter may suddenly find she can't pick up a brush. If this applies to your situation, you can consider trying new forms of expression. Appreciate that your creative self and energy is attending to your grief and your old tools may not work for a while. Avoid judging yourself or viewing this as a failure.

WRITING EXERCISES

In her book *Holding On*, Cathy Sosnowsky writes, "During my first year of grieving I wrote over 140 poems. Every blossom, every falling leaf was imbued with meaning, and I had to write it down—however unclear that 'meaning' was. Writing poetry was a form of therapy, and continued to be a way of expressing my depression, my confusion, and my surprising moments of joy in the years that followed." This highlights what many parents express regarding the healing and therapeutic nature of writing as a tool in the grieving process. Writing can be used to express feelings, release emotions, reflect, voice fears or vent frustrations, angers and uncertainties. Because writing is a private, controlled exercise, it allows you to express difficult emotions. It is your choice whether the writings are shared and as a result it can feel safer to write than to talk. Writing is also helpful for organizing thoughts and solving problems. Here are suggestions for writing exercises you can try:

- **Free Write:** Free writing can seem daunting at first, but once you start it can be hard to stop. Take a piece of paper and write the first thing that comes to mind without using punctuation or considering sentence structure. It is a free flow of thoughts. Purge on the page.
- **Write from Emotions:** If you find an emotion is recurring, it is signaling a need for release. Hold the emotion in your mind and write reflectively on it.
- **Write Your Story:** Write the story of your child's death, your experience, your emotions, your love.
- **Write Stories about Good Memories**: Write about happy or special memories you shared with your child.
- **Write Letters:** Letter writing is a diverse tool. You can write letters to your child, to God, to yourself. Remember that no one will read them unless you choose. Letters provide an opportunity to express disappointments, love, longing, anger, guilt and regret. In letters you can say what you didn't get a chance to say. If you have feelings of guilt or regret, start a letter with "I'm sorry . . ." or "I feel guilty/angry because . . ."
- **Write "What I Miss"**: Start with the phrase "What I miss about you is . . ." and continue from there.
- **Journaling**: Journaling is an ongoing reflective writing practice. Choose a nice journal for yourself to capture your thoughts.
- **Mind mapping**: Mind mapping or brainstorming is a great technique for sorting thoughts and emotions. In the center of a

page, write a word that represents the emotion or problem you are dealing with. Put a circle around it. Draw an attached line and write a related situation, thought or feeling. Continue to create links until you feel finished. Take a moment to reflect on the end result. You may find new understanding regarding the source of your emotions or new ways to address problems you are facing. There are many forms of mind mapping. Search on the Internet for more ideas.

MANAGING DIFFICULT OR SELF-DESTRUCTIVE EMOTIONS

Anger

Anger is often used as a masking emotion to cover deeper feelings of sadness and helplessness. It is important to acknowledge your angry feelings and express them in a safe, supported environment. Once you are able to recognize the emotion that is underlying the anger, it will connect you with the deeper feelings that need acknowledgement and healing. Doing so can move you toward healthier ways of coping with your grief and loss. Some ways to release anger include:

- Writing down your feelings of anger;
- Doing vigorous physical activity;
- Talking with someone;
- Punching a pillow;
- Finding a private place, like in a car or at the beach, to scream;
- Throwing a ball against a wall;
- Hitting a punching bag;
- Pounding nails;
- Chopping wood;
- Throwing stones into a lake or the ocean.

It is important that anger is unleashed in safe ways that do not harm yourself or others. Set safe limits to your expression.

Self-Blame, Guilt or Regret

It is common for bereaved parents to feel self-blame, guilt or regret. These emotions can erode your sense of self-esteem and be destructive. It is crucial to find ways to express and manage these feelings. Some steps to resolve your feelings of guilt, self-blame or regret include:

- Admit your feelings to yourself and/or someone you trust.
- Ask forgiveness or express regrets to your child vocally or in written form.
- Accept the support and love of others.
- Acknowledge that some things are out of your control and the past cannot be changed.
- Work with a therapist or counselor.

The next exercise can be used to express and contain feelings of guilt, self-blame, regrets or unanswerable questions:

BURDEN BASKET AND PEACE OFFERING

Select a nice basket or container with a lid. When thoughts about your relationship history or the circumstances surrounding your child's death invoke regret, guilt or self-blame, write them on pieces of paper and place them in the basket. For example, "I'm sorry I didn't say 'I love you' more often" or "I wish I had picked you up from that party so you didn't get in that car." Acknowledging and externalizing these thoughts and putting them in a safe place for keeping creates emotional space, allowing you to process other aspects of yourself, your grief and the love you feel for your child.

If you have a need to seek forgiveness from your child, a peace offering is a lovely way to externalize and act upon this desire. Think of something that captures your desire for forgiveness and releases it. Pick wildflowers and toss them into the sea or a river, light a candle and let it burn to the end or write a letter seeking forgiveness and burn it or tie it to a helium balloon and release it.

Anxiety

Anxiety is a motivating energy that can help you focus and be attentive to tasks that need to be done. As a result of the trauma response, you may be experiencing excessive anxiety, which is different from generalized worry. Anxiety becomes a problem when worries and fears take over your thinking and interfere with your ability to move through your life effectively. This list outlines signs that anxiety is becoming a problem:

- Frequent periods of excessive anxiousness and worry
- Difficulty controlling worried thoughts, relaxing or enjoying quiet time
- Feeling on edge, keyed up or restless most of the time
- Difficulty concentrating or retaining thoughts
- Irritability

- Racing heart, sweaty or clammy skin, breathlessness
- Pervasive feelings of dread
- Physical or muscle tension most or all of the time
- Difficulty falling and/or staying asleep
- Participation in social, work and other functions is interrupted or prevented

If you are experiencing any combination of these symptoms, it is important that you consult with your doctor or therapist. There are many things you can do to get your anxiety in check and regain control of your life. The breathing exercises provided in the next section of this chapter are effective ways to manage your anxiety.

MANAGING TRAUMA RESPONSE, DEPRESSION AND ANXIETY

Gaining relief from symptoms of anxiety, anxiousness, PTSD and depression is a three-fold process. It requires giving attention to all three spheres of your being: body, mind and spirit. It is important for you to remember that your symptoms do not have to be the controlling force in your life. With a balanced approach and appropriate strategies or treatments, you can recover your mental and physical well-being. There are several approaches to self-management in this chapter. The next two exercises are simple, practical and highly effective in reducing anxiety, helping you to be more grounded and focused and improving your sense of well-being, which are critical to healthy bereavement and recovery from trauma.

Applying mindfulness techniques that interrupt the trauma response cycle is an effective strategy for managing your trauma symptoms. The purpose of the exercises in this section is to quiet the part of the brain that processes language and images. The beneficial effects of using these strategies are:

- Interrupting recurrent negative or worried thoughts
- Arresting flashback cycles
- Reducing internal triggering of physical stress reactions
- Providing a greater sense of calm and focus

The goal of these techniques is to open up mental space and generate conscious awareness and physical functioning that is focused in the present. These mindfulness practices can engender healing within all three spheres. With regular, repetitive practice, you can effectively "rewire" the circuits in your brain that are stuck in overdrive and which cause you to experience uncomfortable and debilitating symptoms.

FOCUSED BREATHING

1. Find a private place/room where you will not be disturbed (by people, phones, etc.).
2. Use a timer to keep track of the practice period (clock radio, egg timer, alarm clock). Using a timer will free you from having to keep an eye on the clock. Set the timer for a minimum of ten minutes to start (you want to work up to about fifteen minutes).
3. Sit comfortably upright, back supported, with your feet flat on the ground.
4. Relax into the chair, close your eyes and take notice of how your body and feet make contact with gravity through the chair and the floor.
5. Keeping your eyes closed, take a few deep "sighing" breaths. This will help you to feel the "bottom" of your lungs and relax your ribcage. Allow yourself to continue breathing comfortably in a relaxed manner.
6. As you continue breathing, silently count your breath on the inhale and exhale using a counting pattern such as:

   a. Inhale: 1,2,3,4; Exhale: 1,2,3,4
   b. Inhale: 1,2,3,4; Exhale: 4,3,2,1
   c. Inhale: 1,3,5,7; Exhale: 8,6,4,2

7. Count each completed inhale-exhale as one breath and repeat until you reach four completed breaths: this is one cycle. Repeat this until you reach a total of four cycles. Example: Inhale: 1,2,3,4; exhale: 1,2,3,4 (one); inhale: 1,2,3,4; exhale: 1,2,3,4 (two); inhale: 1,2,3,4; exhale: 1,2,3,4 (three); inhale: 1,2,3,4; exhale: 1,2,3,4 (four). Return to one.
8. Continue these four-breath cycles until the timer sounds.

You may forget to keep counting because your attention has shifted to thinking or a sound has distracted you. You might even doze off. That's *okay*! Simply notice that you are not counting and start again at one. You can strengthen your concentration by making the choice to return to the count.

Practice this once a day for at least one week and you will notice a significant change. Practice it on an ongoing daily basis and the effect of quieting the "talking brain" and focusing your attention will become more automatic. You are teaching your mind how to calm and focus in the present. Once you have the hang of it, you can use this technique in all kinds of situations. Breathing and silently counting breaths to relax as you feel yourself tense up is a tool you can carry with you wherever you go.

Walking Meditation

This exercise is based on the same basic principles as the focused breathing exercise. It is inspired by walking meditation practices as taught by Thich Nhat Hanh and is highly effective for calming and focusing your mind as well as relaxing your body. The exercise can be done in virtually any environment where you are able to walk for any period of time. It is preferable to set aside at least fifteen minutes and to walk outdoors, down the sidewalk, on a forest trail or even on an indoor track where you can move forward unencumbered. As you grow comfortable with this practice you can adapt it to any environment and any length of time. What is most important is that you walk in a forward motion.

1. Stand with your feet spaced shoulder width apart.
2. Take a few relaxing breaths while allowing yourself to feel your weight on your feet and your connection to the ground where you stand.
3. Begin walking at a relaxed pace in a forward motion.
4. Breathe naturally.
5. As you walk, count how many steps you take on the inhale and how many on the exhale.
6. Allow yourself to observe the things around you passively, without internal comment.
7. Continue counting your steps with your breath until you have finished your walk.

You will notice the step count will change as your pace changes with the terrain. For example: when going uphill you may count more steps as you inhale than as you exhale; on flat terrain the number of steps per breath may be equal.

Remember that you are practicing and the more often you do it, the more effective the exercise will be at helping you to gain greater skill at managing and controlling anxiety and reducing trauma reactions. Once you have the hang of it, you can apply this skill in any situation at any time (for example, walking from car to store, around your office, at the shopping mall, from kitchen to bedroom). You just need to be moving forward.

Replacing Traumatic Imagery

Bereaved parents are often barraged with flashbacks or painful memories of their experiences. Making an effort to counter these mental images with positive or calming imagery is an effective way to manage the response that can follow flashbacks. If you experience a flashback, immediately look at a photograph of your child, recall a happy memory or find something pleasing to observe such as a flower or leaf. Over time, using this strategy of replacing traumatic imagery with alternate memories and images reduces the acute nature and frequency of flashbacks. It can make the flashbacks more manageable and less debilitating or eliminate them altogether.

SELF-REFLECTION

This section outlines some activities you can use to reflect on your grieving process and the changes that have occurred in your life since your child died.

SORT

The intention of this activity is to sort through your emotions. It works to break your experience into smaller pieces so the breadth of your emotional responses can be managed more easily. Take one part of your experience, for example, a statement someone made or a detail of the circumstances surrounding your child's death. List, write or mind map any associated feelings and reactions. Also consider aspects of your history that may have influenced your reaction to the event.

After you have completed this, reflect on what you've written. Continue to work through different, small pieces of your experience. By breaking down your experience into manageable pieces, you can reduce feelings of overwhelm and further understand your emotional and spiritual process.

READ POETRY

There are many beautiful and insightful poems written about grief and the relationship between life and death. Poems often offer "soul nuggets" to which you connect on a deep level. Read poems a few times. Reflect on their meaning in relation to your experience of longing, love and loss. Visit your local library or bookstore or search the Internet for poetry.

ACKNOWLEDGE YOUR PROGRESS

Grief can be such a fog that sometimes it is difficult to recognize how far you have come. It's important to reflect upon the small strides you've made along the way. Grief work is hard work. Acknowledge the steps you have made toward coping with your loss in healthy ways and rebuilding your life day by day, step by step.

CULTIVATE GRATITUDE

Naming the things you are grateful for is a powerful way to find positives in the midst of your grief. There are many ways to cultivate gratitude. Each morning upon awakening you can write or say something for which you are grateful. Throughout the day you can be attentive to things that bring comfort. These can be small things, like "I am grateful for this piece of toast" or more powerful things, like "I am grateful for my health." Practicing gratefulness promotes your reconnection to positive things in your life. This practice can be a touchstone in moments of despair.

Recognize Gifts

The death of a child forces personal growth and transformation. Parents often talk about the lessons they have learned in the process, the changes in their values and interests. Life takes on new meaning. Take time to seek the hidden treasures of your grief and the lessons you have learned about yourself and about life.

REINVEST IN YOUR FUTURE

As the fog of acute grief lifts, you may look in the mirror and be surprised to see a completely new person. Values, concerns and interests change after an experience as profound as the death of a child. Much of the cognitive process of grief is looking back on the past. As the intensity of grief lessens, it is possible to start considering how you want to move forward into the future as this new person. Ask yourself probing questions to determine what your new value set is and what changes you may be interested in making as a result of your experience.

- What do I want?
- What do I feel my purpose is?
- What do I want to keep in my life (physically, emotionally, spiritually)?
- What do I want to let go of (physically, emotionally, spiritually)?
- How do I want to spend my time?
- How can I continue my relationship with my child into the future in a healthy way?
- What do I imagine as an authentic lifestyle for myself?
- What have I learned that I want to share through my actions, attitude or approach to life?

These questions concern making positive changes and choices in your life. Translate your answers to the questions into small, achievable goals. Making a list of goals is one way to set your intentions for the future. Keeping the steps small and achievable will empower you to make changes in your life that reflect the love you continue to have for your child and how you have been changed as a result of his or her death.

What's most important as you work toward recovering a sense of engagement in your life is to take care of yourself and find support. Remember, mourning your child is a systematic process and requires attendance to all parts of your being: mind, body and soul.

CHAPTER FOURTEEN

Creating Personal Rituals and Memorials

Death is the final important life transition and is often marked with ritual. Although rituals involving the larger community are often a part of the immediate aftermath of a death, they do not necessarily signal a completion of the mourning process. Parents have an ongoing need for connection with their child that is often accomplished through personal ritual and ceremony. Personal ritual can help mothers and fathers adjust to their new realities by creating new connections, honoring memories and acknowledging their changed relationships with the deceased. In this chapter we discuss personal rituals and memorials. We also examine ways to manage and transform traditional rituals such as birthdays, anniversaries and holidays. (Body preparation and funeral rites are discussed in chapters 5 and 6.)

RITUALS

Rituals mark change and are a common part of transitions in human experience. In "Creating Therapeutic Ritual in the Psychotherapy of the Bereaved," Therese Rando defines rituals as "specific behavior or activity which gives symbolic expression to certain feelings and thoughts of the actor(s) individually or as a group. It may be a habitually repetitive behavior or a one-time occurrence." Rituals occur in a myriad of forms in cultures across the world. Whether personal or part of a religious or cultural system, rituals "express meaning and significance that extend beyond the ritual itself as participants struggle with complex issues of human existence," Kathie Kobler, Rana Limbo and Karen Kavanaugh explain in "Meaningful Moments: The Use of Ritual in Perinatal and Pediatric Death." The practice of traditional rituals helps us to form a sense of meaning and continuity in the world.

In marking the transition from life to death, rituals take many forms. As long as the act holds meaning for the participants, it will provide an opportunity to express grief, give meaning to life events and maintain an ongoing connection with the deceased. Rituals are a vehicle for expressing and containing strong emotions. They often incorporate the use of symbols that make both conscious and unconscious statements.

The Importance of Personal and Family Rituals

Particularly in child loss, personal rituals act as a means to redefine the relationship between parent and child. Bereavement rituals are not limited to saying goodbye, as traditionally believed, but form an important part of parents' mourning processes and abilities to cope. Rituals express the relationship with the child that continues beyond death. Personal and family rituals result in a number of beneficial outcomes:

- Provide an opportunity to express difficult emotions in a safe and contained environment or time frame
- Acknowledge the reality of the death and the transformation in the relationship as a result of the death
- Recognize an ongoing commitment to the family in its new form
- Acknowledge and calm feelings of crisis
- Allow for continued connection with the deceased child
- Help maintain a sense of continuity in oneself and in the world
- Create an environment to resolve conflicts or feelings of anger, guilt, blame
- Provide an outlet for support and love to be expressed and shared
- Help parents to focus and express mourning
- Allow individuals to recast themselves in the world
- Honor the sacred and precious nature of life's cycles

Individuals and families are free to create and give their own meaning to the rituals they perform. Rituals can be very simple and private, such as saying "good morning" to a photograph of your child every day, or they can be elaborate and include a number of participants, such as holding a gathering on your child's birthday to remember and honor her or his life.

Follow your intuition in deciding how you want to form your personal rituals. The most essential thing is that the rituals you choose to perform feel right for you and hold special meaning. You will find that rituals bring comfort and feelings of connection. If you perform rituals with your family, it provides an opportunity to share feelings and support, to empower surviving children in their grieving process, to recognize your loss as a group and to continue the family bonds with your deceased child.

Your rituals may change over time. How you choose to mark the memory of your child or express your ongoing love for and connection with her or him will evolve as you move through your grief. Do not question or feel guilty about these transformations. They are a symbol that your mourning and continuing relationship with your deceased child are changing.

Ideas for Personal Rituals

Parents with whom we spoke shared many wonderful ideas for personal rituals. Use this list for ideas or transform them and make them your own. Share it with your family members.

- Create a book of letters and correspondence from your child.
- Light a candle every night.
- Hang a wind chime and when it rings think of it as love being sent to your child.
- Visit and bring flowers to the death site.
- Keep a photo of your child on the bedside table and say "good morning" and "good night" each day.
- Write a message for your child on a helium balloon and release it.
- Write to your child in letters or in a journal.
- Light a special candle at your place of worship once a month.
- Visit the cemetery.
- Talk to your child when on morning walks or runs.
- Make a T-shirt or find jewelry to wear that symbolizes your child.
- Keep a plant or bouquet in the house as a symbol of your child.

Rituals can also be a source of movement, a way to mark new endings and beginnings. For example, you may be holding thoughts of anger or guilt or images and memories that are painful for you. Creating a ritual to release you from the hard feelings you have been carrying inside can be very subtle yet powerful. One example is to write down the thoughts, actions and memories that you want to release on small pieces of paper. Then write down the things you want to bring into your life. Mix these together and then burn them to ash. Plant some bulbs in your garden and use the ashes as fertilizer. Rituals like these will not suddenly heal hurting hearts or end your grief. The essence of the ritual act is to mark a transition or threshold that you can step over and move on to the next steps in your journey.

MEMORIALS

Like rituals, memorials are put in place by parents or loved ones as a way to honor and remember the child. They are often based on places, things or values that held meaning for the child or within the relationship. These memorials provide places for parents to visit and find connection. In some cases they also give parents comfort in that they allow for a child's work to continue into the future.

Ideas for Memorials

- Plant a tree in your child's memory.
- Create a piece of art or sculpture to put on display in your home.
- Put together a photo album or video of your child's life.
- Make a quilt out of cloth from your child's clothing.
- Build a pagoda or sitting garden as a meditative space.
- Get a tattoo that symbolizes your child.
- Have a bench placed somewhere in your child's memory.
- Build a Web site with your child's poetry, life, stories, accomplishments.
- Establish a fund for a cause your child was passionate about or affected by.
- Start a nonprofit or charity to continue your child's causes.
- Place a plaque or a symbol of your child at a place in nature that your child had a connection with.

BIRTHDAYS AND ANNIVERSARIES

Bereaved parents look toward birthdays and anniversaries connected to the deceased child with anticipation and dread of a difficult and painful day. Your body as well as your mind will remember the date and its significance. Anniversary days have the potential to be one of those unexplainable days that just don't "feel right."

Cathy shared her own way of remembering her son:

> On birthdays, anniversaries and on other special occasions, my husband and I visit Alex's post by the river where we let go of his ashes. It sits along a forested path by the bank of the river. Walking the path in all kinds of weather, watched by the eagles above and the salmon below, is very healing. We don't talk to each other or even walk side by side, but each of us knows we're walking with Alex.

Be gentle with yourself on these days. Try to keep things simple and do what feels right for you. It is very important that you not force yourself to behave in any way that feels unnatural and discordant with your emotions. You may choose to take a "me" day and move about, listening to your heart and responding to your own natural rhythms. Use the time to relive pleasant memories and talk about your grief. Spend time as a family if possible. Creating personal rituals on birthdays and anniversaries can be a way to focus grief energy in positive ways and bring feelings of connection with your deceased child. Through your own creative process you can give new meaning to these days so that they are not grim reminders of your child's absence, but opportunities to honor your love and the treasures you hold in your heart for your child.

It is advisable to anticipate anniversaries and days that have special connections to your child. Plan ahead, mark your calendar and decide in advance what you might want to do.

Ideas for Birthdays

- Have a birthday party or gathering with your child's friends and/ or family.
- Make or buy a birthday cake.
- Sing happy birthday.
- Give gifts to grandchildren.
- Light a candle.
- Go to the cemetery or a special place outside.
- Try something new you have never tried before.
- Go for a meal at your child's favorite restaurant or make a meal your child enjoyed.

Ideas for Anniversaries

- Go out of town for the weekend.
- Do a reflective exercise and consider how things have changed in the past year.
- Light a candle.
- Visit the cemetery or a place in nature.
- Plant a flower or tree.
- Place an *in memoriam* in the newspaper.
- Make a donation to a special cause.
- Toss flowers into a river or the sea.
- Hold a candlelight vigil.
- Perform a balloon release ceremony.
- Participate in an activity your child enjoyed or that signifies your child in some way.

HOLIDAYS

Holidays are filled with traditions, rituals and obligations that can be very challenging for bereaved parents to face. They remind parents of how things have changed and that things will never be what they were when the child was still living, which can magnify the sense of loss. The idea of facing holidays without the child can be painful and difficult. Again, it is helpful to plan ahead and create new ways of approaching and marking the holidays. Here are some tips for healthy coping during the holidays:

- Plan ahead.
- Only do things you want to do.
- Keep things as simple as possible.
- Allow yourself to talk about your grief and release emotions.
- Consider the needs of the family and make decisions as a group.
- Find a way to create a special tribute to your child.
- Skip the holiday gatherings and traditions if you want to.
- Make sure to take time to be alone if you need it.
- Give yourself permission to have fun.
- Acknowledge that emotional pain on holidays is normal and will likely occur.
- Be vocal about your needs.
- Share stories and reminisce.
- Ignore or change old traditions as feels right.
- Eliminate unnecessary stress.

Here are some ways that parents have chosen to mark their losses and honor their deceased children during holidays:

- Put an extra place setting at the table or a photo on display in the dining room.
- Do something nice for someone else in the child's name.
- Make or buy ornaments or decorations that signify the child.
- Take a trip to a new place.
- Share stories around the table.
- Transform existing traditions or create new ones.
- Spend the day volunteering at a soup kitchen or food bank.
- Explore other holiday traditions from cultures around the world.

EVOLVING RITUALS

Ritual is an important part of creating form for your ongoing connection, relationship and love for your child. The way your valued memories and feelings are expressed in ritual will change over time. For example, perhaps you won't visit the gravesite as often but rather choose to spend time in your memory garden. These changes are normal and need not be judged. Be gentle with yourself and find new ways of your own creation to mark traditional holidays and celebrations that express and incorporate your grief.

CONCLUSION

The Path Ahead

When a child dies, a parent's world is washed by the agony of grief. Much like the impact of a tsunami on a shoreline, the first wave swallows everything in its path, tearing up what was firmly rooted. The wave pulls back, leaving ruin and chaos behind. Relentlessly, another wave comes, not as enormous but still powerful. This cycle of waves, sweeping in and retreating, continues. Over time, the waves become less intense and less frequent, until the sea returns to its usual rhythm with only occasional upsurges of stormy swells.

You may be struggling with many questions about where to go from the place in which you now find yourself. *How can I survive? How do I do this? Will it always be this way? When will I get better? How can I go on? How will I know I'm getting better?*

As time passes, things will change for you in both subtle and obvious ways. The pain of your loss will evolve and change as you move through your grief and mourning. Some indicators that you are gaining ground toward healing are:

- Flashbacks become less acute and less frequent.
- Sleep patterns begin to normalize.
- Appetite is more regular.
- Time between intense grief episodes increases.
- Irritable moods subside.
- Daily challenges become less "derailing."
- New interest in activities arises.
- Libido picks up.
- Focus, concentration and decision making improve.
- Interest in social activities resumes.
- Physical energy increases.

- Less time is spent focusing on the past.
- The need to hold on to mementos or visit the grave lessens.
- There is a shift from "surviving" to "navigating" your grief.
- You experience periods of emotional calm and mental clarity.
- You experience a sense of future.
- You feel more adjusted to new roles in life.
- You feel more flexible and versatile about change.
- You find comfort in happy memories of the child.
- You enjoy laughter and pleasure without guilt.

As we've stressed in this book, self-care and finding outlets for your grief and mourning facilitate your ability to cope with the intensity of your grief. Here are some final reminders we hope will be helpful:

- Care for yourself: lovingly, gently and patiently.
- Trust that your way of grieving is unique.
- Plan for anniversaries (birth, death, firsts) and acknowledge them in ways that are right for you.
- Note your accomplishments, no matter how small.
- Talk about your child.
- Connect with other parents who share child loss.
- Eat and sleep in healthy ways.
- Seek the support of your physician and/or counselor.
- Avoid numbing your emotional pain with alcohol or drugs, as it will only prolong your grief.
- Seek healthy outlets for expressing your pain and grief (exercising, writing, helping others, therapy, etc.).
- Find ways that you can remember and express your child's life creatively.
- Honor that your grief is a measure of your love.

Giving voice and expressing your feelings can help you to understand your process. It is not necessary or helpful for you to remain alone or silent in your grief. You have nothing to be ashamed of; grief and mourning are natural and human.

IN THEIR OWN WORDS

Valuable wisdom comes from bereaved parents who have shared your path. The final question we posed to parents in our interviews was, "What would you say to parents who have lost a child?" Here is a compilation of their replies:

"Time will heal, eventually, believe it or not. [The suffering] does lessen every year, but you are unfortunately in for a very long haul. There is no instantaneous disappearance of the grief. You really have to work through it. [Your child's death] will tap everything that you are, your best and worst self. If it brings out the best in you; that is a positive gift from beyond the grave from the child to parent . . . It's the influence the child has on the rest of our lives."

"There is a law of restoration and one can't lose all hope. Things can be resolved. The law of restoration can bring healing. Find a way to express with someone you feel safe with. Express everything that you can and believe that you will be healed."

"Stay in touch with your child's friends . . . Keep your child's spirit alive through relationships."

"If possible, set up a living trust or fund to carry on the child's work so that what he or she valued can be carried on."

"Be good to yourself. Take care of yourself and do what you need to do."

"Don't let people pressure you to do things or take part in things that are stressful. There are people whom I find difficult to be with now, so I have let some friends go and avoid situations that I know are going to be too hard to deal with, such as birthday parties."

"Exercise is so important and it does help you to feel better physically."

"Find people to whom you can talk openly."

"Going to Compassionate Friends has been very helpful. I have heard so many things that others have said that I hold on to. Those further along in the journey do have wisdom to bestow on the newly bereaved."

"Time marches on and we grow every day with what we are left with. It's not what happened to us but how we handled what happened to us that matters."

"Keep your child's name alive. It is a very special name; use it often."

"You never lose who you are, but you learn to wear a mask—one that helps you cope with the life that you never wanted to be part of."

"Talk, talk, talk; don't bury your grief."

"Keep saying your child's name with your family and friends."

"You will never forget your beautiful child. He or she will always be in your heart and memories. You will never be the same. Your life has been fractured. You will slowly put the pieces back together, but you will develop a new normal and your child will have a place, but a different place . . . You will never 'get over it' but you will learn to live with it."

"Let people help you with whatever they offer to do. Do not try to be like you were before you lost your child. Some people don't know what to do for you. Tell them what you need."

"Do not expect all of your friends to be there. Some will be there for the long haul, but some may not be able to stand your pain. You may make others uncomfortable and they won't know what to say or do. Spend time with those who understand or try to understand. Deal with your feelings for your other friends later."

"Remember to be good to yourself. Do not feel guilty if you find yourself smiling or even laughing. It's hard not to feel guilty but try to allow yourself a break now and then."

"Do not expect to feel better day by day in a continuum, moving from one end to the other. Grief is like waves splashing on the shore and then a [sudden] tsunami; a roller coaster ride that doesn't stop."

"Find a nice, simple book written by someone who has been where you are now and 'gets it.'"

"Try not to hide your grief. Hiding leads to isolation, self-denial (as in denying the real self) and your grief may manifest itself in other negative ways—physical illness, perpetual anger, addiction."

"Listen to your intuition, whether it's telling you about self-care or not. Check in every fifteen or thirty minutes: *What do I need?* It might just be a glass of water or it might be a walk in the garden."

"The most helpful thing someone said to me was it's not my fault. And knowing that so many women do go through miscarriage and have perfectly healthy babies afterwards. You're going to grieve no matter what and everyone deals with it differently."

"Follow your intuition or gut feeling about which people to be around. Less is more for a lot of people. Try to get some professional or peer support. Don't isolate."

"I'd say it's been happening too much. I'd say to them, 'That sucks. I'm so sad for your loss. It's so sad and why does it happen to so many people? What can I do to help you? What do you need? You might not know right now but when you feel like you might need something, even if it's just a hug, I'm here.' That's what I would say and then I would phone and check in."

"Take one day at a time, because it takes several years before you feel better. Honor [your child] by being present to others in life. It's not about me feeling sorry for myself; it's about giving the best that I can to others and to carry [my child's] spirit forward and to be there for others who have lost a child."

"Everybody has his own path and his own relationship and his own background. Be true to yourself."

"The hard part is when you feel like you have to do something for somebody else. Do [things] when you feel like it. Don't let others pressure you or put pressure on yourself."

"[Acknowledge that] the role [your child] plays in your life can't be replaced."

"Do, think, feel, whatever you need to do that is right for you. I'm really grateful that I was given the space to grieve in the way that I wanted to. Take the time and the space to figure out what it is that you need to do. Give yourself permission to be where you're at, however long it takes. Don't feel like you have to do things the way someone else does or follow any kind of rules. Just be in whatever way you need to be."

"Talk about it to whoever will listen. If your friends won't listen or are uncomfortable, tell them you are okay with the fact that they are uncomfortable. Tell them that the best thing they can do is just to listen. They don't have to come with any great ideas or even platitudes. A simple grunt and being able to stare you in the face and acknowledge that this did indeed happen works wonders."

"Parents need to know that this isn't their fault. Sure, they might have been smokers so their kids were premature. Sure, they weren't holding their kid's hand and he or she darted out on the road. Whatever. But ultimately, they did not want this child to die. They would have done anything in their power to have this child survive and live a good life (and the two things have to go together, because you may decide to abort a child or take a child off life support when there is no possibility of a good life). Accept the death without guilt; understand you are not at fault. And if the death results in some sort of relief, that is very okay too."

"There is help out there and it may not be where you expect it to be. Those closest to you may be the ones least able to help."

"Death makes everyone uncomfortable. It is not that people don't want to be supportive but, frankly, it scares them to be reminded of mortality. Leave it be and don't judge them."

"It is okay to be happy. To laugh. To live. It is not an affront to the child who died but a celebration of being human. For most of us, being born and dying have a stretch of time in between . . . If we don't celebrate the fact that we are human, we are throwing away the gift we have been given and that would be an affront to people like my daughters who never got that opportunity."

"Don't ever think that having another child will make up for the one you lost. That isn't fair to the child or to you. You can only fully love a child and properly raise a child if you take that child as a unique, wonderful individual with a unique, wonderful life to live and not as a replacement for someone else."

"It will get better. Honestly, it will never be the same. It will be different, but it will get better. You will get better."

"Seek help in caring for yourself now that this has happened. Oftentimes we think we can do it ourselves. Work at placing yourself in the vulnerable position of getting help."

"Find someone who knows what you're going through. One individual who can cry with you, who can scream with you, who can remember your child. That kind of connection is so wonderful."

REINVESTING IN THE FUTURE

Many bereaved parents with whom we spoke stressed that the most effective words of comfort they received were: "Hang on; this will change; it will get better." Little by little, with each day that passes, there will be changes in how you feel. Some will be small, almost invisible changes and some will be substantial. Take time to notice the little things that are changing in and for you; it is a powerful way to shine light on your journey of grief. As you move along this unfamiliar path, trust that each day is an opportunity to observe your world anew.

Throughout your life there will be times when you experience a resurgence of emotional pain and grief bubbling up. It may be connected to a birth or death anniversary. Sometimes the tears start flowing unexpectedly. These moments validate your ongoing loving relationship with your child and evolving bereavement. Your child will always be in your heart and mind.

Grief is a process and bereavement evolves with time. The day your child died you began a learning process that will continue throughout your lifetime. As time distances you from the intense heartbreak of your loss, you will find you are better able to glean the lessons from your experience that play out over the years. Read this book again in a year or two. Your perspective will have shifted and you may find more helpful suggestions to guide you along your way.

There is no cure for grief; it is a complex, intimate journey that traverses many varied terrains. When faced with tragedy, bereaved parents find wells of strength and resilience they didn't know existed. Facing the pain of child loss and reinvesting in the future are courageous choices that change the course of one's life.

To all bereaved parents, we acknowledge your bravery, strength and love.

They shall grow not old, as we that are left grow old:
Age shall not weary them, nor the years condemn.
At the going down of the sun and in the morning
We will remember them.

—Laurence Binyon

APPENDIX

SUPPORT GROUPS, ORGANIZATIONS AND WEB SITES

General

Bereaved Families of Ontario
Watline Postal Outlet
PO Box 10015
Mississauga, ON Canada L4Z 4G5
info@bereavedfamilies.net
www.bereavedfamilies.net

Bereaved Parents of the USA
National Office
Post Office Box 95
Park Forest, IL 60466
Phone: 708-748-7866
info@bereavedparentsusa.org
www.bereavedparentsusa.org

Center for Loss and Life Transition
3735 Broken Bow Road
Fort Collins, CO 80526
Phone: 970-226-6050
info@centerforloss.com
www.centerforloss.com

The Compassionate Friends
900 Jorie Blvd. Suite 78
Oakbrook, IL 60523
Phone: 877-969-0010 or
  630-990-0010
www.compassionatefriends.org
nationaloffice
@compassionatefriends.org

The Compassionate Friends of Canada
Phone: 866-823-0141
nationaloffice@tcfcanada.net
www.tcfcanada.net

The Dougy Center
PO Box 86852
Portland, OR 97286
Phone: 503-775-5683 or
  866-775-5683
help@dougy.org
www.dougy.org

Griefnet
PO Box 3272
Ann Arbor, MI, 48106-3272
www.griefnet.org

Mental Health and Self-Assessment

**The American Academy of Child
    and Adolescent Psychiatry**
3615 Wisconsin Avenue, N.W.
Washington, D.C. 20016-3007
Phone: 202-966-7300
www.aacap.org

**American Association of Pastoral
    Counselors**
9504A Lee Highway
Fairfax, VA 22031-2303
Phone: 703-385-6967
info@aapc.org
www.aapc.org

**American Counseling
    Association**
5999 Stevenson Ave.
Alexandria, VA 22304
Phone: 800-347-6647
www.counseling.org

**American Mental Health
    Counselors Association**
801 N. Fairfax Street, Suite 304
Alexandria, VA 22314
Phone: 800-326-2642 or
    703-548-6002
www.amhca.org

**American Psychological
    Association**
750 First Street, NE
Washington, DC 20002-4242
Phone: 202-336-5500 or
    800-374-2721
www.apa.org
www.apahelpcenter.org

**American Psychotherapy
    Association**
2750 E. Sunshine St.
Springfield, MO 65804
Phone: 417-823-0173 or
    800-205-9165
www.americanpsychotherapy.com
www.americanpsychotherapy
    .com/services/therapist

**The Association for Death
    Education and Counseling**
111 Deer Lake Road, Suite 100
Deerfield, IL 60015
Phone: 847-509-0403
www.adec.org

**BC Association of Clinical
    Counsellors**
14 – 2544 Dunlevy Street
Victoria, BC Canada V8R 5Z2
Phone: 250-595-4448 or
    800-909-6303
hoffice@bc-counsellors.org
www.bc-counsellors.org

**Canadian Counselling and
    Psychotherapy Association**
114-223 Colonnade Rd S
Ottawa, ON Canada K2E 7K3
Phone: 613-237-1099 or
    877-765-5565
www.ccpa-accp.ca/en

Healthy Place
Online psychological tests
www.healthyplace.com
/psychological-tests

MAYO Clinic
Self-assessment test for depression
www.mayoclinic.com/health
/depression/MH00103_D

Mental Health America
2000 N. Beauregard Street,
6th Floor
Alexandria, VA 22311
Phone: 703-684-7722 or
800-969-6642
info@mentalhealthamerica.net
www.nmha.org

**National Center for Post-
Traumatic Stress Disorder**
U.S. Department of Veterans
Affairs
810 Vermont Avenue, NW
Washington, DC 20420
Phone: 800-827-1000
www.ptsd.va.gov/public/index.asp

United Way
Information and referral
www.211.org

Homicide and Victims of Crime

**Canadian Parents of Murdered
Children**
PO Box 422
Carleton Place, ON Canada
K7C 2P5
Phone: 613-492-1978
admin@cpomc.ca
www.cpomc.ca

**Canadian Resource Centre for
Victims of Crime**
100 - 141 Catherine Street
Ottawa, ON Canada K2P 1C3
Phone: 613-233-7614 or
877-232-2610
http://crcvc.ca/en

**The Center for Victims of
Violence and Crime**
5916 Penn Avenue
Pittsburgh, PA 15206
Phone: 412.482.3240
www.cvvc.org

**Families and Friends of Violent
Crime Victims**
PO Box 1949
Everett, WA 98206
Phone: 425-252-6081 or
800-346-7555
contactus@fnfvcv.org
www.fnfvcv.org

Families of Murder Victims
Anti-Violence Partnership of
Philadelphia
2000 Hamilton Street, Suite 304
Philadelphia, PA 19130
Phone: 215-686-8033
fmv@avpphila.org
www.avpphila.org/fmv.html

**National Center for Victims of
Crime**
2000 M Street NW, Suite 480
Washington, DC 20036
Phone: 202-467-8700
www.ncvc.org

National Organization of Parents
of Murdered Children
100 E. 8th Street, Suite 202
Cincinnati, OH 45202
Phone: 513-721-5683
natlpomc@aol.com
www.pomc.com

National Organization of Victim
Assistance
510 King Street, Suite 424
Alexandria, VA 22314
Phone: 800-879-6682 or
703-535-6682
www.trynova.org

Office for Victims of
Crime Resource Center
National Criminal Justice
Reference Service
PO Box 6000
Rockville, MD 20849-6000
Phone: 800-851-3420
www.ovc.gov/resourcecenter
/index.html
Directory of victim services:
http://ovc.ncjrs.gov
/findvictimservices/

Virginia Mason Medical Center
Separation and Loss
Services
Seattle, WA
Phone: 206-223-6398
www.virginiamason.org
/SeparationandLossServices

Suicide

American Association of
Suicidology
5221 Wisconsin Avenue, NW
Washington, DC 20015
Phone: 202-237-2280
www.suicidology.org

American Foundation for Suicide
Prevention
120 Wall Street, 29th Floor
New York, NY 10005
Phone: 888-333-AFSP (2377) or
212-363-3500
inquiry@afsp.org
www.afsp.org

Suicide.org
www.suicide.org
Support groups:
www.suicide.org/canada-suicide
-support-groups.html
www.suicide.org/suicide-support
-groups.html

Survivors of Suicide
http://survivorsofsuicide.com

Sudden Death

Mothers Against Drunk Driving
(Canada)
2010 Winston Park Drive, Suite
500
Oakville, ON Canada L6H 5R7
Phone: 905-829-8805 or
800-665-6233
info@madd.ca
www.madd.ca

Mothers Against Drunk Driving (US)
511 E. John Carpenter Freeway, Suite 700
Irving, TX 75062
Phone: 877-ASK-MADD or 877-275-6233
www.madd.org

National SUID/SIDS Resource Center
Georgetown University
Box 571272
Washington, DC 20057-1272
Phone: 866-866-7437 or 202-687-7466
info@sidscenter.org
www.sidscenter.org

Perinatal

Babyloss
PO Box 1168
Southampton, UK SO15 8XZ
support@babyloss.com
www.babyloss.com

Center for Loss in Multiple Birth (CLIMB)
PO Box 91377
Anchorage, AK 99509
Phone: 907-222-5321
climb@pobox.alaska.net
www.climb-support.org

Glow In the Woods
www.glowinthewoods.com

Healing Hearts
9866 SE Empire Court
Clackamas, OR 97015
Phone: 503.607.0607
www.babylosscomfort.com

Hygeia Foundation, Inc.
PO Box 3943
New Haven, CT 06525
Phone: 800-893-9198 or 203-389-7700
info@hygeiafoundation.org
www.hygeiafoundation.org

International Stillbirth Alliance
PO Box 46757
Kansas City, MO 64188
www.stillbirthalliance.org

Miscarriage Support Auckland Inc.
PO Box 14 7011 Ponsonby
1144 Auckland, New Zealand
Phone: 09-360-4034
support@miscarriagesupport.org.nz
http://miscarriagesupport.org.nz/

Sands Stillbirth and Neonatal Death Charity
28 Portland Place
London, W1B 1LY
Phone: 020-7436-7940
support@uk-sands.org
www.uk-sands.org

Share Pregnancy and Infant Loss Support
The National Share Office
402 Jackson Street
St. Charles, MO 63301
Phone: 636-947-6164 or 800-821-6819
www.nationalshare.org

Terminal Illness

Hospice
401 Bowling Avenue, Suite 51
Nashville, TN 37205-5124
info@hospicenet.org
www.hospicenet.org

Hospice Foundation of America
1710 Rhode Island Ave, NW,
        Suite 400
Washington, DC 20036
Phone: 202-457-5811 or
        800-854-3402
hfaoffice@hospicefoundation.org
www.hospicefoundation.org

Military Death

**Helping Others by Providing
        Empathy (H.O.P.E.)**
Phone: 800-883-6094
HOPE-ESPOIR@forces.gc.ca
www.familyforce.ca/sites
        /shouldertoshoulder/EN
        /peersupport/Pages
        /HOPE.aspx

Shoulder to Shoulder
www.familyforce.ca/sites
        /Shouldertoshoulder/EN
        /Pages/default.aspx

**Tragedy Assistance Program for
        Survivors (TAPS)**
National Headquarters
1777 F Street NW, Suite 600
Washington, DC 20006
Phone: 202-588-TAPS (8277) or
        800-959-TAPS (8277)
info@taps.org
www.taps.org

BIBLIOGRAPHY

This section is divided into two parts, with the first containing readings that are suggested for parents and the second containing works that are intended for professionals.

FOR PARENTS

Bernstein, Judith. *When the Bough Breaks: Forever After the Death of a Son or Daughter*. Kansas City: Andrews McMeel Publishing, 1997.

Bolton, Iris and Curtis Mitchell. *My Son, My Son: A Guide to Healing After Death, Loss, or Suicide*. Atlanta: Bolton Press, 1998.

Colgrove, Melba, Harold Bloomfield and Peter McWilliams. *How to Survive the Loss of a Love*. Los Angeles: Prelude Press, 1991.

Doka, Kenneth J., ed. *Living with Grief: Children, Adolescents, and Loss*. Hospice Foundation of America's *Living with Grief* Series. Bristol, PA: Taylor & Francis, 2000.

Doka, Kenneth J. and Joyce Davidson, eds. *Living with Grief: When Illness is Prolonged*. Hospice Foundation of America's *Living with Grief* Series. Bristol, PA: Taylor & Francis, 1997.

———, eds. *Living with Grief: Who We Are, How We Grieve*. Hospice Foundation of America's *Living with Grief* Series. New York: Routledge, 1998.

Ericsson, Stephanie. *Companion Through the Darkness: Inner Dialogues on Grief*. New York: HarperPerennial, 1998.

Fitzgerald, Helen. *The Grieving Child: A Parent's Guide*. New York: Fireside, 1992.

———. *The Grieving Teen: A Guide for Teenagers and Their Friends*. New York: Simon and Schuster, 2000.

——. *The Mourning Handbook: The Most Comprehensive Resource Offering Practical and Compassionate Advice on Coping with All Aspects of Death and Dying.* New York: Simon & Schuster, 1995.

Frankl, Viktor E. *Man's Search for Meaning.* Translated by Isle Lasch. Boston: Beacon Press, 2006.

Grollman, Earl. *Talking About Death: A Dialogue between Parent and Child.* Boston: Beacon Press, 1990.

Ilse, Sherokee. *Empty Arms: Coping with Miscarriage, Stillbirth and Infant Death.* Maple Plain, MN: Wintergreen Press, 1996.

Kubler-Ross, Elisabeth. *On Death and Dying.* New York: Macmillan, 1969.

Kubler-Ross, Elisabeth and David Kessler. *On Grief and Grieving: Finding the Meaning of Grief Through the Five Stages of Loss.* New York: Scribner, 2005.

Kushner, Harold S. *When Bad Things Happen to Good People.* New York: Avon, 1981.

Lord, Janice Harris. *No Time For Goodbyes: Coping with Sorrow, Anger and Injustice after a Tragic Death.* Ventura, CA: Pathfinder Publishing, 1990.

Lothrop, Hannah. *Help, Comfort and Hope after Losing Your Baby in Pregnancy or the First Year.* Tucson: Fisher Books, 1997.

Maguire, Thomas V. "A Recovery Bill of Rights for Trauma Survivors." April 1997. http://www.drpattilevin.com/educational/recovery_bill_of_rights.pdf.

Marcus, Eric. *Why Suicide?: Answers to 200 of the Most Frequently Asked Questions About Suicide, Attempted Suicide, and Assisted Suicide.* San Francisco: HarperCollins, 1996.

McCracken, Anne and Mary Semel, eds. *A Broken Heart Still Beats: After Your Child Dies.* Center City, MN: Hazelden, 1998.

Nhat Hanh, Thich. *Creating True Peace: Ending Violence in Yourself, Your Family, Your Community and the World.* New York: Simon and Schuster, 2003.

——. *The Long Road Turns to Joy: A Guide to Walking Meditation.* Berkeley, CA: Parallax Press, 1996.

Noel, Brook and Pamela Blair. *I Wasn't Ready to Say Goodbye: Surviving, Coping & Healing After the Sudden Death of a Loved One.* Naperville: Sourcebooks, Inc., 2008.

O'Hara, Kathleen. *A Grief Like No Other: Surviving the Violent Death of Someone You Love.* New York: Marlowe and Company, 2006.

Rando, Therese. *How To Go On Living When Someone You Love Dies.* Lexington, MA: Lexington Books, 1988.

Rathkey, Julia Wilcox. *What Children Need When They Grieve: The Four Essentials: Routine, Love, Honesty and Security.* New York: Three Rivers Press, 2004.

Redfern, Suzanne and Susan K. Gilbert. *The Grieving Garden: Living With the Death of a Child.* Charlottesville, VA: Hampton Roads Publishing, 2008.

Rinpoche, Sogyal. *The Tibetan Book of Living and Dying.* Edited by Patrick Gaffney and Andrew Harvey. New York: Harper Collins, 1992.

Rosenbloom, Dena and Mary Beth Williams. *Life After Trauma: A Workbook for Healing,* 2nd ed. New York: Guilford Press, 2010.

Rosof, Barbara. *The Worst Loss: How Families Heal from the Death of a Child.* New York: Henry Holt and Company, 1994.

Schaefer, Dan and Christine Lyons. *How Do We Tell the Children? A Step-By-Step Guide for Helping Children Two to Teen Cope When Someone Dies.* New York: Newmarket Press, 1993.

Schiff, Harriet Sarnoff. *The Bereaved Parent.* New York: Penguin Books, 1977.

Sosnowsky, Cathy. *Holding On: Poems for Alex.* Vancouver: Creative Connections Publishing, 2001.

Staudacher, Carol. *Men and Grief: A Guide for Men Surviving the Death of a Loved One.* Oakland, CA: New Harbinger Publications, 1991.

Wolfelt, Alan. *Healing a Child's Grieving Heart: 100 Practical Ideas for Families, Friends and Caregivers.* Fort Collins, CO: Companion Press, 2001.

——. *Healing a Teen's Grieving Heart: 100 Practical Ideas for Families, Friends and Caregivers.* Fort Collins, CO: Companion Press, 2001.

——. *Mourner's Bill of Rights.* http://www.hlebmf.org/billofrights.pdf.

——. *Understanding Your Grief: Ten Essential Touchstones for Finding Hope and Healing Your Heart.* Fort Collins, CO: Companion Press, 2003.

Wylie, Betty Jane. *New Beginnings: Living Through Loss and Grief.* Ontario: Key Porter Books, 1991.

FOR PROFESSIONALS

Aho, Anna Liisa, Marja-Terttu Tarkka, Päivi Astedt-Kurki and Marja Kaunonen. "Fathers' Experience of Social Support after the Death of a Child." *American Journal of Men's Health* 3, no. 2 (2009): 93–103.

Al-Gamal, Ekhlas and Tony Long. "Anticipatory Grieving Among Parents Living with a Child with Cancer." *Journal of Advanced Nursing* 66, no. 9 (2010): 1980–1990.

American Psychiatric Association. *Diagnostic and Statistical Manual of Mental Disorders*, 4th ed. Washington, DC: American Psychiatric Association, 2000.

Armour, Marilyn. "Meaning Making In the Aftermath of Homicide." *Death Studies* 27 (2003): 519–40.

Attig, Thomas. *How We Grieve: Relearning the World.* Rev. ed. New York: Oxford University Press, 2011.

——. "Relearning the World: Making and Finding Meanings." In *Meaning Reconstruction and the Experience of Loss*, edited by Robert A. Neimeyer, 33–53. Washington: American Psychological Association, 2001.

Barrera, Maru, Kathleen O'Connor, Norma Mammone D'Agostino, Lynlee Spencer, David Nicholas, Vesna Jovcevska, Susan Tallet and Gerald Schneiderman. "Early Parental Adjustment and Bereavement after Childhood Cancer Death." *Death Studies* 33 (2009): 497–520.

Binyon, Laurence. "For the Fallen." In *The Oxford Dictionary of Quotations*, 2nd ed. London: Oxford University Press, 1955.

Breen, Lauren J. and Moira O'Connor. "Family and Social Networks after Bereavement: Experiences of Support, Change and Isolation." *Journal of Family Therapy* 33 (2011): 98–120.

Brier, Norman. "Grief Following Miscarriage: A Comprehensive Review of Literature." *Journal of Women's Health* 17, no. 3 (2008): 451–464.

Buckle, Jennifer L. and Stephen J. Fleming. *Parenting After the Death of a Child: A Practitioner's Guide.* New York: Routledge/Taylor & Francis Group, 2011.

Children's & Women's Hospital. "Autopsy Information for Parents." Children's & Women's Health Centre of BC. September 2007. http://www.cw.bc.ca /library/pdf/pamphlets/CW020Autopsy.pdf.

Davies, Ruth. "Mothers' Stories of Loss: Their Need to Be with Their Dying Child and Their Child's Body after Death." *Journal of Child Health Care* 9, no. 4 (2005): 288–300.

Doka, Kenneth J., ed. *Living with Grief: After Sudden Loss: Suicide, Homicide, Accident, Heart Attack, Stroke.* Hospice Foundation of America's *Living with Grief* Series. Bristol, PA: Taylor & Francis, 1996.

Doka, Kenneth J. and Terry L. Martin. *Grieving Beyond Gender: Understanding the Ways Men and Women Mourn,* rev. ed. New York: Routledge, 2010.

Emswiler, Mary Ann and James P. Emswiler. *Guiding Your Child Through Grief.* New York: Bantam Books, 2000.

Everly, George S., Jr. "Psychotraumatology: A Two-Factor Formulation of Posttraumatic Stress." *Integrative Physiological and Behavioral Science* 28, no. 3 (July-September 1993): 270–78.

Everly, George S., Jr. and Jeffrey M. Lating. *A Clinical Guide to the Treatment of the Human Stress Response.* New York: Plenum Press, 1989.

———, eds. *Psychotraumatology: Key Papers and Core Concepts in Post-Traumatic Stress.* New York: Plenum Press, 1995.

Gilbert, Kathleen R. "Religion as a Resource for Bereaved Parents." *Journal of Religion and Health* 31, no. 1 (Spring 1992): 19–30.

Goodrum, Sarah. "When the Management of Grief Becomes Everyday Life: The Aftermath of Murder." *Symbolic Interaction* 31, no. 4 (Fall 2008): 422–442.

Grout, Leslie A. and Bronna Romanoff. "The Myth of the Replacement Child: Parents' Stories and Practices after Perinatal Death." *Death Studies* 22 (2000): 93–113.

Harrington-LaMorie, Jill and Meghan E. McDevitt-Murphy. "Traumatic Death in the United States Military: Initiating the Dialogue on War-Related Loss." In *Grief and Bereavement in Contemporary Society,* edited by Robert A. Neimeyer, Darcy L. Harris, Howard R. Winokuer and Gordon F. Thornton, 261–272. New York: Routledge/Taylor & Francis Group, 2011.

Herman, Judith. *Trauma and Recovery: The Aftermath of Violence—From Domestic Abuse to Political Terror.* New York: BasicBooks/Perseus, 1997.

Himebauch, Adam, Robert M. Arnold, MD and Carol May. "Grief in Children and Developmental Concepts of Death #138." *Journal of Palliative Medicine* 11, no. 2 (2008): 242–243.

Hinds, Pamela S., Lisa Schum, Justin N. Baker and Joanne Wolfe. "Key Factors Affecting Dying Children and Their Families." *Journal of Palliative Medicine* 8, no. 1 (2005): S70-S78.

Klass, Dennis. *The Spiritual Lives of Bereaved Parents.* Philadelphia: Taylor and Francis, Brunner/Mazel, 1999.

Kobler, Kathie, Rana Limbo and Karen Kavanaugh. "Meaningful Moments: The Use of Ritual in Perinatal and Pediatric Death." *MCN, The American Journal of Maternal/Child Nursing* 32, no. 5 (2007): 288–295.

Lang, Ariella, Andrea R. Fleiszer, Fabie Duhamel, Wendy Sword, Kathleen R. Gilbert and Serena Corsini-Munt. "Perinatal Loss and Parental Grief: The Challenge of Ambiguity and Disenfranchised Grief." *OMEGA Journal of Death and Dying* 63, no. 2 (2011): 183–196.

Leon, Irving. *When A Baby Dies: Psychotherapy for Pregnancy and Newborn Loss.* New York: Yale University Press, 1990.

Lichtenthal, Wendy G., Joseph M. Currier, Robert A. Neimeyer and Nancy J. Keesee. "Sense and Significance: A Mixed Methods Examination of Meaning Making after the Loss of One's Child." *Journal of Clinical Psychology* 66, no. 7 (2010): 791–812.

Lobb, Elizabeth A., Linda J. Kristjanson, Samar M. Aoun, Leanne Monterosso, Georgia K.B. Halkett and Anna Davies. "Predictors of Complicated Grief: A Systematic Review of Empirical Studies." *Death Studies* 34, no. 8 (2010): 673–698.

MADD Victim Services. "Grandparent's Grief: The Double Grief." MADD. http://www.madd.org/victim-services/finding-support/victim-resources /grandparents-grief.pdf.

Martin, Terry L. and Kenneth J. Doka. *Men Don't Cry . . . Women Do: Transcending Gender Stereotypes of Grief.* Philadelphia: Brunnel and Mazel/Taylor and Francis, 2000.

———. "Revisiting Masculine Grief." In *Living with Grief: Who We Are, How We Grieve,* edited by Kenneth J. Doka and Joyce D. Davidson, 133–42. New York: Routledge, 1998.

Milo, Elizabeth Moulton. "The Death of a Child with a Developmental Disability." In *Meaning Reconstruction and the Experience of Loss,* edited by Robert A. Neimeyer, 113–136. Washington: American Psychological Association, 2001.

Nehari, Miri, Dorit Grebler and Amos Toren. "A Voice Unheard: Grandparents' Grief Over Children Who Died of Cancer." *Mortality* 12, no. 1 (2007): 66–78.

Neimeyer, Robert A. and Diana C. Sands. "Meaning Reconstruction in Bereavement: From Principles to Practice." In *Grief and Bereavement in Contemporary Society* edited by Robert A. Neimeyer et al., 9–13. New York: Routledge Taylor and Francis Group, 2011.

Okun, Barbara and Joseph Nowinski. *Saying Goodbye: How Families Can Find Renewal Through Loss.* New York: Penguin Group, 2011.

Oliver, Luis E. "Effects of a Child's Death on the Marital Relationship: A Review." *OMEGA Journal of Death and Dying* 39, no. 3 (1999): 197–227.

Prigerson, Holly, Ellen Frank, Stanislav Kasl, Charles Reynolds, M. Katherine Shear, Jason Newsom and Selby Jacobs. "Complicated Grief as a Disorder Distinct From Bereavement-Related Depression and Anxiety: A Replication Study." *American Journal of Psychiatry* 153, no. 11 (November 1996): 1484–86.

Prigerson, Holly, Paul K. Maciejewski, Charles F. Reynolds, Andrew J. Bierhals, Jason T. Newsom, Amy Fasiczka, Ellen Frank, Jack Doman and Mark Miller. "Inventory of Complicated Grief: A Scale to Measure Maladaptive Symptoms of Loss." *Psychiatry Research* 59 (1995): 65–79.

Prigerson, Holly, M. Katherine Shear, Ellen Frank, Laurel C. Beery, Rebecca Silberman, Joyce Prigerson and Charles F. Reynolds. "Traumatic Grief: A Case of Loss-Induced Trauma." *American Journal of Psychiatry* 154, no. 7 (1997): 1003–9.

Rando, Therese. "Bereaved Parents: Particular Difficulties, Unique Factors, and Treatment Issues." *Social Work* (1985): 19–23.

———. "Complications in Mourning Traumatic Death." In *Living with Grief after Sudden Loss: Suicide, Homicide, Accident, Heart Attack, Stroke,* edited by Kenneth J. Doka, 139–59. Bristol: Taylor & Francis, 1996.

———. "Creating Therapeutic Ritual in the Psychotherapy of the Bereaved." *Psychotherapy* 22, no. 2 (1985): 236–240.

———. *Treatment of Complicated Mourning.* Champaign, IL: Research Press, 1993.

Read-Johnson, David, Susan C. Feldman, Hadar Lubin and Steven M. Southwick. "The Therapeutic Use of Ritual and Ceremony in the Treatment of Post-Traumatic Stress Disorder." *Journal of Traumatic Stress* 8, no. 2 (1995): 282–98.

Rilke, Rainer Maria. *Letters to a Young Poet.* Translated by Stephen Mitchell. New York: Random House, 1984.

Rini, Annie and Lillia Loriz. "Anticipatory Mourning in Parents with a Child Who Dies While Hospitalized." *Journal of Pediatric Nursing* 22, no. 4 (2007): 272–282.

Romanoff, Bronna D. and Marion Terenzio. "Rituals and the Grieving Process." *Death Studies* 22 (1998): 697–711.

Rosen, Helen. *Unspoken Grief: Coping With Childhood Sibling Loss.* Lexington, MA: D.C. Heath & Co, 1986.

Rosenblatt, Paul. *Parent Grief: Narratives of Loss and Relationship.* Philadelphia: Taylor and Francis Group, 2000.

Rynearson, E.K. "Bereavement after Homicide: A Descriptive Study." *American Journal of Psychiatry* 141, no. 11 (November 1984): 1452–54.

———. "Bereavement after Unnatural Dying." In *Advances in Bereavement,* edited by S. Zisook. Washington, DC: American Psychiatric Press, 1987: 77–93.

———. "Psychological Effects of Unnatural Dying on Bereavement." *Psychiatric Annuals* 16, no. 5 (May 1986): 272–75.

———. "Psychotherapy of Bereavement after Homicide: Be Offensive." *In Session: Psychotherapy in Practice* 2, no. 4 (1996): 47–57.

———. "Recovery From Unnatural Death." Gift From Within—PTSD Resources for Survivors and Caregivers. Last updated January 2012. http://www.giftfromwithin.org/html/recovery.html.

Rynearson, E.K. and J.M. McCreery. "Bereavement after Homicide: A Synergism of Trauma and Loss." *American Journal of Psychiatry* 150 (1993): 258–61.

Sanders, Catherine M. "Gender Differences in Bereavement Expression Across the Life Span." In *Living With Grief: Who We Are, How We Grieve* edited by Kenneth J. Doka and Joyce D. Davidson, 121–32. New York: Routledge, 1998.

Shear, Katherine, MD, Ellen Frank, Patricia Houck and Charles Reynolds. "Treatment of Complicated Grief." *Journal of the American Medical Association* 293, no. 21 (June 2005): 2601–08.

Sormanti, Mary and Judith August. "Parental Bereavement: Spiritual Connections with Deceased Children." *American Journal of Orthopsychiatry* 6, no. 3 (1997): 460–469.

Torbic, Holly. "Children and Grief: But What About the Children? A Guide for Home Care and Hospice Clinicians." *Home Healthcare Nurse* 29, no. 2 (2011): 67–77.

Van der Kolk, Bessel A. "Posttraumatic Stress Disorder and the Nature of Trauma." In *Healing Trauma: Attachment, Mind, Body, and Brain*, edited by Marion F. Solomon and Daniel J. Siegel. New York: W. W. Norton, 2003.

Wordon, J.W. "Tasks of Mourning." In *Grief Counseling and Grief Therapy: A Handbook for the Mental Health Practitioner*, 2nd ed. New York: Springer, 1991.

Zayfert, Claudia and Jason C. DeViva. *When Someone You Love Suffers from Posttraumatic Stress: What to Expect and What You Can Do.* New York: Guilford Press, 2011.

ACKNOWLEDGEMENTS

RANDIE'S ACKNOWLEDGEMENTS

This book is the culmination of a journey that began on a December night in 1995. To those who first held a light on the path to guide me through the darkest hours, Peg Blackstone, Dr. Ted Rynearson and Cindy Sinnema, I will be ever grateful for your kind wisdom and loving shelter. Kay Kukowski, my respected mentor, guide and teacher, your spirit calms the most terrifying tempest. For the gift of remembering that Nature is the mother who embraces us all, thank you Skatman. My deepest love and gratitude to my daughter Diedra for her bright spirit and love that reaffirms life's purpose. To my husband Ken, your constancy, patience, encouragement and support have been the anchor that has made it all possible. Thank you Big Sisser, you have never let me stop believing in myself. It is with joyous gratitude that I acknowledge my writing partner, Avril, without whom this book would still be only wished for and imagined; what an endearing taskmaster you are! Thank you to Evelyn White for the wise words, "The only way a book gets written is to sit down and put words on paper." And last but not least, my humble gratitude to all who have offered the love, support, stories and guidance that have made this book possible.

AVRIL'S ACKNOWLEDGEMENTS

Dave, my husband, thank you for the support, love and learning you bring to my life. Your encouragements to trust my intuition and to seek self-improvement constantly have made this book possible. To my children, you are my touchstones and my mirrors. Sam, Auntie Anne and Alaya, thank you for your guidance and expertise along the way. Aja, thank you for nurturing my writing and editing skills. Ken, thank you for opening your home and for the vital dark chocolate runs. To family and friends who grieved for Alden along with us, thank you. Your support helped me through. And finally, thank you, Randie, for this miraculous partnership and friendship.

Our combined thank you to Dr. Joan Dunphy and New Horizon Press for having the insight and persistence to know this book is needed. Thank you to JoAnne Thomas, Joanna Pelizzoni and Charley Nasta for your support and editing prowess.

Most important, our heartfelt gratitude goes out to all the parents who shared their stories with us. May your journeys know love and comfort along the way.

INDEX

CHAPTER FOUR:
Taking Your Child Off Life Support

CHAPTER FIVE:
Seeing Your Child's Body

CHAPTER SIX:
Handling End-of-Life Rituals

CHAPTER SEVEN:
Dealing with the Criminal Justice System and the Media

CHAPTER EIGHT:
Surviving with Your Partner

CHAPTER NINE:
Healing the Family System

CHAPTER TEN:
Managing Social Relationships

CHAPTER ELEVEN:
Experiencing Identity Loss and a Shattered Worldview

CHAPTER TWELVE:
Facing Spiritual Emergencies

CONCLUSION:
The Path Ahead